'Look to Your Front'

Studies in the First World War
by The British Commission for Military History

'LOOK TO YOUR FRONT'

Studies in the First World War
by The British Commission for
Military History

Brian Bond et al

SPELLMOUNT
Staplehurst

British Library Cataloguing in Publication Data:
A catalogue record for this book is available
from the British Library

Copyright © Individual contributors 1999

ISBN 1–86227–065–1

First published in the UK in 1999 by
Spellmount Limited
The Old Rectory
Staplehurst
Kent TN12 0AZ

1 3 5 7 9 8 6 4 2

Typeset by Palimpsest Book Production Limited,
Polmont, Stirlingshire
Printed in Great Britain by TJ Press International, Padstow, Cornwall

Contents

BRIAN BOND
Foreword

The British Commission for Military History has been in existence for about thirty years and draws its members from many walks of life including university teachers, lecturers from the Royal Military Academy Sandhurst, serving and retired officers, and the staff of the Imperial War Museum. Although in principle our field of interest has no chronological, national or Service boundaries, the majority of our members are students of late nineteenth- and twentieth-century warfare with a definite leaning towards land operations.

Furthermore, if there is one special focus of interest and expertise it is the First World War and particularly, though by no means exclusively, the Western Front. Our members have numerous and wide-ranging publications to their credit, from the raising of the Kitchener Armies via the development of the tank to the culminating victories of 1918; our ranks contain some of the best-known guides on the extremely popular battlefield tours; and we are pioneering a database on the performance of all British divisions on the Western Front.

The present collection of essays, with its ingenious punning title, consequently provides an admirable showcase for the stimulating research conducted by our members, many of whose essays were originally presented in draft at BCMH conferences. While there has been no attempt to enforce a uniform view on the many persisting controversial issues of the war, our contributors broadly incline to the positive interpretation of the British Army's role (siding for example with John Terraine rather than Alan Clark), and are more concerned with apportioning credit for the 'learning curve' rather than denying its existence. What they certainly do have in common is a conviction that the time is at last coming when the First World War can be treated as history (like earlier wars) rather than being approached emotionally and polemically in terms of 'futility', 'horror' and 'national trauma'. The recent media coverage of the eightieth anniversary of the ending of the war suggests that military historians must continue to campaign vigorously to convey to the wider public a sense of 'the real war' in all its complexity.

Professor Brian Bond

President, British Commission for Military History 1999

IAN F W BECKETT

Hubert Gough, Neill Malcolm and Command on the Western Front

Writing to his niece on her 7th birthday not long after the battle of Loos, Hubert Gough, commanding I Corps, in alluding to Sir John French, concluded: 'You must ask Mummie what a Field Marshal is – I am not sure I know! But he wears a cocked hat and feathers'.[1] It is hardly a revealing description of the functions of a commander-in-chief but it is tempting to suggest that it is only comparatively recently that understanding of the true nature of command on the Western Front has progressed much beyond this elementary level.

This may seem an extraordinary statement given the countless books which have constantly repeated the familiar 'westerner' and 'easterner' arguments for and against Haig's strategy. Indeed, if it has done nothing else, Brian Bond's recent edited collection, *The First World War and British Military History*, has usefully served to demonstrate how the parameters of this seemingly endless exercise in polemic were set even before the war had actually ended. Nothing said, for example, by Leon Wolff's *In Flanders Fields* in 1959 or John Terraine's *Douglas Haig: The Educated Soldier* in 1963 substantially differed from what had been said already in the 1920s and 1930s.[2] Consequently, scholarship and understanding were simply not materially advanced by most of these publications, the tradition of which lingers.[3]

In the meantime, many historians positively shunned the battlefield in favour of investigating the social aspects of the British presence on the Western Front. Indeed, while oral history and what Peter Simkins has described as the 'everyman at war' approach have focused increasing attention on the experience of war for the ordinary soldier, Simkins is quite right to call for more 'operational histories and studies of battlefield performance'.[4] Thus, it is the operational level of war with which this article will be concerned, being defined in modern military parlance as that area between strategy and tactics which denotes the conduct of battle in a given theatre of operations in pursuit of the war's political objectives, or to achieve goals set by theatre strategy. Effectively, in contemporary armies, this means the decision-making process at corps and divisional level but, for the Great War, this might be defined as decision-making at army and corps level.

1

Fortunately, a number of historians are working in this field and the studies so far produced by Tim Travers, Dominick Graham, Robin Prior and Trevor Wilson have already begun to re-arrange the historiographical landscape of the Western Front.[5] What will be attempted here is a contribution to the debate in the context of one particular army on the Western Front, namely Fifth Army as commanded by Hubert Gough from its creation as Reserve Army in May 1916 until its absorption by Fourth Army in April 1918.

I

Neither Gough nor his chief of staff from May 1916 to December 1917, Neill Malcolm, have had a good press. It is not surprising to find Gough one of the 'fallen stars' in a recent book on command. As recounted in the book's chapter on Gough by Anthony Farrar-Hockley, the Secretary of State for War, Lord Derby, suggested Gough's removal to Haig on 5 March 1918 on the grounds that 'he does not have the confidence of the troops he commands'. Derby and Lloyd George had said much the same in December 1917 and Derby was to repeat the formula in ordering Gough's dismissal in April 1918.[6]

Edward 'Moses' Beddington, who was GSO2 in Fifth Army from May to November 1916, and again from December 1917 to April 1918 and was Malcolm's temporary successor as Gough's chief of staff, claimed in his memoir that he had confronted Gough and Malcolm in December 1917 to tell them that: 'Fifth Army was very unpopular with divisions and that only divisional commanders who were quite confident in themselves and their divisions were happy to serve in it. Others all dreaded it especially those whose nerves were not strong and those who were not sure they were filling the bill or were doubtful . . .'[7] He went on to state that Gough acknowledged this himself and said he had been told the same by Haig two days earlier. This kind of comment finds an echo in the recollection of Major-General Wace, wartime GSO1 of 32nd Division, that his divisional commander, Major-General Sir William Rycroft, was 'terrified of Gough' following an earlier failure on the Somme in July 1916 and 'knew he'd "got it in for us", and when at Bethune we got orders to go back to the Somme in October he turned to me and said wryly this would be his undoing unless he went to Rawlinson's army'. Rycroft did lose his command in November 1916, and one of the assistants of the official historian, Sir James Edmonds, concluded, with respect to Gough's demand that Lieutenant-General Claud Jacob's II Corps continue to attack Grandcourt in the same month, that Gough's subordinates were less than happy. Similarly, an old friend of Gough, Major-General Llewellyn Pope-Hennessy, told Basil Liddell Hart in 1933 that an 'atmosphere of terror' had existed in Fifth Army during the Passchendaele campaign.[8]

Neill Malcolm's diary confirms that the close of the Somme and Passchendaele campaigns were both defining moments for Gough and Fifth Army. Referring to Rycroft's dismissal, Malcolm noted, 'I am afraid that Hubert is inspiring rather an atmosphere of fear in his subordinates, making them shy of expressing their opinions & perhaps forcing them into acts against their better judgement.' Almost exactly a year later, Malcolm wrote, 'Am a good deal distressed about Hubert's unpopularity. Am hearing more of it now we are resting. There is a great deal of jealousy in it, and as he makes enemies by his frank speech, it is only natural that they should get their own back now & then. Many stories are told against him most of which are entirely untrue, and that makes them more difficult to combat.'[9]

In essence, three main charges were laid against Gough. As suggested by the Grandcourt affair, the first was that he was careless of the lives of his men. Thus, Adrian Hodgkin, who was temporarily attached to Fifth Army as gas and chemical adviser from November 1916 to March 1917, recorded of losses at Bucquoy in March 1917 through alleged lack of artillery support, 'very typical of Gen. Gough, who apparently does not care a button about the lives of his men'. In September 1917, by which time he was serving in Third Army, Hodgkin reported a rumour that Gough would be dismissed 'chiefly, I believe, because of the large and unnecessary number of casualties among our artillery. Everybody seems delighted.'[10] Certainly, this was a view which increased over the summer and autumn of 1917 despite the fact that Gough counselled the cancellation of the Passchendaele offensive after the failure at Langemarck on 16 August, and again in company with Plumer commanding Second Army on 7 October.[11]

The second charge was that Gough was all too ready to dismiss commanders who failed to be sufficiently optimistic or enthusiastic in attack. Gough himself remarked in his memoir, *The Fifth Army*, that some commanders did dislike coming to him but this never applied to 'the bold, the energetic, the resolute'. In his later autobiography, *Soldiering On*, Gough also made the point that he had brought on younger men of ability such as Arthur Asquith, Bernard Freyberg, Tom Cubitt and Adrian Carton de Wiart. However, in both *Soldiering On* and post-war correspondence with Edmonds, Gough made no apologies for being 'very severe towards inefficiency, especially in high places which undoubtedly created much soreness and sometimes jealousy'. The case of Rycroft has been cited and there are similar examples. Lieutenant-General Morland's X Corps was withdrawn from the Somme at Gough's request while Malcolm's diary often notes the perceived faults of divisional commanders such as Major-Generals A B Scott of 12th Division in August 1916 and W de L Williams of 30th Division in August 1917. Another well known case is the dismissal of G McK Franks from 35th Division in the chaos of March 1918.[12] But clashes did not always result in dismissal. Malcolm refers to 'rather outspoken language on both sides' between Gough and Major-General Robert Fanshawe of 48th Division during the Pozières operation in August 1916, but Fanshawe survived as did Scott and Williams. Similarly, Major-General Colin Mackenzie of 61st Division survived when he expected to be sacked in September 1916.[13]

The third charge was poor staff work in Fifth Army as suggested by Walter Guinness, Brigade-Major of 74th Brigade. Australians had formed a particularly poor view of Gough on the Somme and, according to Haig and his chief of staff, Kiggell – who blamed Malcolm – this disenchantment spread to the Canadians in October 1917. Relying on the evidence of Beddington's memoir, Farrar-Hockley ascribes most of the problems to Malcolm for undermining Gough and exceeding his powers. As Farrar-Hockley expresses it, through his own inexperience of high command, Gough did not perceive that 'the executive who is loyal, able and friendly to oneself may be, for a wide variety of reasons, a perfect tyrant to those lower down the scale.[14] Gough did later suggest to Lloyd George and Liddell Hart in 1936 that Malcolm had not proved a good chief of staff. However, Gough had been sorry to lose Malcolm in December 1917 and he had written in 1931 that the real problem had been taking Malcolm with him on all visits to units since 'it prevented subordinates pouring out to him [Malcolm] all their troubles, which they often concealed from me, but which they would not have hidden from him if he had been alone'. This, of course, is a very different version of the situation from that suggested by Farrar-Hockley. Moreover, Charles Bonham-Carter, who had been BGGS for Staff Duties and Training at GHQ, told Liddell Hart in 1935 that his view was that Malcolm had been too ready to carry out Gough's orders and was often exhausted from lameness.[15]

Malcolm's diary suggests surprise at his removal and, while this might indicate a lack of perception, it is not obvious from the tone of the diary as a whole. Interestingly enough, Malcolm also makes no mention of the confrontation remembered by Beddington. Moreover, A J H Smith, who served in Fifth Army's Intelligence Branch from March 1917 to April 1918, recorded of Malcolm's departure that he 'will be a great loss as he was universally liked in the Army'. In contrasting Rawlinson's Fourth Army staff unfavourably with that of Gough, Smith also recorded his distaste for Beddington.[16]

Whatever the truth of the charges popularly held against Gough and his staff, there is no doubt that he had acquired plenty of enemies during his rapid rise to high command. Henry Wilson, with whom Gough had been on particularly bad terms since the Curragh incident in March 1914, was certainly deeply implicated in Gough's dismissal. Gough was well aware of Wilson's animosity but he was also on bad terms with many at GHQ.[17] Gough's post-war conversations and correspondence with Lloyd George, Liddell Hart and Edmonds show that he had no time for Haig's successive chiefs of staff, Butler, Kiggell and Lawrence, although his wartime correspondence is more ambivalent with respect to Kiggell.[18] Clearly, there was no love lost between Gough and Haig's DMO, Brigadier-General John Davidson, and Edmund Ironside, who had commanded 99th Brigade in 1918, later recorded that Gough was utterly contemptuous of GHQ.[19] Fellow army commanders were equally viewed with suspicion, especially Rawlinson – like Wilson, he was described by Gough as 'crooked' – but Allenby, Byng and Monro were also criticised.[20]

Tim Travers has amply illustrated the growing antipathy of Edmonds for Gough in the course of the preparation of the Passchendaele volumes of the official history between 1939 and 1948, although the earlier volumes dealing with March 1918 and published between 1935 and 1937 were more sympathetic. Gough also waged his own successful campaign for the rehabilitation of his conduct of the March retreat after the war and he was unfortunate in the manner of his dismissal. As the Deputy CIGS, Robert Whigham, expressed it to the King's assistant private secretary in April 1918, 'They say that whatever was the feeling before, he handled a difficult situation against enormous odds in a very efficient manner.'[21]

Clearly, it is difficult to discuss Fifth Army's reputation without reference to the personality of Gough[22] but it is equally important to view it against the background of the understanding of command within the army as a whole.

II

It is generally recognised that, once deadlock had occurred on the Western Front, soldiers in all armies were confronted with both new technical and managerial problems requiring a process of adjustment and learning. Whilst some historians have tended to separate the two, the technical and managerial problems are intimately related and, in the British Army, overcoming the managerial problems was arguably the key to achieving a solution to the technical difficulties. It must be remembered that the regular army was but 247,432 strong in August 1914, the intended strength of the BEF of just six infantry divisions requiring full mobilisation of army and special reservists. Even with the addition of the Territorials and other reserves, disposable manpower was still only 733,514 officers and men. The numbers who enlisted in August and September alone were over double the latter figure and, in all, there were 4.9 million wartime enlistments. At peak there were 3.9 million men in the army in 1917, of whom 1.5 million served on the Western Front in fifty-six divisions (out of seventy-five) formed into seventeen corps and five armies.[23]

This was an extraordinary and rapid expansion necessitating an equivalent increase in the number of officers. There were only 12,738 regular officers in 1914 and, ultimately, some 229,316 wartime commissions were granted although only 16,544 were permanent, regular commissions. Even without the prejudice which manifested itself towards the 'temporary gentlemen', it would have taken time for the new officers to acquire the necessary command skills. Much then rested on the abilities of the small regular cadre, but 3,627 had become casualties by November 1914 alone. Moreover, these included a significant proportion of the 908 graduates from the staff colleges at Camberley and Quetta: 134 were subsequently killed or died of wounds including fifty-six in 1914 and thirty-four in 1915. Yet, there was an increasing need for trained staff officers. A typical corps staff in 1914 had eighty-nine officers and men in 1914, but 183 by 1918 and, in all, there were an estimated 12,000 officers in staff appointments or almost as many as in the entire regular officer corps four years previously.[24]

The qualification of Passed Staff College, or *psc*, had only been effectively established as an essential qualification for staff appointment in September 1906. Camberley had produced only forty-nine graduates a year, and it was closed in August 1914 with no systematic staff courses again until April 1916. But, in any case, pre-war staff training had been deficient, Rawlinson's future chief of staff, Archibald Montgomery, contending in January 1914 that so much staff training had been undertaken in syndicates that too few officers were used to making individual decisions. The belated development of the general staff in Britain had also resulted in a staff serving commanders rather than the system pertaining on the continent in which the staff and not the commanders were the real centre of authority.[25] It will be recalled, for example, that a German staff colonel, Hentsch, determined that the German First and Second Armies should begin to retreat from the Marne in September 1914. In the British Army, staff officers could not issue orders on their own authority although they were the only official channel for the communication of orders between commanders and their subordinates. Thus, CRAs and CREs were purely advisers to their commanders and a highly capable professional such as Gough's CRA in Fifth Army, Uniacke, was not consulted at all in the planning for Passchendaele.[26]

As Dominick Graham has argued, at the heart of this problem lay an absence of doctrine. Co-ordination of the different arms of service was no one's specific responsibility, and the prevailing assumption was that all else existed to support the infantry. Rigid demarcation also existed in the Army which, in staffing terms, saw a division between the G branch, responsible for operations and intelligence, and the A and Q branches tasked with personnel and supply functions. Despite the conclusion of the post-war Braithwaite committee that the staff system had worked well, it should not be a matter of surprise if staff work was often sloppy given the small percentage adequately trained for such appointments.[27]

If the level of staff expertise was one significant drawback for the Army, then what of the commanders whom staff served? Naturally, it was also the case that few regulars had commanded higher formations before the war other than during the short annual manoeuvres revived only in 1898. In 1914 the only corps headquarters in peacetime was that at Aldershot and, apart from Haig as its current incumbent, only French and Smith-Dorrien among serving soldiers had previously held the command; by contrast, the French and German Armies had twenty and thirty-five such peacetime commands respectively. By and large army commanders in 1916 had only commanded divisions in 1914, corps commanders only brigades, and divisional commanders only battalions. Gough, of course, was less experienced than other army commanders in having commanded only a brigade in 1914.

In fact, the lack of command experience had been recognised before the war in the last of the annual staff officers' conferences in January 1914 with a paper by Hubert's brother, Brigadier-General John Gough, entitled, 'Can more be done to render officers competent commanders in war?'. In the words of Robertson, then DMT, it was generally agreed that 'something more ought to be done than is done' to achieve this result, Robertson having concluded from the 1913 manoeuvres that what he called the 'duties of command' were not sufficiently well understood. Again, the crux was a lack of doctrine. As John Gough expressed it, commanders needed to find an essential balance: 'In other words, superior commanders should command in the true sense of the word. The practical difficulty, however, is that some commanders are so anxious to leave subordinates a free hand that they forget their own duty of control and guidance while others go to the opposite extreme and interfere with the methods of their subordinates. It does not appear easy to hit off the happy mean.' At one point during the Somme, Neill Malcolm made the same point, noting that 'Troops must be given a free hand & yet we must not lose control at all costs. I hope we have discovered a fairly happy medium.'[28]

In reality, of course, the 'happy medium' remained elusive. As is known, Haig was well aware of the need for a commander-in-chief 'to prepare for battle, not to execute on the battlefield'. Unfortunately, while fully adhering to the idea that his strategy should not be challenged, Haig was wholly inconsistent in his approach to the authority to be delegated to subordinates. Haig could not stop interfering in operational planning as evidenced, among other examples, by the planning for Passchendaele in which Gough became totally confused as to whether or not a breakthrough was intended. Yet, there were other occasions when Haig should have intervened but did not do so, as in the failure to co-ordinate Third and Fifth Armies during the German March offensive. In that sense, Gough was correct in maintaining after the war that Haig did not actually command.[29]

Not only did confusion in command exist at the highest level but throughout the Army as the situation within Fifth Army clearly demonstrates. On the one hand, Gough and other Army commanders expected that corps and divisions would follow orders without dissent. Thus, Gough wrote to his sister-in-law in September 1916: 'We have so many very incompetent Divisional Generals and Corps Commanders, & owing to their previous slackness & weakness, no one is accustomed to obey orders & they seem to look on orders as a basis of protest & argument as Neill M expressed it. It requires a considerable exercise of firmness to get one's orders carried out sometimes & one has to closely supervise the plans of everyone!'. Similarly, Malcolm had complained in July 1916 that there was 'too much tendency not to command units – that is to say to look upon command as interference. This is not Hubert's line and as he insists on commanding I think some corps don't quite like it. However, they must lump it as it is all rot.' Again, with particular reference to Morland's X Corps, Malcolm wrote: 'There is still this wretched idea of command being interference which we must abolish.'

Jacob's II Corps also came in for criticism from Malcolm, although both he and Gough believed the problem was not Jacob himself but the chief of staff, Philip Howell. According to Malcolm, Howell, who had fallen out with Gough during the Curragh incident, was under the impression that an order 'is a proposal to be discussed – a bone to be worried – to be set aside when done with – perhaps buried. This is not exactly Hubert's idea so there is to be trouble.' In precisely similar terms, Gough described Howell as a 'great thorn' who 'always tries to argue, he produces the most complicated schemes, he always wants to avoid fighting, & he never loyally carries out his orders'.[30]

It can be seen how such a total concept of command as entertained by Gough and Malcolm might be unpopular when they themselves detected far less direction being applied elsewhere. Malcolm complained on one occasion (prior to Tim Harington's appointment as Plumer's chief of staff at Second Army) that Plumer's 'system of command merely appears to be to tell the corps to carry on'. Similarly Gough complained that, when Henry Wilson commanded IV Corps, subordinates 'were neither guided, nor controlled nor driven'. There were similar criticisms of Allenby and Rawlinson although, ironically, Gough had complained in 1914 that Allenby as his then divisional commander was 'the most interfering I ever served under'. Gough's own willingness to obey orders might also be questioned in the light of the Curragh.[31]

Yet, as at the higher level and as Gough's reference to Allenby implied, there was a different side to the command concept in Fifth Army existing simultaneously with the notion of total control. In the long-running battle over the preparation of the official account of Passchendaele, for example, both Gough and Malcolm were adamant that corps were always fully consulted. Gough specifically stated that he held conferences on the evening of every major attack and that he could not recall any occasion when the decision reached was not unanimous. Malcolm similarly wrote that he could not 'remember any case where the decision was other than unanimous'. Obviously, one explanation might be that, since dissent was unacceptable, none was offered but, with the exception of Lieutenant-General Sir Herbert Watts of XIX Corps, Gough and Malcolm appear to have had the greatest respect for their other corps commanders such as Jacob, the Earl of Cavan (XIV Corps), Walter Congreve (XIII and VII Corps) and Ivor Maxse (XVIII Corps). The evidence suggests that the corps commanders, in turn, were equally supportive of Gough, Malcolm recording of the growing criticism of Gough in November 1917 after a visit to Maxse that 'not one of the Corps Commanders under us this year have one word to say to it'.[32]

It must also be emphasised that, in Fifth Army as elsewhere, there was the same inconsistency in, and frequently a lack of, command where it could have been exercised profitably. Over the winter of 1917–18 ideas for a defence in depth not only differed between Third and Fifth Armies but within each army. Maxse's XVIII Corps opted for defence in depth but Butler's III Corps resolved to hold the front line in strength. When requested to adjudicate between the corps, Fifth Army's response was 'to the effect that we should have to settle it amongst ourselves'.[33] In mitigation, there was no system for army training schools in France until Monro established one in Third Army in late 1917 and corps and other lower formations moved from army to army frequently. Furthermore, control was not assisted by the often primitive state of communications until late into the war. In March 1918, of course, those communications broke down entirely in both Third and Fifth Armies and, once they had done so, corps in particular appeared to flounder under the responsibility of acting on their own initiative in a highly mobile and volatile situation.[34] It is not the purpose of this article to consider formations lower than corps but it is sufficient to observe that command was not exercised below corps level with any more consistency.

III

For much of the Great War, the Army was both hierarchical and anti-intellectual, its habits of deference and loyalty and the practice of patronage equally hard to throw off. Yet, while suffering from the effects of such a personalised command structure, the Army simultaneously felt the lack of any coherent doctrine for command. This resulted in considerable confusion not just in Fifth Army but throughout the Army as a whole.

The Army did triumph in 1918 but largely, it would seem, without any solution being found to managerial problems.

It is the case that younger men were increasingly reaching divisional command. Moreover, Haig had been compelled to change personnel at GHQ and, either through choice or default, increasing freedom of action was accorded down the chain of command in what Travers has characterised as 'useful anarchy'. Similarly, Prior and Wilson have concluded that Rawlinson was even more of a spectator as Army commander in 1918 than he had been in 1916. Yet it is difficult to explain how commanders were suddenly capable of exercising flexibility and initiative in the summer of 1918 when they had so demonstrably failed to do so as recently as March and April although, conceivably, the chaos of the retreat itself and the necessity to improvise ad hoc formations during it was significant in effecting a transformation. Prior and Wilson see success in terms of sheer weight of Allied material while Travers suggests that the explanation lies primarily in the German Army being its own worst enemy.[35] There may or may not have been improvements in British tactical methods by 1918 but, certainly, there was little real improvement in the understanding of command. Given the confusion over the concept and its practice, this is hardly surprising. In that sense, not just Gough and Malcolm but the British Army as a whole was also its own worst enemy.

Notes

1   Diana Gough Mss, Hubert Gough to Diana Gough, 8 October 1915
2   Brian Bond (ed.), *The First World War and British Military History* (Oxford University Press, 1991)
3   See, for example, John Laffin, *British Butchers and Bunglers of World War One* (Stroud: Alan Sutton, 1988) and Denis Winter, *Haig's Command* (London: Viking, 1991)
4   Peter Simkins, 'Everyman at War' in Bond, *The First World War and British Military History*, pp.289–313
5   Shelford Bidwell and Dominick Graham, *Firepower* (London: Allen & Unwin, 1982); Dominick Graham, 'Sans Doctrine: British Army Tactics in the First World War' in Tim Travers and T Archer (eds.), *Men at War* (Chicago: Precedent, 1982), pp.69–92; Tim Travers, *The Killing Ground* (London: Allen & Unwin, 1987); ibid, *How the War Was Won* (London: Routledge, 1992); Robin Prior and Trevor Wilson, *Command on the Western Front* (Oxford: Blackwell, 1992)
6   Anthony Farrar-Hockley, 'Sir Hubert Gough and the German Breakthrough, 1918' in Brian Bond (ed.), *Fallen Stars* (London: Brassey's, 1991), pp.65–83; ibid, *Goughie* (London: Hart-Davis, MacGibbon, 1975), pp.262–3, 311–12
7   Kings College London, Liddell Hart Centre for Military Archives (hereafter LHCMA), Beddington Mss pp.121–2. Haig's diary indicates his meeting with Gough was on 9 December 1917 – see Robert Blake (ed.), *The Private Papers of Douglas Haig* (London: Eyre & Spottiswoode, 1952), p.272
8   PRO, Cab 45/138, Wace to Edmonds, 30 October 1936; Travers, *Killing*

Ground, p.187; LHCMA, Liddell Hart Mss, 11/1933/23, conversation with Pope-Hennessy, 14 October 1933

9 Malcolm Mss (hereafter Malcolm), diary, 21–22 November 1916 and 27 November 1917

10 I(mperial) W(ar) M(useum), Hodgkin Mss, P.399, diary, 14 March and 12 September 1917

11 Farrar-Hockley, *Goughie*, pp.207, 237; LHCMA, Edmonds Mss, II/2/274, Gough to Edmonds, 19 August 1933; Malcolm, Gough to Malcolm, 4 March 1951; Hubert Gough, *The Fifth Army* (London: Hodder & Stoughton, 1931), p.205. Doubt has been cast on the events of 7 October in Robin Prior and Trevor Wilson, *Passchendaele: The Untold Story* (New Haven: Yale University Press, 1996) p.160

12 Gough, *Fifth Army*, p. 133; Hubert Gough, *Soldiering On* (London: Arthur Barker, 1954), pp.129–30, 149; LHCMA, Edmonds Mss, II/1/43, Gough to Edmonds, 3 May 1923; Malcolm, diary, 2/3 and 4 August 1916, 4 August and 19 September 1917; Congreve Mss (hereafter Congreve), diary, 26 March 1918; PRO, Cab 45/192, Sandilands to Edmonds, 14 August 1923

13 Malcolm, diary, 25 August 1916; Farrar-Hockley, *Goughie*, p.232. For a survey of dismissals from command, see John Bourne, 'British General Officers and the Somme: Some Career Aspects' Part II (*Gunfire* 39, 1997, pp.12–25)

14 Brian Bond and Simon Robbins (eds.), *Staff Officer* (London: Leo Cooper, 1987), p.162; Blake, *Private Papers of Douglas Haig*, p.257; Farrar-Hockley, *Goughie*, pp.227–9

15 LHCMA, Liddell Hart Mss, 11/1936/31, conversations with Lloyd George and Gough, 27 January 1939 and 11/1935/14, with Bonham-Carter, 12 December 1935; Gough, *Fifth Army*, pp.134–5

16 Malcolm, diary, 16 December 1917; IWM, Smith Mss, Smith to mother, 17 December 1917 and 16 May 1918

17 LHCMA, Edmonds Mss, II/1/43, Gough to Edmonds, 3 May 1923; Ian Beckett, *The Army and the Curragh Incident, 1914* (London: Bodley Head for Army Records Society, 1986), passim; ibid, *Johnnie Gough VC* (London: Tom Donovan, 1989), pp.147–73; Dorothea Gough Mss (hereafter DAG), Hubert to Dorothea, 18 March 1917 and 22 February 1918; Hubert Gough Mss (hereafter HPG), Gough to Blumenfeld, 25 December 1918; LHCMA, Liddell Hart Mss, 11/1935/72, conversation with Gough, 9 April 1935; R(oyal) A(rchives), Geo V, Q.1377/1, Gough to Wigram, 12 October 1918

18 LCHMA, Edmonds Mss, II/2/239, Gough to Edmonds, 19 March 1931; Liddell Hart Mss, 11/1935/72 conversation with Gough, 9 April 1935; 11/1936/31, conversation with Gough and Lloyd George, 27 January 1936; House of Lords Record Office, Lloyd George Mss, G/215, Gough to Lloyd George, 3 May 1936; RA, Geo V, Q.832/2/299, Gough to Wigram, 21 January 1918; DAG, Hubert to Dorothea, 30 December 1915

19 HPG, Edmonds to Gough, 24 May 1945; PRO, Cab 45/140, Edmonds to Gough, 24 March 1944; Travers, *How the War Was Won*, p.63

20 LHCMA, 11/1935/72 and 107, conversations with Gough, 9 April 1935 and with Gough and Lloyd George, 28 November 1935; HPG, diary, 6 May 1930; DAG, Hubert to Dorothea, 30 December 1915, 9 March 1936 and 22 April 1917; PRO, Cab 45/134, Gough to Edmonds, 16 June 1938

21 Travers, *Killing Ground*, pp.203–17; Ian Beckett, 'Frocks and Brasshats' in Bond, *The First World War and British Military History*, pp.89–112; RA, Geo V, Q.2522/6/236, Whigham to Wigram, 29 April 1918. See also PRO, Cab 45/193, Maxse to Edmonds, 7 October 1934; and Congreve, diary, 7 April 1918

22 For contrasting views of Gough's character (and temper), see Travers, *How the War Was Won*, pp. 15–16; IWM, Butler Mss, PP/MCR/107, Butler to father, 23 March 1918; PRO, Cab 45/33, Edmonds to Wynne, 17 February 1944 and Cab 45/192, Sandilands to Edmonds, 14 August 1923; IWM, Hodgkin Mss, p.399, diary, 10 January 1917

23 Ian Beckett, 'The Nation in Arms' in Ian Beckett and Keith Simpson (eds.), *A Nation in Arms* (Manchester University Press, 1985), pp.1–36

24 Keith Simpson, 'The Officers' in Beckett and Simpson, *Nation in Arms*, pp.64–96; Brian Bond, *The Victorian Army and the Staff College* (Eyre Methuen, London, 1972), pp.299–329; Peter Scott, 'The Staff of the BEF', *Stand To 15*, 1985, pp.44–61

25 Staff College Library, *Reports of the General Staff Conferences, 1906–14*, Conference of 12–15 January 1914; Graham, 'Sans Doctrine', pp.69–92

26 See, for example, Malcolm, diary, 24 September 1917

27 Bidwell and Graham, *Firepower*, pp.44–6; Bond, *Victorian Army and Staff College*, pp.299–329. For Gough's view of Braithwaite, see DAG, Hubert to Dorothea, 22 February 1917

28 Beckett, *Johnnie Gough*, pp. 148–9; Malcolm, diary, 29 June 1916

29 Travers, *Killing Ground*, pp.85–97, 127–46, 203–17; Prior and Wilson, *Command*, pp. 52–73, 137–53, 222–3; Tim Travers, 'A Particular Style of Command: Haig and GHQ, 1916–18', *Journal of Strategic Studies* 10, 3, 1987, pp. 363–76; LHCMA, Liddell Hart Mss, 11/1936/31, conversation with Gough and Lloyd George, 27 January 1936

30 DAG, Hubert to Dorothea, 23 September 1916; Malcolm, diary, 6 and 13 July, 28 August, and 17 September 1916

31 Malcolm, diary, 10 June 1916; RA, Geo V, Q.832/296, Gough to Wigram, 3 March 1917; DAG, Hubert to Dorothea, 22 April 1917; PRO, Cab 45/134, Gough to Edmonds, 16 June 1938; DAG, Hubert to Dorothea, 25 January 1915

32 HPG, Gough to Edmonds, 3 May 1944 and Malcolm to Gough, 24 and 29 April 1944; LHCMA, Edmonds Mss, II/1/45a, Gough to Edmonds, 22 May 1923; Farrar-Hockley, *Goughie*, p.228; Malcolm, diary, 13 and 28 August 1916 and 28 November 1917; DAG, Hubert to Dorothea, 21 August 1916; RA, Geo V, Q.832/294, Gough to Wigram, 7 January 1917; Congreve, diary, 7 April 1916; PRO, Cab 45/193, Maxse to Edmonds, 7 October 1934; Gough, *Fifth Army*, pp.143, 151–2, 228; Gough, *Soldiering On*, pp.131–2

33 PRO, Cab 45/193, Hodgson to Edmonds, 1 December 1926

34 Travers, *How the War Was Won*, pp.50–109.

35 ibid, p.149, 175–82; Prior and Wilson, *Command*, pp.394–8

Quotations from the Royal Archives appear by gracious permission of Her Majesty the Queen. Quotations from other Crown Copyright material in the Public Record Office appear by permission of the Controller of Her Majesty's Stationery Office. Grateful acknowledgment is also given for permission to consult and quote from archives in the care of the Trustees of the Imperial War Museum; the Trustees of the Beaverbrook Foundation; the Clerk of the Records and the House of Lords Record Office; the Staff College Library; and the Trustees of the Liddell Hart Centre for Military Archives, King's College, London. Particular acknowledgment is given to the assistance of Mrs Denise Boyes (Hubert Gough Mss); the late Mrs Diana Pym (Diana and Dorothea Gough Mss); Captain Dugald Malcolm (Malcolm Mss); and Major A C J Congreve (Congreve Mss) in enabling consultation of archives remaining in private hands.

BRIAN BOND
Liddell Hart and the First World War

When the First World War began Basil Hart had just completed his first year at Cambridge reading History. In his initial reactions he was typical of thousands of middle-class, ex-public schoolboys: patriotic, idealistic and anxious to prove himself in combat before the war's anticipated early conclusion. On his own admission a spoilt 'mother's boy' who had outgrown his strength, Basil at first enjoyed the rigours of officer training in England and was fortunate to arrive on the Somme, still 'all quiet', in the autumn of 1915. 'It reminds one most of a great picnic,' he wrote cheerfully to his parents in September. In mid-October he was struck low by a sudden fever and had difficulty in persuading the doctors not to send him home. His second tour of duty later that winter introduced him to the mud and nerve-shattering noise of the Ypres salient. After a brief spell in the front line, which he privately transformed into heroic mode, he was concussed by a shell exploding above the entrance to his shallow dugout. This time he raised no objection to an immediate return to England.

As with so many of his contemporaries who survived combat, the war made a profound impression on Basil's conception of his own character (which he was already analysing in 'notes for history'), and his attitude to armed conflict. Yet, when he came to write his memoirs in the 1960s, he devoted only a few pages to the critical experiences in 1915 and 1916 which had fundamentally shaped his outlook and his career[1]. Moreover, his surprisingly brief account of his experiences in the front line, and particularly the reasons for his rapid evacuation to the rear on all three occasions, is cool, detached and – in modern parlance – economical with the truth. What was the precise nature of Basil's wounds and disabilities? Was the damage he suffered more psychological than physical? What were the immediate and more lasting effects of experiences seemingly bordering on the traumatic? These questions preoccupied and baffled Liddell Hart's only son, Adrian, in his later years and have recently been subjected to close and imaginative scrutiny by his biographer, Alex Danchev[2].

Danchev rightly devotes the most thorough discussion to Liddell Hart's third and final experience of front-line combat – on the Somme near Fricourt between mid-June and 18 July 1916. Liddell Hart was fortunate indeed to be in reserve for the first attack when his battalion, 9th KOYLI suffered very heavy casualties, but he went up later that day and fifty years later was still disputing Lance Spicer's right to temporary command of the company rather than himself. His physical and mental ordeal occurred – or culminated – between 16 and 18 July at the northern end of the devastated charnel house of Mametz Wood. In the darkness of the wood Liddell Hart suffered flesh wounds in a heavy bombardment and then was badly gassed with phosgene, though unaware of this until later. The effects of gassing were quite sufficient to explain Liddell Hart's subsequent collapse and evacuation to England but, scrutinising his contemporary accounts and later hints – notably in correspondence with General Ironside – Danchev speculates boldly and persuasively that he also experienced a devastating psychological revelation which affected his whole outlook on war and, more specifically, on command. To summarise a complex matter: Liddell Hart had a nightmare vision of being left alone on the battlefield, and in Mametz Wood he apparently yielded to the fear of being afraid. He discovered that he was not physically brave or, in Danchev's phrases, 'he lacked intestinal fortitude. In and out of Mametz Wood the liver had been searched, painfully, and found wanting'[3]. This self-discovery that he lacked physical and mental robustness of the storybook variety is not a matter for censure, particularly for those of us who have not endured a comparable trial, but it was a catastrophic blow to the immature but ambitious subaltern who dreamt of becoming a great commander. Liddell Hart found consolation in becoming a famous writer instead and a demanding critic of commanders ancient and modern (in Ygal Allon's perfect phrase 'The Captain who teaches Generals'), but he was too self-critical and introspective not to be naggingly aware that he had failed to 'hack it' in his brief opportunity on the Somme. Danchev speculates, in my view persuasively, that Liddell Hart was henceforth handicapped in dealing with a profession which prizes physical courage above all other virtues. He was obliged to dispute this priority in his writings and to award the palm to moral courage. I would also invoke in this context his lifelong tendency to lay stress on the role of the individual genius as against the mass; on the crucial importance of surprise and psychological unsettling of the enemy; and on the ideal of winning battles without bloodshed. He was reluctant to admit that, even when his ideals were most nearly realised, for example in France in May 1940, a great deal of hard fighting and bloodshed was still unavoidable.

During the war, however, Liddell Hart's obligatory withdrawal from combat did not entail a sudden evaporation of patriotic idealism and uncritical reverence for the British high command. Quite the contrary, as is now well-known, though the booklet remained unpublished, while convalescing in the autumn of 1916 he wrote a eulogy entitled 'Impressions of the Great British Offensive on the Somme by a Company Commander who saw three and a half weeks of it'. As I commented when writing on Liddell Hart's military thought in 1977, 'there could hardly be a more comprehensive catalogue of the assumptions about British generalship in the First World War which he would denounce with increasing severity for the remainder of his career'[4].

A few phrases must suffice to convey the tone of this youthful effusion: he praised 'the amazing perfection of our organisation which in its generalship and staff work were super German'. The Somme area was well chosen for the offensive and the strategy was masterly. Sir Douglas Haig was 'the greatest general Britain had ever owned'. 'Whilst not all our staff are brilliant, it is safe to say that 90 per cent of our general staff officers are really brilliant men, with quite a large number amongst them who have a genius for war . . . We have produced fully a hundred first-rate generals.' While he acknowledged that war, as waged on the Western Front, is 'horrible and ghastly beyond all imagination of the civilian', he was still able to conclude that 'with all its faults and horrors, it is above all a man's life, in the fullest and deepest sense of the term[5]'. How can we account for the complete sea-change in his views of British strategy and tactics, and above all of British generalship, which occurred in the 1920s, hardened in his intensive writing on the war in the early 1930s and never significantly changed thereafter?

It could be argued that in his own brief experience, particularly on 1 July 1916, he had seen enough tactical ineptitude with its horrific cost in lives, to justify an obsession with improving the quality of professional officers and the theoretical and practical development of tactics. These concerns he shared with a whole generation of surviving junior officers including Bernard Law Montgomery, though going beyond most of them in his emphasis on tanks as a war-winning weapon which would also be more economical with soldiers' lives.

We must surely, however, take into account a number of other factors relating to Liddell Hart's post-war career and the influence of individuals in explaining his transformation from near-idolatry of the generals to harsh and unremitting criticism. The following seems to me a significant, but not necessarily exhaustive, list.

Soon after the war Liddell Hart came under the powerful influence of the Army's most original, irreverent and iconoclastic thinker, J F C Fuller, already a colonel and his senior by twelve years[6]. Fuller had little patience with senior officers less intelligent than himself (i.e. nearly everybody), and few were spared his scathing sarcasm. Liddell Hart, though possibly less arrogant, was also unimpressed by the intellectual shortcomings of senior officers whom he met, penning for example a belittling description of General Horne's inability to understand a simple sand-table exercise.

He was also very reluctant to abandon a touching but naive belief in the moral integrity and gentlemanly code of behaviour of senior officers. Thus he was one of those who declared himself shocked by the posthumous publication of Field Marshal Sir Henry Wilson's edited diaries in 1927 –

despite the fact that Wilson had long been known as a notorious gossip, a 'political soldier' and an arch-intriguer.

A quite different consideration is that Liddell Hart shared the conviction common to virtually all military writers and historians of that era that operations should be studied primarily for the 'lessons' that they yielded. He readily took a further step in arguing that it was more rewarding to concentrate on failures and shortcomings since they would produce more valuable lessons. His role as a professional military journalist from 1925 onwards surely reinforced this tendency; indeed he would protest to critics that he had to avoid at all costs appearing to be an apologist or propagandist for the Army or the War Office.

One can only speculate about the precise effects of his enforced departure from the Army on health grounds in 1924, but it clearly freed his egotism and natural critical bent from the severe restraints prevalent within the Service. As Danchev brings out well in his biography, Liddell Hart reluctantly abandoned his dream of becoming a 'Great Captain' and substituted that of 'Great Writer'. By 1930, still aged only 35, he had achieved an international reputation as a military theorist, critic and historian. As Fuller told him, he now had the power to shake the Army Council to its roots[7].

Finally, by 1925, in his little book *Paris* subtitled 'The Future of War' he already displayed the main elements of his methodology or 'keys' to historical development. In his approach, the First World War was depicted as the negation of classical strategy and the fatal aberration from Britain's traditional strategy in particular. In short, Britain's leaders in 1914 had wilfully abandoned her traditional – and economical – maritime strategy in favour of a total commitment to continental war waged by mass conscript armies. One may suggest that it was Liddell Hart's Whig or Liberal sympathies which were appalled as much as his military sensitivity[8]. He saw it as part of his duty as a military critic to warn against the dangers of repeating such a catastrophic mistake; the corollary being that Britain would fight a Second World War with a group of generals who had learnt as little from the First as had Frederick the Great's mule from its campaigns.

Let us turn now to Liddell Hart's sources. The British Cabinet and War Office Papers remained closed throughout his working life, but he enjoyed some unofficial access to them via Brigadier-General Sir James Edmonds and other official historians. He did not read German and even his command of French is uncertain. He therefore depended mainly on published books and journals, especially *The Army Quarterly* (established in 1920) with its summaries of foreign accounts of the war; supplemented by innumerable interviews with participants or witnesses – a source which he exploited brilliantly throughout his life.

Although the thrust of this article is deliberately critical, it needs to be stressed that, given his limited sources and busy working life as a journalist, Liddell Hart's early attempts to provide a structure and an outline for the war as a whole were very successful. His bibliography was impressive; he provided a fair narrative coverage of fronts other than the Western; and above all he developed an attractive style with a plethora of images and metaphors; and with his confident personal judgements well to the fore. But he conspicuously lacked some notable scholarly attributes, such as an interest in past events for their own sakes or a willingness to make substantial alterations in the light of later evidence. Indeed, given his stance as the widely recognised authority whose personal philosophy was bound up with his historical judgements, he found it increasingly difficult to admit to shortcomings in matters of fact or perspective. In his later decades he was committed to a somewhat dogmatic and, on some sensitive issues, even ruthless defence of positions adopted by the early 1930s.

The main works under discussion are *Reputations* (1928), *The Real War* (1930) and *A History of the World War* (1934). The war was depicted, in the latter two volumes, chronologically and geographically in a series of episodic scenes and sketches rather than by an attempt at a sustained narrative of the war as a whole. In this respect he compares unfavourably with C R M F Cruttwell (an Oxford don and ex-combatant) whose substantial single volume treatment, *A History of the Great War*, was first published in 1934[9]. Surprisingly even major campaigns such as the Somme and Passchendaele receive progressively shorter treatment with striking images and phrases substituting for analysis. Above all, the fundamental error of Britain's primary commitment to the Western Front, the unwisdom of the strategy of attrition waged there and the inadequacy of the high command (i.e. Generals Haig and Robertson as Commander-in-Chief and Chief of the Imperial General Staff respectively) are taken as established facts.

If a personal reminiscence may be inserted here, I was flattered, in the 1960s, by Liddell Hart's meticulous 'vetting' of my early forays into the history of the First World War, but also embarrassed by the pressure he placed on me to alter even moderately sympathetic or favourable statements about Haig or Robertson. In some cases I decided to risk his angry reaction by sending off articles or contributions to volumes without first showing them to him. As I now approach the age he was then, I have more understanding of the natural tendency to identify ever more defensively with positions one has taken in print; but even so I must say that Liddell Hart carried this tendency to unusual extremes, perhaps reflecting more deep-seated feelings of insecurity about his career and reputation.

In a perceptive critical essay[10], Hew Strachan has noted the unintentional irony of Liddell Hart's title *The Real War*, published in 1930 during the spate of trench memoirs which really did try to recapture the conditions and experiences of ordinary soldiers. Here, as in his other works, Liddell Hart resolutely (and puzzlingly) set his face against dealing with such emotive personal aspects. Rather he aimed to view the war, loftily, 'as an episode in human history', and to argue that 'the decisive impressions were received and made in the cabinets and the military headquarters'. As Strachan aptly comments, by omitting any glimpse of operations at the tactical level or any depiction of hardship and suffering, Liddell Hart was effectively helping to perpetuate a false image of the war, resting on the wartime claims of politicians and generals. Lord Beaverbrook's volumes might be cited as the supreme example in this genre; namely of the 'battles' waged in Whitehall and at Westminster by politicians to whom the nostalgic line of the wartime song might be applied: 'There was a Front, but damned if we knew where'. In contrast to the generals, however, the politicians who were ultimately responsible for Britain's strategy largely escape Liddell Hart's censure.

By this time (1930), Liddell Hart's main interest in the war and its 'lessons' was clear. He had moved beyond his wartime and early post-war concern with tactics, and had never been much concerned with the broader considerations underlying operations such as munitions, logistics, manpower and morale on the home front. No, his overriding concern was with British strategy (essentially Army or land-based) and the terrible error which he traced back to Sir Henry Wilson (as Director of Military Operations between 1910 and 1914), of committing the small British Expeditionary Force to a mass continental war of attrition. Wilson's original error had been compounded – from December 1915 – by an obstinate and unimaginative Commander-in-Chief, Sir Douglas Haig, abetted by an excessively loyal and single-minded CIGS Sir William Robertson. Liddell Hart's sympathies seem to have lain increasingly (in the post-war 'battle of the memoirs') with David Lloyd George, in the compilation of whose multi-volume account he played an influential role.

Hew Strachan has accurately described *The Real War* as 'a sustained strategical critique'[11], but even as such it is flawed by its emphasis on the (long) period of British failures almost to the exclusion of the final phase of outstanding success in the summer and autumn of 1918. As mentioned earlier, this approach was defended on the grounds that more is to be learned from the study of failures, but one cannot avoid the suspicion that he found British failures more congenial, and was reluctant to confront the awkward facts that the British Army (and the newly constituted Air Force) had improved markedly in 1918, and that Haig and his general headquarters had contributed significantly to the eventual victory.

One explanation for Liddell Hart's concentration on the years of British failure, in the sense that little ground was gained and enormous casualties incurred, might be that he had left the Western Front in July 1916 before the debut of the tank and before the 'learning curve' in such aspects as the roles of artillery, airpower, and combined all-arms tactics had become apparent. But against this, he had ample post-war evidence that such positive improvements had occurred, and indeed made his reputation largely by concentrating on one dramatic facet of British operational innovation – the tank.

A more persuasive insight is Hew Strachan's suggestion that a more sophisticated gambit was adopted[12]. By largely ignoring the successful culminating battles of 1918, Liddell Hart was able to imply a natural progression from the British commanders' incompetence on the Western Front to their conservatism and failure to learn lessons in the 1920s and 1930s. In short, the British Army and its leaders were not up to continental standards and never would be. Britain had been drawn into a continental struggle based on material and manpower attrition rather than on psychological effect and the optimum exploitation of new technology. The obvious inference or 'lesson': that such a costly strategic error must not be repeated, exercised considerable appeal in the 1930s. David Low's cartoon caricature of the Army's leaders as 'Colonel Blimps' reinforced this message. Liddell Hart's alternative national policy was clearly outlined in *The British Way in Warfare* (1932), in which he urged a return to the primacy of a maritime strategy whose main features were economic blockade and reliance on superior naval power to mount amphibious operations in an 'indirect approach' to the enemy's vulnerable coast.[13]

It would be pedantic and 'academic', in the popular sense of 'pointless', to place so much emphasis on the omissions and limitations in Liddell Hart's coverage of the First World War were it not for the pretensions – and enduring influence – of the theories based upon such faulty foundations. Liddell Hart's relative lack of interest in the Eastern Fronts, or other peripheral aspects from a British viewpoint, may be excusable, but it is very strange indeed that he should make such high claims for the decisive effects of the blockade of Germany (in comparison with attrition on the Western Front) without subjecting the whole operation to careful scrutiny[14].

Again, given his youthful eulogy of British generals and staff officers, it is surprising that as a mature writer he should display so little sympathy for commanders confronted with the unexpected conditions of siege warfare on a vast scale, maintained by the near-total mobilisation of industry and manpower. In these conditions the learning process was likely to be slow and costly, but Liddell Hart contended that the principles of military leadership were eternal and could be derived from a study of the 'Great Captains' such as Scipio Africanus ('greater than Napoleon' in Liddell Hart's league table), Maurice de Saxe or Napoleon himself. Sherman was a more recent and more relevant model, but there was much more scope for strategic mobility and an indirect approach in the western theatre of the American Civil War. Also Sherman's deliberate policy of undermining Confederate morale by destroying crops, buildings and communications was at odds with Liddell Hart's essentially humane and moderate philosophy.

Were there, then, any generals or commanders in the First World War who found favour with Liddell Hart? General Sir John Monash appealed to him as an 'outsider' whose background contrasted sharply with the standard British commander. He was Australian, Jewish and a civil engineer. Far from being a handicap, his lack of a Staff College education and failure to jump the usual hurdles of the regular officer's career were believed to bring a fresh and original 'business mentality' to the problems of the Western Front. Danchev also interestingly develops the point that Monash's alleged lack of physical courage in the Gallipoli campaign provided Liddell Hart with a plausible example of a successful commander who lacked the traditional physical leadership qualities but made up for them 'by an uncanny mastery of what was reported and by a masterly organisation of his intelligence'. Above all he displayed moral courage[15].

Two senior British commanders retained Liddell Hart's admiration: Sir Edmund Allenby because he had achieved victory by a brilliant example of strategic mobility in Palestine; and Sir Ian Hamilton because he had failed gallantly in the campaign (Gallipoli) which might have transformed the whole course of the war. But the commander, or at any rate leader, who most closely approached Liddell Hart's ideal was T E Lawrence[16]. His personal qualities and achievements were as remote from those of Haig and other Western Front commanders as could be imagined. Here was a completely unmilitary intellectual and scholar who had proved himself a brilliant leader through strength of character and intelligence; had achieved strategically significant victories through boldness, cunning and mobility rather than in attrition by protracted battles; and had aspired to literary fame by writing his war memoirs, *The Seven Pillars of Wisdom*, on an epic scale. Liddell Hart was too intelligent and too well informed to suggest that Lawrence would have succeeded in a high command on the Western Front (and Lawrence himself stressed that his methods were peculiarly suited to Arabia/Palestine and not of universal validity). Nevertheless, through Liddell Hart's (and others') idealisation of Lawrence and his romantic operations, the notion was firmly implanted that his was the 'real war' or war as it should have been conducted had intelligence and genius been allowed wider play than the sordid, unimaginative slogging match on the Western Front.

One further puzzle or paradox needs to be discussed. As mentioned earlier, Liddell Hart, with one outstanding exception, displayed little interest in the materiel or 'sinews of war' such as guns, munitions and the enormous quantity of stores which had to be transported and replenished in order that the armies could survive, let alone advance. The great exception was, of course, the tank whose utility in the recent war and revolutionary potential Liddell Hart began to extol, under the influence of J F C Fuller, from the early 1920s. The paradox, only to be suggested here, is that in his military career and in civil life alike, Liddell Hart was notoriously unmechanical and impractical. He also, surprisingly, neglected the tactical application of airpower. Such limitations do not necessarily of course invalidate theories based upon observation, reading and reflection, but they should cause us to examine more critically the relationship between the available technology and means of waging war and the theories built upon them. Liddell Hart was by no means unique in his hope that mechanisation would restore mobility and decisiveness, while at the same time greatly reducing casualties, but did he perhaps come to see tanks almost as chess pieces or symbols which would again make possible a conflict between small, high-quality forces in which there would be the opportunity for the superior mind to triumph over matter?

Liddell Hart did not write much specifically on the First World War after 1939 except for the long-gestating first volume of his history of the Royal Tank Corps, *The Tanks* (1959). However, in the same year, he published an important revisionist article 'The Basic Truths of Passchendaele', which served to re-awaken slumbering controversies before the volcanic eruption of these issues in the 1960s[17]. Here was Liddell Hart at his best in puncturing, or at least challenging, myths and errors. He argued convincingly that Haig had not been pressured by the French into launching his ill-fated offensive, nor had he felt obliged to continue it into the autumn to prevent a general French collapse. These were excuses put forward by Haig's supporters after the war. Charteris's reputation was again questioned for providing over-optimistic reports on German casualties which Haig had accepted. More generally, the article raised the complicated issue of comparative casualty statistics on which the chief culprit was said to be the senior British official historian, Sir James Edmonds, who had deliberately 'cooked the books' to suggest that attrition had in fact worked in the Allies' favour[18].

Although he never revisited the First World War to produce a significant publication, Liddell Hart continued to publicise and inculcate his views in various ways. Though some might detect a veiled and calculating motive, it must also be stressed that he was an extremely generous host and a brilliant teacher manqué who delighted in encouraging young scholars and writers to pursue the numerous controversies in military history which had enthralled him for so many years[19]. He thus opened for many of us the dazzling prospect of making our own contributions to living issues whose protagonists we might meet (as I, for example, on one occasion was left alone to entertain 'Boney' Fuller), or at least study their private correspondence in his vast and haphazardly organised archives.

In my own experience, as mentioned earlier, I do not think he found it easy to follow Clausewitz's advice that the wise teacher should be content to guide and stimulate his students' intellectual development but be careful not to lead them by the hand for the rest of their lives[20]. All teachers experience this dilemma in some degree with promising pupils, and Basil was not good at letting go, particularly where the acolyte reached opinions contrary to his own on issues which he regarded as critical and on which his judgement represented 'The Truth'. Nevertheless, while it would be invidious to name names, I can assert with confidence that several of my contemporaries derived tremendous benefits from Liddell Hart's enthusiasm, encouragement and practical help without forfeiting their integrity and independence of mind. This reflection applies even to the highly emotive issues discussed here; namely British strategy and generalship in the First World War.

On the wider 'front' of popular opinion it must be acknowledged that Liddell Hart's unremitting efforts to propagate his interpretation of the First World War have been remarkably successful. In the 1960s his controlling hand and distinctive authorial 'voice' seemed to be omnipresent. Thus he was the consultant or adviser for the BBC's celebrated 'Great War' series, Joan Littlewood's play 'Oh! What a Lovely War', the screening of 'Lawrence of Arabia' and the play 'Ross'. His was the chief inspiration behind Purnell's best-selling part-work series on the First World War.

Moreover in this radical, revisionist decade it was almost obligatory to obtain Liddell Hart's approval and imprimatur for publications on the First World War. Thus he vetted the drafts of Alan Clark's *The Donkeys* and A J P Taylor's irreverent *History* which depicted British Western Front generals as donkeys and the war itself as meaningless; praised Leon Wolff's poignant dirge about the Passchendaele campaign ('In Flanders Fields'), and passed an anathema on John Terraine for his heretical presumption in daring to write sympathetically about Haig. Clinching evidence is provided by Raymond Fletcher, a self-confessed fan of Liddell Hart and a significant contributor to the script of 'Oh! What a Lovely War', who revealingly described the play's message as 'one part me, one part Liddell Hart, the rest Lenin!'[21] Interestingly, in the 1960s Liddell Hart's personal contacts were mostly with Labour politicians concerned with defence issues such as Denis Healey, George Brown, Reginald Paget and Richard Crossman.

Liddell Hart died in January 1970. Nearly thirty years on he is beginning to take his place as an historical figure as distinct from a ubiquitous brooding presence. We can begin to place him as a late Victorian autodidact with a polemical approach to history, grandiose ambitions and excessive confidence in his own judgement. If his various overlapping accounts of the First World War were generally seen to be outdated and of mainly historiographical interest like, say, the war histories of Conan Doyle or John Buchan, there would be no problem. But, due to his immense readability, his Olympian tone and his politically appealing message for a generation which assumes the First World War to be the epitome of vain slaughter and pointlessness, his histories are still reprinted, widely translated and read uncritically. This is anomalous because in the last twenty years or so, since the opening of the Cabinet and War Office Papers, a new generation of scholars such as David French, Peter Simkins, Robin Prior, Trevor Wilson, David Woodward and Ian Beckett (the list could easily be doubled), have truly begun to delineate the 'real war' and, though by no means reaching consensus on the great issues, have moved the debates forward onto ground where archival evidence, historical perspective and reasoned argument are in the ascendancy[22].

Unfortunately, with some honourable exceptions, many popular authors and producers of television documentaries seem to be more than ever obsessed with the Somme, Passchendaele, Haig's generalship and the historical significance of the 'War Poets', or to be more precise, two of them. To hold Liddell Hart primarily responsible for late twentieth-century interpretations of the meaning and relevance of the First World War would be as unreasonable as his indictment of Clausewitz as post-humously responsible for the actual nature of the war itself. Nevertheless, whether we approve or not, it is in large part Liddell Hart's remarkable achievement and legacy that so much of the British discussion of the First World War still takes place in the arena and under the guidelines which he established more than sixty years ago.

Notes

I am grateful to Professor Hew Strachan and Dr Brian Holden Reid for their comments on this paper in draft.

1 B H Liddell Hart, *Memoirs Vol I* (Cassell, 1965) pp.11–28
2 Alex Danchev, *Alchemist of War, The Life of Basil Liddell Hart* (Weidenfeld & Nicolson, 1998)
3 Danchev, pp.47–67
4 Brian Bond *Liddell Hart: A Study of his Military Thought* (Cassell, 1977) pp.15–21
5 Bond, p.18
6 See Brian Holden Reid, 'Fuller and Liddell Hart: a Comparison' in his *Studies in British Military Thought* (Lincoln: University of Nebraska Press, 1998) pp.168–82
7 Fuller quoted in Danchev, p.73
8 For a discussion of Liddell Hart's political inclinations see Brian Holden Reid op cit, pp.187–93

9   Hew Strachan, 'The Real War: Liddell Hart, Cruttwell and Falls' in Brian Bond (ed), *The First World War and British Military History* (Oxford: The Clarendon Press, 1991) pp.41–67

10 ibid, pp.46–7

11 ibid, p.47

12 ibid

13 For criticisms of 'The British Way in Warfare' see Bond, *Liddell Hart* pp.65–85

14 In *The Real War* for example, there are only passing references to the naval blockade of Germany on pp.94, 227 and 336

15 Danchev, pp.66–7. B H Liddell Hart, *Through the Fog of War* (Faber & Faber, 1938) pp.149–51

16 Allenby was allotted an essay in *Reputations* (1928), and all three (Allenby, Hamilton and Lawrence) were discussed in *Through the Fog of War* (1938)

17 Liddell Hart, 'The Basic Truths of Passchendaele' in RUSI *Journal*, November 1959, and my brief comments in Peter H Liddle (ed.), *Passchendaele in Perspective* (Leo Cooper, 1997) p.481

18 M J Williams, 'Thirty Percent: a Study in Casualty Statistics' RUSI *Journal*, February 1964, pp.51–5

19 See the list in Danchev, p.251

20 Michael Howard and Peter Paret (eds), *Carl Von Clausewitz on War* (Princeton University Press, 1976) p.141

21 See Alex Danchev, 'Bunking and Debunking' in Brian Bond (ed.) *The First World War and British Military History*, p.282

22 See Brian Bond 'A Victory Worse than a Defeat?', Liddell Hart Lecture at King's College, London 17 November 1997 (printed 1998)

RICHARD BRYSON
The Once and Future Army

Time present and time past
Are both perhaps present in time future,
And time future contained in time past . . .
. . . And do not call it fixity,
Where past and future are gathered.[1]

INTRODUCTION

Britain largely holds to a popular view of the First World War rooted in the truisms of mud, blood and red-tabbed donkeys[2]. There has rarely been a sense of victory associated with the war's conclusion. Nevertheless, a victory it was, and a victory in which the British Army played a leading role. This summer and autumn, as we have passed the 80th anniversaries of the nine great battles with which the German Army was finally defeated, the British Army might justifiably have chosen to commemorate the climacteric events of 1918 with pride and conviction. It did not do so. Indeed, one garrison opted instead to host a National Theatre revival of Joan Littlewood's 'Oh! What a Lovely War', a fine piece of theatre, but a flawed and superficial piece of history telling us more about the prejudices of the 1960s than ever it does about the First World War[3].

Today, as the British Army continues a vast and accelerating process of reorganisation, at the heart of its conceptual approach to Force Development lies the tenet that its core role should remain one of 'warfighting'[4]. During the Second World War, the Army played second fiddle to the RAF and, to a very large extent, was spared the need to face the main weight of the enemy[5]. The demonstrable warfighting successes of 1918, however, *were* achieved against the main weight of the German Army – a first class opponent – representing an unparalleled scale of effort for the British Army and the only time in modern history when it has acted as the principal focus for national effort in a continental war[6]. And yet, the First World War is generally only mentioned within the modern British Army as shorthand for a style of warfare deemed to be the antithesis of our current doctrine. The inflexibilities of mind and procedure associated with the attritional warfare of the Western

25

Front form a canvas on which is painted a view of future conflict that seeks to shatter the opponent's will to fight without necessarily attacking his strengths, thereby achieving success for the least cost in blood and treasure.

Modern British doctrine is vested in the 'Manoeuvrist Approach to Operations' and its command philosophy in 'Mission Command'[7]. In essence, this approach was arrived at during the 1980s and was, in many important ways, an interpretation of American doctrinal development during the 1970s, which had initially centred closely on studies into German Army doctrine and tactical methods in the Second World War. Such studies underpinned the American Army's physical and spiritual *renaissance* following the disasters of Vietnam[8]. However, it is clear that the principles and language of German doctrine, which may be traced back to 1806, were largely developed, formalised and refined during (and immediately after) the First World War[9]. Hence, and with the deepest irony, the genealogy of the British Army's Manoeuvrist Approach may be traced back to its German adversary on the Western Front. The First World War merits careful and objective study within the British Army, since it is critical to any evaluation of the British Army's current doctrine and its associated command philosophy. Without such evaluation, doctrine becomes dogma.

WORLD WAR ONE: THE STRATEGIC CONTEXT

Britain approached the First World War seeking to avoid a continental commitment for her Army. The unofficial Haldane reforms of 1906 provided the capability to deploy a small Expeditionary Force, but its strength was diluted as it fulfilled its primary task of training drafts for service around the Empire, leaving Home Service battalions 'squeezed like lemons'[10]. The Army was hampered in its preparations for war through lack of a '. . . clarity of purpose . . . A new General Staff [formed 1908], new infantry divisions [the division was adopted as a warfighting structure only in 1907], falling budgets and lack of a strategic direction from the top were conditions under which this excellent British Army prepared for the war.'[11] Even as late as November 1913 Lord Esher was warning the Cabinet that '. . . the British Army existed for garrison duty, overseas reinforcement, and for use as an auxiliary of the Royal Navy.'[12]

The Army's need for a unifying sense of purpose has long been felt. When Field Marshal Lord Milne became CIGS in 1926, one of his first actions was to draft a memorandum asking the Secretary of State for War to define the tasks for which the Army existed. It was not forthcoming, leading one reviewer to comment that: 'The most important cause of

26

the Army's unpreparedness at the start of the Second World War lay in protracted military and political indecision over its role.'[13] Similarly, the Army asked, in 1995, for '. . . a clear and publicly stated view of the Army's purpose.'[14] Policy in the current strategic environment does not provide this, adding new language to the debate but providing no solution to the often conflicting demands of warfighting and the plethora of activities associated with Britain's 'wider security interests'[15]. The tension between the 'continental strategy' and the 'maritime strategy' was manifest before and during the First World War in the division between 'easterners' and 'westerners'[16].

Three British war aims evolved between 1914 and 1916: to hold the Entente together; to vanquish the Central Powers (Germany in particular), and to be the strongest of the belligerents at the peace table. These aims were intended to avoid the much-disliked necessity of conscription and to permit the possibility of pursuing the 'British way' wherever possible[17]. Kitchener raised the volunteer New Armies to a timetable designed to ensure that they would be committed in 1917 to deliver the *coup de grâce* to the Germans once France and Russia had weakened them sufficiently.

Events were to prove, however, that although the war would be difficult to win on the Western Front, it would be very easy to lose it there. French losses in 1914 and the Russian 'great retreat' of 1915 brought Kitchener's timetable forward, and the Battle of Loos in September 1915 is significant as the 'halfway point' in the progressive conversion of British policymakers to the belief that the Western Front was the point of main effort. Coalition war, therefore, entailed Britain's gradual assumption of more and more of the burden of land fighting and, in 1916, ensured that the New Armies were committed on the Somme to relieve German pressure on the French at Verdun. Kitchener did not like this, but saw that it could not be avoided, drawing from him the resigned assertion that 'we must make war as we must; not as we should like'[18]. By the end of 1916 the United States dictated that the Western Front was to remain the main theatre if a large American Expeditionary Force was to be deployed[19]. The need to hold the Entente together after November 1914 became almost the driving force behind the British war effort as hope – or the possibility – of pursuing any alternative strategy receded. Britain was drawn inexorably into the provision of a major continental army without the mechanisms in place for doing so.

Space precludes a chronological history of the BEF's operations on the Western Front. It is helpful, however, to outline a number of significant precepts here before moving on to look more closely at the development of British fighting methods during the war. Perhaps the most important factor to be remembered is that the British Army was the nation's major effort in World War One, and fought to defeat the main weight of the German Army in what became the principal theatre of war. It is a common misconception that British commanders were uniquely profligate with the lives of their British and Dominion soldiers, often unnecessarily so. However, the BEF's loss rate is not significantly different, for example, to that of Montgomery's Army Group in the North West European campaign from 1944 to 1945. What is markedly different is the scale of its commitment. At El Alamein, the eleven British divisions of the Eighth Army faced four weak German divisions and a further eight Italian divisions of varying strength and quality, at a time when 171 German and sixty-one other Axis divisions were operating on the Eastern Front. The BEF of 1914–1918 deployed at its peak up to sixty-six divisions, in five armies, with a total manpower sometimes over two million. During the German offensives of March-April 1918 the British armies engaged a total of 109 German divisions, and ninety-nine divisions during the final offensive from August 1918 to the Armistice[20].

The lack of any precedent or mechanism for the tremendous growth of the BEF (the largest and most comprehensive single organisation of any sort that Britain has ever created) was deeply problematical in itself. Critically, the New Armies were largely required to train themselves, bringing to the task strong civilian preconceptions as to how an army should operate and behave. This was often at odds with the ethos, character and capabilities of the Regular Army and the demands of warfighting. Training necessarily concentrated on the specific requirements of trench warfare, at the expense of the principles and skills needed in mobile warfare.

Only once the New Armies were committed to operations on the Somme were their shortcomings exposed, ensuring that their subsequent progress and development would come the hard way – in action. After the disaster of the first day of the Somme, the learning curve accelerated rapidly, much of the technical improvement simply following from the re-introduction of established tactics, as the realisation grew that these were still relevant to the new conditions as well as the new technologies of warfare. It should also be remembered that the First World War saw commanders deprived both of a truly mobile arm and, in ever more dispersed and protracted battles, largely bereft of the communications essential to facilitating situational awareness and timely decision-making[21]. Seldom has the critical interaction between weapons technologies and information technologies been so markedly out of step, as firepower forged ahead both in range and lethality, whilst wireless communications were at best rudimentary even in 1918. The repercussions caused by technological mismatch during the First World War were considerable, those for the future – as information technology rapidly outpaces weapons technology – have been little explored. This drift between technological capabilities is loosely represented in the following schematic:

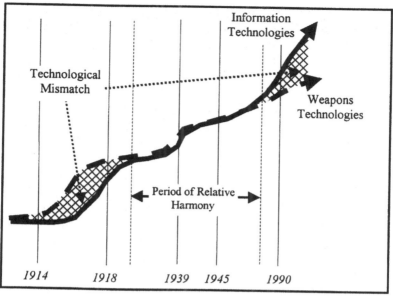

The Mismatch Between Information and Weapons Technologies 1914–1918, and in the Present Day.

In general, the rate of technological change during World War One is widely acknowledged to have far outstripped the pace of change through World War Two and the Cold War. Indeed, the first two decades of the twentieth century witnessed the development of what has been termed the 'Modern Style of Warfare'[22]. Consideration of the British Army's performance in the First World War must recognise, therefore, that it was in the midst of '. . . its transformation from a colonial defence force to one capable of defeating a first-class continental opponent and that its institutions were under a particular strain because of the rapid changes in fire-tactics that followed the experience of the war in Manchuria.'[23]

TACTICAL AND OPERATIONAL DEVELOPMENTS

On 1 September 1918 Major General John Campbell, GOC 31st Division held a conference with his brigade and battalion commanders to discuss operations over the last two days of August, during which the Division had taken part in operations around Ypres in XV Corps, with the Second Army. His brief speaking notes survive, and highlight succinctly his thoughts on the differences between trench and open warfare. He speaks of using the seeing eye rather than the blind eye, and of maintaining a

29

concentrated rather than a diffused mind. He explains that trench warfare stultifies and limits initiative, is characterised by artillery barrages and waves, rigid boundaries and a concern for flanks, and leads to a general cramping of style. It is the province of synchronisation and timetables. In contrast, for the new conditions of open warfare, he emphasises artillery *support*, flexible formations, flexible boundaries, initiative and a general flexibility of style. There should be no asking for or waiting on orders. Platoons should use their scouts to find ways of outflanking the enemy to take positions in rear, with units moving fast and striking hard[24].

The 31st Division is not generally one of the Western Front's most notable formations. It had suffered one of the greatest disasters on 1 July 1916, in front of Serre. It had been used sparingly through 1917 (not being involved at 3rd Ypres at all). Yet by 1918 its commander encapsulates in one set of bullet points a marked change in doctrinal emphasis that had been effected in the BEF between 1916 and 1918. It is not simply a list of the characteristics of trench and open warfare. It summarises the essential differences in philosophy between our modern views of the Manoeuvrist Approach to warfare and the costly attritional warfare it seeks to avoid, reminding us that both are essential and inseparable elements of warfighting.

The November 1918 reissue of the Army Stationery Store's publication SS135[25], 'The Division in Attack', echoes the truth at the heart of GOC 31st Division's notes, warning that there had been: '. . . a tendency in the present war to look upon trench warfare and open warfare as two separate things. This has led to a disregard of many of the fundamental principles, laid down in the training manuals issued before this war, as being inapplicable to trench warfare. Most noticeable have been the neglect of the principle of distribution in depth both in attack and defence, the loss of individual initiative, and the exaggeration of the value of ground for its own sake.'[26]

It is significant that the first iteration of SS135 in December 1916 had divided offensive operations into action against prepared positions, action against hasty defensive positions, and open warfare. This attitude reinforced the New Army tendency to concentrate in its early training on the special conditions of trench warfare. Much of this training underestimated the value of initiative and self-reliance on the battlefield, substituting firepower in its place. On July 1916 the payback for these shortcomings was catastrophic. However, the reaction was swift and the British Army learned and rediscovered a great many things through the remainder of the Somme fighting. New technologies and methods emerged and the process of trial, experimentation, rediscovery and dissemination began to reap rewards.

Much of this development may be followed through the activities of one senior commander, General Sir Ivor Maxse[27]. Maxse merits close attention for three principal reasons:

- He was an avid hoarder and his files in the Imperial War Museum contain a rich record of his life as a brigade commander before the war and as a brigade, divisional and corps commander during the war itself, on the Somme, at 3rd Ypres and in the centre of Gough's Fifth Army during the German Offensive in March 1918.
- He was influential in doctrinal debate and reform both before and during the war, although he is far from being unique in this respect. His penchant for visiting neighbouring formations, to garner their commanders' ideas and to spread his own, made him the natural choice to create and fulfil the new appointment of Inspector General Training in July 1918 to develop and co-ordinate tactical concepts and training across the Armies[28].
- After the war, Maxse was an important early patron to Liddell Hart. Indeed, the latter's 'man in the dark' and 'expanding torrent' theories of infantry tactics drew heavily on Maxse's 'Soft Spots' paper, which will be examined later.

A number of key issues closely identified with Maxse and central to consideration of the BEF's fighting power will be discussed in this section, with close reference to current concepts for the Future Army[29].

The 'Principle of Four': Maxse held a vested interest in a structural principle common to both periods, which may be referred to as the 'Principle of Four'. In its current form, this states that 'As a general principle one force element is required to provide covering fire, or fire potential, while the other moves – thus requiring two force elements. If more than a single tactical option is to be available to a commander and momentum developed, then a third force element, a second echelon, is required. Finally, a fourth element is needed to provide a true reserve, a need reinforced by the wide dispersion that will be a feature of the future battlefield. It may be possible and desirable to substitute indirect fire for one of the force elements . . . ('3+1') . . . therefore a formation or unit will consist of a minimum of four force elements – one of which might be an indirect fire element at formation level.'[30] This principle has provoked considerable and often heated debate in its present form, drawing the frequent criticism that it is too prescriptive, yet as a doctrinal concept it is mirrored closely by debate before the First World War and borne out by subsequent developments in the BEF.

In December 1911 Maxse (then commanding the 1st Guards' Brigade in Aldershot) presented in an RUSI lecture a view of battalion organisation as developed by a growing reform movement of, primarily, regimental officers[31]. The basis of their argument was that the contemporary eight-company organisation was inefficient and curtailed the development of true leadership qualities in regimental officers and NCOs. The presentation was detailed and thorough, with General Sir John French in the Chair. Maxse outlined what he termed 'seven platitudinous military axioms', which the existing organisation could not accommodate in practice. These axioms reflect timeless concerns, and at their core are the related beliefs that the object of organisation in peace is to facilitate a smooth transition to war with the minimum of disruption, while those who will command any unit from the section upwards in war must be responsible for training it in peace. These thoughts were elaborated in the body of the presentation:

> At the present moment I submit that our battalion organisation is many years behind our fire tactics, that the latter are as good as or better than any in Europe, but that we are failing to develop them along progressive lines, because we are hampered and thrown back [by the current system] which destroys the initiative of subordinates . . . It is unsuitable to the wide and deep formations which modern weapons compel a battalion to assume in an attack, and it is positively detrimental to co-operative fire tactics, which are based upon the initiative of individuals . . .

Maxse continued with a critique showing how the Army 'unconsciously' organised in peace for disorganisation in war, through cadreisation and through not allowing those who would fight together in war to live and train together in peace. The proposed solution was a four-company organisation, each containing four platoons of four sections – a system held to represent the optimum span of command[32]. It ensured that officers commanded *units* in battle, leaving the NCOs to command *men* (although this was in no way meant to weaken the special relationship between platoon commanders and their platoons). All the specialists, bandsmen and others who did not fight in the companies in war were extracted to create a headquarters 'section' some two hundred or more strong. Maxse claimed for the proposed four-company organisation '. . . a capacity to strike hard, and strike with cumulative intensity throughout an attack . . .' and concluded his presentation with the thought '. . . either do this thing quite thoroughly or do not touch it at all.' The proposed structure was tested through the formation of experimental companies at Aldershot. The Army Council, following the autumn manoeuvres of 1913 and the enthusiastic reports submitted by the relevant commanders, subsequently endorsed it and the re-organisation was largely completed throughout the Regular and Territorial Armies by the outbreak of the war.

In battle, the system of fours proved robust and flexible, adapting to changing circumstances and new technologies. A truism emerged, that

'. . . a single line will fail; two lines will usually fail; three lines will sometimes fail, but four lines will usually succeed'.[33] This maxim is representative of the early fighting on the Somme but, as new techniques emerged and the creeping barrage was developed, we can identify the substitution of mutually supporting *elements* in more flexible, looser formations rather than inflexible waves. The initial publication of SS135 'Instructions for the Training of Divisions for Offensive Operations' in December 1916 and SS143 'Instructions for the Training of Platoons for Offensive Operations' in February 1917 emphasised the platoon as the principal building-brick and established a system whereby each section specialised, either as a rifle, Lewis gun, rifle grenade or bomber section. Additionally, a minimum of two riflemen per section were to be trained as scouts.

The system of fours extended up to the brigade level, with brigades consisting of four battalions. The perennial problem of communications largely denied the brigade commander access to timely, flexible artillery fire and the option of '3+1' did not exist. As the emphasis on the infantry fighting their way with their own weapons gathered pace in 1917, the four-battalion structure was found to assist with the maintenance of momentum. Better communications were available at divisional level, and '3+1' was very much the basis for operations, since the artillery provided the fourth element around which the commander could manoeuvre his three brigades. Only one division – the New Zealanders – had four brigades, its commander finding this problematical both in trench routine and on the battlefield. In trenches, the fourth brigade was routinely called on by higher formations as a source of labour, to the detriment of morale. More significantly, on the battlefield the division was awkward to handle[34]. As wireless communications became more capable in the later stages of the war – and certainly thereafter – '3+1' would become a real possibility at brigade level and a reality in World War Two[35].

By 1918 the pattern of offensive operations was well established, embodying true all-arms cooperation and based on the ability of the infantry's looser, more flexible formations to manoeuvre to exploit success. The platoon was by now established for two sections of riflemen and two sections of Lewis guns and instructed, in the updated SS135 'The Division in Attack' of November 1918 to '. . . fight its way forward by means of its own weapons, making use of all cover available to facilitate its advance'.[36] Rifle grenades, rifle smoke grenades and Stokes mortars (attached from the brigade light TM company) completed the platoon armoury.

It seems bitterly ironic that, as the British armies in France were establishing the means for successful offensive operations, continued political intriguing aimed specifically at 'keeping the War Office short of men' should break up the proven structure of fours at brigade level during the winter of 1917–18. The government rejected Haig's recommendation as to how the restructuring should be implemented, but delayed the establishment of its own plan, with near-fatal results. The bulk of the reorganisation was undertaken in February 1918 – within days of the German spring offensive. A recent study of the War Cabinet's dissembling draws a stark conclusion:

> Brigades were now of a different size (three battalions instead of four), of different composition, with unfamiliar men mixed up in units. New rosters of duty had to be drawn up; new friendships had to be made; new feelings of implicit trust would need time to grow; the ease which comes from familiarity between commanders and staff, officers, NCOs and men all had to be renurtured.[37]

The net effect on the British formations (the Commonwealth formations were not affected) was that, having brought the art of generating fluidity and momentum on the battlefield to a high state of efficiency, they lacked the fourth element vital to the maintenance of momentum and to the provision of endurance. This acted as a significant constraint on British formations in their development of techniques for *exploitation*, an area in which experimentation was beginning to bear fruit through increased mechanisation allied to a growing willingness to push on into the enemy's depth.

Mission Command: Mission Command is now the established command philosophy of the British Army, and '. . . has three enduring tenets: timely decision-making, the importance of understanding a superior commander's intention, and, by applying this to one's own actions, a clear responsibility to fulfil that intention'.[38] Modern doctrine acknowledges earlier examples of Mission Command at work, but identifies the style of command of the First World War closely with rigid, centralised control, contrasting this unfavourably with the decentralisation and initiative required by Mission Command[39]. This is a false picture, since British commanders in the First World War undoubtedly understood the central elements of what is now called Mission Command before the war, but would take time to bring the wartime volunteers and conscripts up to the level of ability required to implement it on the battlefield. The language of the First World War centres on the word 'initiative', but the principles expressed are markedly similar to those contained within Mission Command.

In November 1914 the RUSI *Journal* published the text of a lecture delivered by one of Maxse's subordinates to London units of the Territorial Force entitled 'The Four-Company Battalion in Battle'. It describes a battalion on an offensive operation and is interesting from two points of view. In the first instance, the commanding officer issues a clear scheme of manoeuvre to his company commanders, and the author notes that '. . . there is no stereotyped form of attack.' Secondly '. . . the colonel does not tell a company officer <u>how</u> he wants a thing done. He simply tells him <u>what</u> he wants done and leaves it to him how to do it.'[40]

Haig gave his view on initiative in a written critique of orders that Maxse and his brigade staff had produced as Syndicate 4 on a Command Staff Exercise in May 1914: 'While on the one hand it is right not to interfere with the initiative of subordinate commanders, on the other hand you as C-in-C Expeditionary Force must take your share of responsibility and tell your subordinates what your plan is and what you want him to do.'[41] During the war, as the Army grew at an alarming rate, many publications sought to pass on something of the ethos of the pre-war Regular Army to the 'duration only' men. One such publication was directed at young officers on joining their regiment, and included, in a chapter 'On the Art of Command', the comments that:

> What we should aim at is cheery and willing obedience, and not the slavish fulfilment of the letter of the order. When you have received an order which your platoon is to carry out, I am sure that you resent being told what to do, but prefer to perform it your own way. Do as you would be done by, and don't interfere too much with your Section commanders . . . the principal object of all tactical instruction is to train officers and men to act when they have no superior on the spot to refer to . . . always encourage initiative and love of responsibility on the part of your subordinates . . . If you are ever in doubt as to whether an order still holds good, ask yourself: Was the officer responsible for the order in possession of the main facts as I now know them to be when he issued it?[42]

Maxse aired his views on the subject before the war in a suggested amendment to the draft of 'Infantry Training 1914': '. . . Subordinates should be given definite tasks and made to accomplish them by their own methods . . . Those company commanders who deliberately create tactical opportunities which, in peacetime, compel their subordinates to think and act for themselves, produce self-reliant leaders of men who will prove invaluable in war.'[43] This was to be the cornerstone of his vigorous approach to training throughout the war. It is manifest in the emphasis placed upon low-level initiative within the November 1918 reissue of SS135, which states:

> The successful conduct of a battle depends upon the rapidity with which local successes are gained and exploited . . . It is absolutely essential, therefore, that commanders of all grades should be able

quickly to grasp the salient features of a tactical situation and to act with boldness and decision. Training must aim at the production of commanders and leaders . . . Initiative must not be cramped by too rigid orders and methods of instruction . . . The initiative, self-confidence and offensive power of the infantry must be developed to the utmost.[44]

Recce Pull: Developing doctrine within Future Army work emphasises the value of infiltration and exploitation tactics in the concept of 'Recce Pull'. This is provisionally defined as 'A concept inherent in the manoeuvrist ethos by which the enemy's vulnerabilities and weaknesses are identified and exploited rapidly in order to maximise the effect of our own combat power and shatter the enemy's cohesion. In simplistic terms it could be defined as: "The considered exploitation of opportunity".'[45]

Similarly, as the BEF increasingly achieved the ability to break into defensive positions and set the battlefield in motion, commanders began immediately to explore methods of exploiting initial successes in the absence of universal communications or an effective manoeuvre arm. GOC 31st Division's views, discussed earlier, were commonplace in 1918 and found expression in a growing emphasis on penetration and exploitation, with commanders realising the value of assigning wider frontages to units and formations, in order to allow greater freedom of manoeuvre[46]. These tactics placed a high premium on initiative at all levels and the ability to 'stalk' and outflank points of resistance, as it was found that the Germans tended to 'chuck it' when in danger of being cut off[47].

Such tactics developed and prospered under different names in different formations, but eventually evolved into a full-blown doctrine, though this was not published formally until January 1919 when Maxse, as IGT, issued Training Leaflet 13, 'Soft Spots – an Example of Minor Tactics'.[48] Its essence lay in the finding and infiltration of gaps or weaknesses in the enemy's defences, a determination to avoid reinforcing against resistance or delaying to organise a 'set piece', and the development of confidence in pushing on and allowing flanks to be protected by following units:

In attack, the enemy's defences will not be equally strong along the whole front. There will be 'soft spots'. These we must find, penetrate and exploit. We cannot expect to find the 'soft spot' without fighting for it, unless favoured by ground or mist . . . The IMMEDIATE EXPLOITATION of these 'soft spots' influences the course of the battle on the whole front. Originally found by a company, platoon or even a section, and widened into gaps by bold and skilful exploitation, they admit the advance of the reserves and provide the suitable moment for the decisive attack.

The 'soft spots' tactic had begun to formalise on the Somme, when it was found that bold and aggressive reconnaissance or patrolling by section and platoon scouts beyond the objective following a successful assault could often be followed up with further, opportunistic advances while the enemy was off-balance. It was also beneficial in identifying enemy strongpoints prior to subsequent advances. One early reference to such tactics is made in a 'Tactical Memorandum' circulated by GOC XIV Corps dated 3 August 1916 which states 'Every advance except the first assault should be preceded by Battle Patrols to avoid "fire surprise".'[49]

The publication of SS119 in July 1916, 'Preliminary Notes on the Tactical Lessons of the Recent Operations', gave additional impetus with a section on patrol work stressing the value of active patrolling and reconnaissance, commenting that 'superiority in patrol work will greatly facilitate a further advance.' In December 1917, SS195 'Scouting and Patrolling' stated that 'Every Section of the Platoon should, if possible, maintain a pair of men who have received further training in Scouting, Observing and Sniping.' It provided a full syllabus of training for the battalion scout officer, sergeant and corporal, and for company and section scouts. The pamphlet noted that 'it is with the advent of more open warfare that their sphere of usefulness increases, until it becomes of vital importance.'

During the middle period of the war, the infantry lacked integral firepower and relied heavily on protective artillery barrage fire. As the infantry consolidated on a captured objective they would often require *pre-arranged* protective fire tasks from the artillery to disrupt enemy counter-attacks, and this necessarily prohibited exploitation beyond the objective. Only as the infantry acquired greater firepower, and artillery began to focus more on depth objectives, reserves, command centres and counter-battery work would infiltration and exploitation tactics come into their own. Thus, by April 1917, the 12th (Eastern) Division emphasised in its training for the Arras battles the '. . . exploiting [of] success using patrols, and using the platoon as a "self-contained fighting unit."'[50] In the final battles of 1918, mechanisation assisted the maintenance of momentum and the process of exploitation as 'light' tanks, armoured cars, motorcycle machine guns and ad hoc APCs were pressed into service to improve the rate and depth of penetration.

Deep Battle: Current doctrine identifies a framework for battle of deep, close and rear operations[51]. Such definitions are lacking in pre-First World War publications, although the nature of rear operations is implicit in contemporary considerations of 'strategical security' within the principles of war. Close battle would have required little clarification at the time, being the essence of warfare as it was then taught and studied. Deep operations, however, require closer scrutiny. Modern deep operations are a balance of deep fires and deep manoeuvre, applied against the opponent's centre of gravity[52]. Their growing significance is diminishing the traditional emphasis upon the primacy of close operations. World War One has a pivotal significance in the historical development of deep operations. Before the war, deep operations consisted primarily of deep manoeuvre – from the 'ordinary' and 'extraordinary' forces of Sun Tzu, to the Grande Chevauchée of the Plantagenet kings across the heartlands of France to the irregular actions of the American Civil War. The special conditions of the First World War brought a temporary end to such operations, certainly on the Western Front. Firepower was the key to the re-establishment of mobility during the war, and this was based primarily on deep fire, as the technological means became available – especially through developments in air support, counter-battery and locating capabilities. Ironically, the ability to develop mobility into exploitation was limited by the relative immobility of artillery and its cumbersome logistic support.

On 31 July 1916 Maxse (as GOC 18th Division) submitted a short report to HQ Fourth Army in response to a private request from Rawlinson for divisional commanders' views on the Somme fighting to date. Maxse included the comment that 'I rather feel we are trying to do every attack by barrage . . . it would sometimes be preferable to attack without a preliminary intensive bombardment, and only put a barrage on *when* the attack has commenced, and then only to stop reinforcements being sent up to the point attacked.'[53] The improvements in artillery techniques that would eventually facilitate such tactics are amply covered elsewhere[54]. It is significant, however, that the requirement to implement such improvements was being voiced at this relatively early stage. Birch, Haig's artillery commander, maintained that his role as given by Haig had been to re-organise and strengthen the artillery such that it could defeat the German artillery through surprise attack at any point in the line, without the attendant need to undertake any obvious artillery reinforcement beforehand[55]. The key to the development of deep battle was the shift in emphasis from 'destruction' to 'neutralisation' and from 'barrage fire' to 'artillery support'.

Tempo: In current doctrine, the key to shattering the opponent's cohesion is tempo, '. . . the rate or rhythm of activity relative to the enemy, within tactical engagements and battles and between major operations. It incorporates the capacity of the force to transition from one operation of war to another.'[56] Tempo was a critical factor in Haig's choice of Ypres for his 1917 offensive, since the difficulty of reinforcement and resupply on the limited lines of communication available to the Germans entailed their vulnerability to a series of short, sharp actions delivered by fresh British forces against increasingly stale German formations[57].

In the operations of the 'One Hundred Days', tempo was a key consideration, the summation of the tremendous wartime advances made in the science of firepower, allowing Haig the ability to switch the point of attack repeatedly. The in-place forces at a given point of attack were able to switch to offensive operations with a minimum of reinforcement, facilitating maximum surprise. The guns could achieve the neutralisation and suppression of enemy batteries, anti-tank guns and command centres for the period of the operation, without a lengthy preliminary bombardment or an obvious build-up of ammunition. The break-out was more difficult to achieve – the required mobility was simply not present in 1918. Instead, as the pace of operations began to slow in one area, the focus would shift elsewhere, achieving multiple surprises and the cumulative dislocation of the German Army's fighting power. The rate of advance, at around thirty miles per month from August to November 1918, compares favourably with the rates of twenty-five miles per month achieved in Italy from September 1943 to May 1945, and fifty miles per month in North West Europe from June 1944 to February 1945 (with a fully mechanised force)[58].

Tempo required a highly developed all-arms capability, a condition outlined in Maxse's vision for battle of August 1917:

(a) The ideal to which we should work is to obtain temporary command of the air in front of our offensive with sufficient aeroplanes to attack strong points, nests of machine guns, infantry advancing or massing for counter attack, and the personnel of enemy's batteries.
(b) . . . If these conditions obtain [sufficient aeroplanes to deal with anti-tank guns and forward batteries, battlefield not made impassable by artillery and smoke to screen enemy observation posts], Tanks should be used in sufficient numbers to neutralise strong points, nests of machine guns, and generally to facilitate the task of infantry. Tanks should be given definite objectives, and definite infantry units should be told off to co-operate in attacking each tank-objective, but not necessarily to accompany the Tank . . . The infantry formation (already practised) aims at stalking the tank-objective under a barrage and assaulting it simultaneously with the Tank.[59]

Linked to his earlier views on artillery support, this represents a well-developed view of all-arms tactics. Such tactics were the ideal in 1917, when other factors often conspired to prevent these elements working in close harmony, but were commonplace the following year. Their development was essentially a bottom-up process, but this benefited from the willingness of commanders at all levels to utilise and disseminate good ideas. Linked to the growing emphasis on initiative and the emerging 'Soft Spots' tactics, they laid the foundations for success at the operational level.

OPERATIONAL ART AND THE MANOEUVRIST APPROACH

British operational art traditionally lacks the focus that, for example, the German Army is able to bring to the discipline, because British defence policy tends to be pulled in two directions; between, on the one hand, defence against direct threats to the homeland and, on the other, the protection of Britain's 'wider security interests'. Despite such uncertainty over its purpose before the First World War, the Army prepared vigorously against the possibility of a continental war. If much of the Army's thinking and development was empirical and pragmatic, it was necessarily so, for it took place then – as it often does now – in a strategic vacuum. Although doctrinal debate at the Staff College may have been in the doldrums[60], there was no lack of debate, reform and development throughout the Field Army and the Arms and Services: '. . . indeed, the flood of published material showed that talented men were leading a renaissance in military science in the six years before 1914.'[61] Many of the talented and determined individuals at the heart of this renaissance would rise to key command and staff appointments during the war.

The reforming zeal was widespread. It has been seen that Maxse's drive for reform of the infantry involved the ideas and active participation of his subordinates. Maxse raised support for his proposals through the circulation of his draft RUSI paper, not only to the military hierarchy, but also among the 'great-and-good' outside the Army. General French chaired the RUSI meeting, and the favourable reception for Maxse's lecture led directly to the initiation of trials and experimentation in the field. This was in the face of considerable resistance to change, not least at grass-roots level, where four company commanders per battalion would lose their command as the number of companies reduced from eight to four. Eventually, the concept was demonstrated to the Army Board during the autumn manoeuvres of 1913, when the performance of the new 'double-companies' and the enthusiasm of their commanders impressed the Board sufficiently for the new structure to be endorsed.

The foregoing reforms were primarily concerned with tactics, whereas much of the criticism levelled at British commanders of the First World War concerns their perceived lack of understanding of the *operational* level of war, which provides the critical link between national strategic objectives and all tactical activity within the theatre of operations. Critics frequently regard the pragmatic outlook of pre-war commanders as having prevailed at the expense of operational theory[62]. Although it is increasingly acknowledged that 'Field Service Regulations, 1909' represents a coherent doctrine, its content is often condemned for its

40

focus on 'destruction' of the enemy's forces through decisive battle: the Clausewitzian *Vernichtungsprinzip*. Indeed, the First World War has been portrayed as a period of 'operational ignorance', characterised by a largely unsuccessful extension of tactical concepts to accommodate the scale and scope of contemporary warfare and flawed through belief in pitting strength against strength. The resulting impasse would only be overcome through the systemic thinking of Soviet researchers, based largely at the Frunze Academy in the 1920s and 1930s, who developed the theory of deep operations. This school of thought identified the critical nature of the role of operational shock, which engenders the opponent's paralysis through instilling in him the realisation that his aims are no longer achievable. These theories were further developed in the American concept of 'Airland Battle'[63].

The theory of operational manoeuvre to create shock forms the basis of manoeuvrist theory. The British Army currently defines it as follows:

> The Manoeuvrist Approach to Operations is one in which shattering the enemy's overall cohesion and will to fight, rather than his materiel, is paramount . . . it aims to apply strength against identified weakness; significant features are momentum and tempo . . . It calls for an attitude of mind in which doing the unexpected and seeking orginality is combined with a ruthless determination to succeed . . . Such an indirect approach offers the prospect of rapid results, or of results disproportionately greater than the resources applied.[64]

The Army will seek to find, fix and then strike the opponent's centre of gravity to shatter his will and cohesion through disruption, dislocation and pre-emption. The language and scope of the Army's current doctrine owes much to the legacy of Fuller and Liddell Hart and, as such, it re-emphasises their claims to have distilled truths from the First World War that commanders had failed to recognise, or ignored, both at the time and subsequently. It has been suggested in a recent study that it is Fuller and Liddell Hart's *theories* that should be studied by the British Army today, given that their historical works are increasingly subject to criticism[65]. However, this is no easy task given the degree to which their theories and their histories are inextricably entwined.

Fuller and Liddell Hart portrayed the blinkered, managerial style of 'Château Generalship' as being alleviated only by the tank-heavy success delivered by Fuller's plans for Cambrai and the German use of *Stosstruppen* tactics in the spring 1918 *Kaiserschlacht*. Taken in combination, Fuller and Liddell Hart saw, in their post-war assessments of these phenomena, the harbingers of *Blitzkrieg*, a concept which Liddell Hart later claimed as his own.

Their views have come under increasing criticism in recent years. One study of the development of British thinking on the role of armour cites the '. . . scale of historical deception and distortion for which Liddell Hart was responsible.'[66] Similarly, a modern, comprehensive study of operational theory says of Liddell Hart's role in formulating the myth of *Blitzkrieg* that: '. . . by imposing retrospectively his own perceptions of mobile warfare upon the shallow concept of Blitzkrieg he created a theoretical imbroglio that has taken 40 years to unravel.'[67] Liddell Hart's deceptions have influenced many other writers and his '. . . long reign and tentacular patronage extended deep into the bunking and debunking of generals which afforded him such pleasure.'[68]

Although both Fuller and Liddell Hart wrote extensively over a long period, their collective theories (though they were often far from being in agreement) have been summarised as follows:

- The theory of the 'offensive-defensive', regarded as the strongest form of war, by which forces operating from a secure base would seek to absorb the momentum of the enemy's assault while awaiting the moment for a decisive riposte.
- The theory of the 'indirect approach'. This required that the main assault should be concentrated at the enemy's most vulnerable spot and his 'line of least expectation'. Breakthrough should lead, through an 'expanding torrent', to progressive psychological dislocation of the enemy as the advance penetrated rapidly into his rear areas. This psychological element reduced the emphasis upon decisive battle, making manoeuvre the supreme military activity.
- The 'indirect approach' was predicated on economy of force with the maximum effect being derived from the minimum of effort.
- Mobile defence should be the most effective form of defence, allowing the defender to protect his fighting power and installations without surrendering the initiative.
- The main aim of military operations should be the dislocation of the enemy's command and organisation, rather than the destruction of his forces.
- The pursuit should be the most important and decisive act of battle. The commander should, therefore, husband his reserves in such a manner as to be able to organise and commit them to guarantee annihilation of the enemy and the attainment of the political objective of the war.[69]

However, it is simplistic to ascribe the formulation of these concepts to them alone and the theories outlined above were certainly not new, being discernible in pre-First World War British and French writing. In 1907 Kiggell, Haig's Chief of Staff for much of the war, anticipated Fuller's consideration of the offensive-defensive: 'The most important subject to consider is the relationship between offensive and defensive action in battle . . . These terms are misleading, and some words other than "offensive" and "defensive" are sorely needed to express the situation more clearly, as regards a battle in which both sides equally aim at decisive victory. In such a case, under generals who know their business, neither side has any monopoly of defensive or offensive. Each aims at a final, decisive, offensive stroke. Each uses the power of the defensive, as it may suit him, in preparing the way for that stroke, and in gaining the time necessary for it to take full effect.'[70]

Debate about direct and indirect approaches was equally familiar before the First World War, when the emphasis upon *decisive battle* gained favour in France and Britain. The *Entente* view has been criticised for its narrow focus and an emphasis on 'human tonnage'[71]. However, decisive battle was not seen merely as *guerre à outrance*, a doctrine of attack that disregards losses. Within his lectures to the French Staff College early in the century, Foch provides a considered exposition of decisive battle that displays far greater subtlety, arriving at a framework of understanding of future war that appears remarkably prescient. It anticipates many of the arguments that Fuller and Liddell Hart would deploy many years later, particularly Fuller's analogy of the 'shot through the brain' and Liddell Hart's analogy of 'the expanding torrent'[72].

Foch's book *The Principles of War*, based on his Staff College lectures, was well known to British officers and undoubtedly had an influence on British military thinking[73]. In it, Foch elaborated a theory based on the enduring principles of war, aimed at achieving 'direction, convergence and a result.' Foch outlined his view of operational art, stating that '. . . in order to create [a result], you must have artistic adaptation of the means to the end, an adaptation which involves a very clear understanding of the means and of the end: in other words, you cannot create anything before knowing the component elements of art.'[74] He developed a process of campaign planning designed to permit the dispersion of forces operating with 'special missions' towards an end whereby '. . . that mobile enemy [can be] discovered; then fixed, or pinned, so that the play of our forces may strike him . . .' through rapid concentration at the decisive point. To the functions of find, fix and strike, Foch added exploitation, believing that the destruction of the enemy would be achieved through pursuit, when the pursuer would finish off '. . . forces which are no longer a force.'[75]

Foch also analysed the 'psychological phenomenon of battle', believing it better to break the enemy's spirit in a clash of wills than to annihilate his combatants. This would be achieved primarily through surprise, aimed at '. . . depriving the enemy of the possibility of reflection and therefore of discussion. Here we have a novel instrument, and one capable of destructive power beyond all knowledge.'[76] He sums up his consideration of decisive attack with the comment that:

Mechanics as well as psychology lead us to the 'battle of manoeuvre.'

43

The means provided by the first consist in <u>applying superior forces on one point</u>; the means provided by the latter consist <u>in producing a peril, an attack that cannot be parried</u> . . . Theoretically too, in order to be stronger than the enemy on a given point and at a given moment, <u>all</u> forces must be <u>simultaneously</u> applied on that point, and this in an <u>unforeseen</u> manner . . . in view of which, therefore, the <u>maximum</u> of forces and of <u>manoeuvring</u> troops must be <u>kept in reserve</u>. Hence <u>the economy</u> of forces, that is, their distribution and use in battle.[77]

In effect, Foch considers the decisive attack to be an attack on the enemy's cohesion, utilising surprise, simultaneity, tempo and superior firepower. In an earlier chapter, 'Intellectual Discipline – Freedom of Action as a Function of Obedience', he illustrated his command philosophy to accompany these principles: 'To <u>passive obedience</u>, such as used to be in favour under the absolute systems of the past, we oppose <u>active</u> obedience; it is an implicit consequence of the appeal constantly made to initiative . . . this notion of freedom of action [is] <u>fundamental</u> to all acts of war.' In a footnote, he quotes Von der Goltz's definition of initiative as the '. . . manifestation of personal will helped by judgment and acting in compliance with the schemes of the high command.'[78]

Foch would have condemned his modern critics as specious, since he believed a capable and numerous enemy would not collapse until thoroughly beaten. Decisive battle might be costly, but in achieving a result, it would prevent repetition of the even costlier defeats inflicted on France by Prussia in 1870, when he felt his predecessors had fallen foul of the expectation that they could defeat the Prussians through manoeuvre alone. He stated, in characteristically uncompromising fashion, that '. . . manoeuvre in itself = 0.'[79] Modern operational theory requires that manoeuvre, at the operational level, should be directed at the opponent's centre of gravity. The distinction between the Manoeuvrist Approach and the dilemmas facing commanders on the Western Front is their differing interpretation of the accessibility of the opponent's centre of gravity at that level.

The 'westerners' view of the German centre of gravity was essentially Clausewitzian, and was illustrated by Kitchener in 1915 when he said 'You are not fighting the troops in front of you. You are fighting the manhood of a great power.'[80] Similarly, Haig had said the same year that 'we cannot hope to win until we have defeated the German Army.'[81] Maxse himself held typically forthright views on the subject, and in his opening address to the XVIII Corps School for Platoon Commanders on 14 May 1917 restated his view that:

The strongest thing about the German people is their belief in the German Army, and so long as they continue to believe in the invincibility of their Army, so long will they <u>endure any hardships</u> of blockade to enable the Army to win. They have made a God of the Army, and it is no good telling them that the Army is <u>a bad God, or a weak God, or not a God at all.</u> Belief in the Army is <u>ingrained in the German nation,</u> and they will not change that belief until the Army itself <u>breaks down,</u> You have then <u>to defeat the German Army. You cannot measure this task by miles any more than you can measure a man's courage by his height.</u>[82]

In marked contrast, Lloyd George believed it would be impossible to force a result on the Western Front, and favoured instead a policy of 'knocking away the props' of the Central Powers (the 'indirect approach'). This belief, and the political intrigue and deception that accompanied it, runs like a cordite trail of destruction throughout the period of the BEF's primacy on the Western Front from April 1917 to the end of the war. The 'eastern' view is flawed in two important respects; firstly, it overlooks the point that Germany's allies were far from being her 'props' and, secondly, that if the allies did not force a decision in the west then, ultimately, the Germans would. Foch emphasised his mistrust of the indirect approach by quoting von der Goltz:

. . . The mistake made was the giving to war as its object the execution of nicely combined manoeuvres, instead of the object of annihilating the adversary's forces. The military world has always fallen into such errors whenever it has abandoned a simple and straightforward notion of the laws of war and attempted to make abstraction of matter.[83]

Perhaps manoeuvrist operational theory is no more correct than Foch is wrong. War is a blend of attrition and manoeuvre. In the crunching battles of 1914 and 1915, the French did not achieve a decisive victory, nor did the Germans achieve victory through manoeuvre and envelopment. The defensive had briefly gained an overwhelming ascendency and it would take a tumultuous advance in the science of firepower to restore manoeuvre to its rightful place on the battlefield. The British Army progressed farthest along the road in combining modern firepower with manoeuvre, re-learning the fundamentals of war as it did so. Fuller, Liddell Hart and the *Wehrmacht* extended the primacy of manoeuvre in their post-war doctrines but, as the *Wehrmacht* discovered on the Eastern Front in World War Two, if the enemy does not allow you to avoid his strengths or to shatter his will, there is left only the 'ruthless determination to succeed.'[84]

In this light, there is a danger that the Manoeuvrist Approach 'makes abstraction of matter', ignoring Shelley's observation that 'what is new is not true, and what is true is not new'. If the fundamental principles underpinning the Army's modern doctrine were known and applied during the First World War, the critical question becomes that of why success still came at such a cost. The answer, as has been seen, involves a mix of: political prevarication before and during the war; inadequate resources and the difficulties inherent in a rapid and unplanned expansion; the skill and determination of the enemy; and the rate of technological advancement. What matters is not simply doctrine itself, but the people, structures and training required to apply it. Hence, a successful warfighting army must be a learning organisation, challenging and refining its doctrine continually through historical and contemporary lessons learned and always seeking the means to apply its doctrine efficiently and effectively. It must live and train for war in the organisations in which it will fight, and must be able to make the transition to war and to undergo expansion with the minimum of disruption. To regard our current doctrine as the *antidote* to past ills, rather than examining it objectively against the conditions and lessons of past conflicts, implies a complacency based on 'camouflaged history [which] not only conceals faults and deficiencies that could otherwise be remedied, but engenders false confidence – and false confidence has underlain most of the failures that military history records. It is the dry rot of armies.'[85]

This section has dwelt upon the writings of Foch because they offer a detailed insight into the meaning of 'decisive battle' to commanders of the time. Foch demonstrates a clear support for a 'manoeuvrist approach', tempered by a practical concern for the difficulty of applying it on the battlefield. It is for this reason that he warned his students not to expect his praise simply for *saying* that they intended to '. . . undertake <u>outflanking</u> operations or operations on the <u>rear</u> of the enemy which draw all their assumed value from the mere <u>direction</u> in which they will be made . . .'[86]

Rather than a period of 'operational ignorance', the First World War represents a period of rapid change in the nature of conflict, during which the principal elements of the 'modern style of warfare' came together to create a step-change in military capability. Operational art was stretched severely through such turmoil, and doctrine had to develop constantly to reflect new conditions and technologies. Operational art was also severely constrained by lack of mobility and effective communications, making a decision in battle difficult to achieve between closely matched protagonists. The restoration of mobility was contingent upon developments in the science of firepower, but artillery and its huge logistic support chain were themselves inherently *im*mobile due to the primitive state of mechanisation at the time. This also ensured that breakthroughs could not be developed into breakouts, a problem exacerbated by the slow passage of information, which would only be resolved as wireless technology matured – a process that is far from complete even today.

It perhaps behoves the Army to consider the degree to which modern formation staffs could realistically overcome the constraints of 1914–18 and, commensurately, to what degree modern theory and doctrine would have enabled First World War commanders to apply fighting power with any greater degree of success than was achieved. Much of our modern doctrine represents only a greater definition and codification of long established principles and procedures. General Hamley's rueful observation of 1866 still has, perhaps, some resonance today:

> Now, most military terms are easy enough to understand; and they do not require to be defined formally, because the solution of military problems does not depend upon the exactitude of the definitions. Thus the subject is at the very outset uselessly encumbered – worse than uselessly indeed, for the definitions are often much more difficult to understand than the original phrase, and are therefore confusing . . . It is the method which, in exchange for a good shilling, gives you a pocket full of bad halfpence.[87]

THE LEARNING ORGANISATION

The British Army of 1918 could no more shake off the legacy of its pre-war history than the Army today can escape from the equipment and cadreisation legacies that hang over from the Cold War. In 1914 the Army was not a warfighting army, because it had focused perforce on small-unit operations around the Empire at the expense of thorough training against the eventuality of a war on the continent. When that war came, the Army was ill-equipped and under-resourced, both in materiel and in trained soldiers, commanders and staff. In 1916 the process of learning its job (the conceptual component of fighting power) began in earnest, but the technological means to apply the emerging solutions effectively were lacking. By 1917 both the conceptual and physical elements of fighting power had advanced considerably, but any mismatch between them was ruthlessly exposed by the enemy and, at 3rd Ypres, the weather. The author is drawn to the hypothesis that, freed from political intrigue and able to choose the time and place of its operations, the BEF might have achieved startling results that year[88]. By 1918 the offensive means were readily to hand. But further political meddling and the arrival of significant German reinforcements fresh from victory in the east meant that the BEF had first to stem the onslaught of successive German offensives before wresting back the initiative and opening up the road to victory.

On the battlefield, the British Army was most certainly imbued with a warfighting ethos by 1918, displaying many of the attributes to which the Future Army now aspires. Critical to the achievements sketched out above was the role of training and, when weighing up the 'ifs' and 'might-have-beens' of the BEF's capabilities, the pressing problems of effective training in war, and of disseminating lessons-learned, are recurring themes. The warfighting ethos is hard to inculcate in war if it is not fully developed in peace. After 1914 new formations and drafts were trained in trench warfare, often by officers and NCOs who themselves knew little or nothing of warfighting. When, on the Somme, conditions of semi-open or open-warfare occasionally arose, the ability to exploit the new conditions to the full was slow to be grasped, since the skills were simply not there. Maxse commented on this in his letter to Rawlinson of 31 July 1916, already referred to:

> The total casualties in my Division in the Battle of the SOMME amounted to 6754. This is not a figure to boast about, because I am convinced that perhaps 30% of these casualties would have been avoided if the officers and men had been trained to move in open country . . . No Corps commander or Corps staff could possibly have done more for my Division to give it TIME to train, during the four months preceding 1st July. Plan after plan for battalion and brigade training was made; every device was thought out; all were alert to getting training accomplished. But, our training programme came to nothing; every plan was necessarily vetoed on account of our manual labour being required day and night whenever battalions were out of the trenches . . . No rest and no training were possible for Infantry, except during the one week.[89]

Even as the Somme fighting continued, the 'lessons-learned' process was hard at work, with preliminary lessons published in SS119 in July 1916, and instructions for the future training of divisions and platoons detailed in SS135 (December 1916) and SS143 (February 1917) respectively. What was required in 1917 was some system for co-ordinating training across the armies in France, where army and corps schools had sprung up in response to a multitude of specialist needs. To meet the requirement, a training branch was established in GHQ under the command of Brigadier Solly-Flood. The department published SS152, 'Instructions for the Training of the British Armies in France' in June 1917, 'the object of which is to co-ordinate policy and system, and so to arrive at a uniformity of doctrine.'[90] This was only an interim version, however, and the authoritative draft was not issued until January 1918. SS152 also re-emphasised the golden rule that commanders should train the troops they lead into action: 'this is a principle that should never be departed from.' The publication included detailed syllabi for courses of instruction at corps and army schools across the full range of requirements.

The 'Soft Spots' tactics previously referred to represented the culmination of developments in a number of related and inseparable areas. The conditions necessary for such techniques to prosper were unattainable until these component strands were in place. The limited firepower available to battalions in 1916 meant that much of it was vested in specialists who were formed and trained at battalion level. This avoided the necessity of training all infantrymen in special skills when time to train in even the most basic skills was at a premium (even in early 1917 there was continued debate as to whether Lewis guns were company or platoon weapons). After the Somme fighting, the emphasis focused on the further development of the platoon as a self-contained fighting unit. Having been instrumental in reorganising the Army in 1911–13, Maxse was consulted throughout the drafting of SS143, 'Instructions for the Training of Platoons for Offensive Operations'. Asked to comment on a draft of the publication, Maxse replied in January 1917 that: 'My ideal would be that . . . they [the sections] should all be armed with rifle, bayonet, bomb and rifle grenade . . . But I recognise that in our backward state of training . . . it might be advisable to have one section trained as bombers and another as rifle grenadiers, but I don't like it . . .'[91].

The necessity for specialisation at this stage was expressed in a letter to Maxse from one of his divisional commanders: 'The starting point from which I arrived at this organisation is the principle that those who live together and are trained together, fight best together.'[92] In essence, the divisional commander did not wish to implement 'all-arms' sections that would need to split up in order to train within their specialities, given the limited time available to units for training when on 'rest'. Only by 1918 would the armies reach a state of training sufficient to approach Maxse's ideal, with all infantrymen trained in the various roles and weapons required in the platoon.

As tactical commanders began to refine the art of all-arms co-operative fire and movement, fluidity and momentum were restored to offensive operations. Greater freedom of action and a growing self-reliance at the tactical level freed commanders at the operational level from the micro-management that had been so necessary to raise, train and equip the huge organisation that the British Armies in France became. One authority states that '. . . Haig, again like Rawlinson, proved far more effective as a commander once the sphere of his activities began to diminish . . .'[93]. In essence, commanders were empowered to get on with the business of commanding, fighting soldiers to get on with the business of fighting.

In the lessons-learned process that followed the German spring offensives of 1918, a paper from Major General Dawnay at GHQ to the Director of Military Operations in London outlined the system of training in France and how the inability to conduct formation-level training had added to the problems in March and April 1918. The paper reiterated briefly the problems caused by reorganisation and the extension of the front, then detailed in full the great difficulties in finding time for formations to rest and train – and of establishing the necessary training areas in the face of French bureaucracy. It made the telling point that 'It is not possible to bring a division to a thorough state of efficiency unless it remains in a back area and devotes its whole time to training for a period of at least six weeks. In one case only was a division as long as six weeks in a back area [over the winter 1917/1918] and this division, the 55th, had practically to be entirely reformed after the heavy casualties at CAMBRAI. On the 21st March, therefore, we had less than half our divisions who had done even a month's training in a back area undisturbed and there were a certain number who had had practically no training at all.'[94] This is a sad reflection on the circumstances the BEF had been placed in – primarily by the British government – at a time when it was in the throes of adopting new defensive doctrine that required thorough re-training at all levels.

The 'eastern' tendency in the War Cabinet's policies led not only to a constant diminution of effort on the Western Front, but added to the burden of troops and formations deployed there, denying them the reserves of strength necessary for preparation and to allow formations to rest and train. How much this protracted the war may never be accurately assessed, though we may note here Maxse's oft-asserted maxim that 'Every day's good training that you do is a day off the duration of the war.'

The BEF was a learning organisation, but began the critical period (1916–18) needing to 'unlearn' many of the preconceptions the New Armies and other wartime recruits brought to France with them and, especially, their belief in the military stereotype of 'passive obedience' rather than 'active obedience'. Although the process of implementing lessons learned and of re-instilling the skills needed for open warfare was generally swift, it was often fairly informal and constrained by the slower rate at which the necessary weapons and the full supporting cast of enabling technologies could be developed. Dawnay's paper (referred to earlier) and the earlier General Staff paper 'Notes on Recent Fighting' of April 1918[95] shows the shock engendered by failure at formation level to interpret and implement extant doctrine effectively and a determination to resolve the problem in future. The resulting requirement to give Solly-Flood's training department greater teeth was recognised and, as a direct result, the IGT was established. As the Inspector-General of Training, Maxse was able to promote direct and open discussion with formation commanders to speed the acquisition and dissemination of lessons learned. These were then incorporated into divisional training packages run by Maxse's training teams, each led by a brigadier. Maxse shifted the focus on 'uniformity of doctrine' to include the teaching of tactics as drills, which enabled units to be 'elastic in battle . . . companies and platoons can quickly modify a FAMILIAR system to suit the ground and the resistance encountered, but they cannot learn a new one in a day.'[96]

In one of the boxes of the Maxse papers in the Imperial War Museum, there is a sheaf of handwritten letters contained in a buff folder. They are thank you notes to Maxse from the BEF's divisional and corps commanders following the issue by IGT of the 'Soft Spots' Training Leaflet in January 1919. They offer a poignant testimony to the brief work of Maxse's Inspectorate, at a time when demobilisation was reaching full swing and the BEF was ebbing swiftly away. Nearly all of them contain a variation on the theme of 'if only your Inspectorate had been established two years earlier!' It is worth noting that in 1999, as the Army finds it increasingly difficult to reach collective performance and readiness levels, there is again no single authority responsible for training policy and its implementation, let alone able to include the establishment of 'uniformity of doctrine' within its remit.

CONCLUSIONS

Peacetime ambiguity as to the Army's purpose has underpinned its problems in two world wars and, in trying to resolve its difficulties, political imperatives and prevarication have trumped military judgment all too frequently. Yet, despite the strategic uncertainties within which it prepared for war prior to 1914, the Army was able to undertake many important reforms. Its pre-war doctrine – both formal and informal – played a significant role in informing debate and development. During the war years, the Army struggled to complete the processes of reform and modernisation already in being, while implementing an unexpected and overwhelming expansion programme without the necessary mechanisms for training in place and following the loss of much of the pre-war Regular Army. The solutions to the tactical problems of the war – on which operational success could eventually be built – were largely based upon principles known and understood by the pre-war Regular Army. These principles are enduring and are reflected both in our doctrine today and in our concepts for the future.

This study has attempted to achieve two ends: to show that the First World War is something more than a source of bad lessons for the Army today; and to highlight the similarities in doctrinal thinking within the Army in the first twenty years of this century and again, at the century's end. The Manoeuvrist Approach to Operations is not new, nor does it claim to be. However, it is commonly misconstrued as being new, and with this misconception comes the belief that 'New Doctrine' will be tough on friction, tough on the causes of friction, and this at minimal cost in blood and treasure. Much of this perhaps false confidence is based on the success enjoyed by coalition forces against the supine and largely irrelevant Iraqi forces of the Gulf War. However, the Army should continue to look beyond the establishment of doctrinal cliche dominance, to the strategic, organisational, training and endurance issues that must be addressed continually if doctrine is to be deliverable in action.

The essential conclusion that this article has sketched out, through a study of British fighting methods during the First World War, is that the principal elements of the Manoeuvrist Approach were integral to operations by 1918. If the cost of success in that war was high in terms of blood and treasure, the Army must look elsewhere for the causes. It is clear that the ethos and procedures associated with a successful warfighting army are, like the principles of war themselves, timeless and enduring. There are, therefore, valid lessons to be drawn for the Army's current doctrine and future concepts from a more rigorous approach in its understanding of the First World War and all that flows from it. Doctrine is not an end in itself, and cannot of itself defeat the enemy. An avowedly warfighting army must not rest on the laurels of its theory and writings, rather, it should prepare, structure and train for war at all times as if it really means it. If, in some future conflict, the Army is to avoid being reminded painfully of Kitchener's warning that 'we must make war as we must, not as we would like to', it needs greater clarity of purpose, the resources to train collectively as it means to fight, and the mechanisms to manage a relatively seamless expansion should this ever again prove necessary.

Footnotes to Chapter 3

1 T S Eliot, 'Burnt Norton', *The Four Quartets*, Faber & Faber, London, 1944

2 A view epitomised in the front-papers to Clark, Alan: *The Donkeys*, London, Hutchinson, 1961. This gives a quotation, supposedly from Falkenhayn's *Memoirs*, in which British troops are characterised as 'lions led by donkeys'. The quote was suggested to Clark by Liddell Hart. It is now clear that no such comment appears in Falkenhayn's *Memoirs* and that the quotation almost certainly refers to French troops during the 1870 Franco-Prussian War and may well be a recurrent 'chestnut' over a longer timeframe – see Terraine, John: *The Smoke and the Fire – Myths and Anti-Myths of War 1861–1945*, London, Leo Cooper, 1992, pp.170–81 and Baynes, John: *Far From a Donkey – The Life of General Sir Ivor Maxse KCB, CVO, DSO'*, London, Brassey's, 1995, pp.viii-ix. Alex Danchev refers to Clark's '. . . much inferior evocation of 1915, *The Donkeys*', claiming that it was written primarily for financial gain under the patronage of Lord Beaverbrook, '. . . for his own vindictive purposes in 'Bunking and Debunking: the Controversies of the 1960s', in Bond, B. (ed.) *The First World War and British Military History*, Oxford, Clarendon Press, 1991, pp.263–88. Denis Winter defends Clark, claiming that his work '. . . remains

the single most accurate book in print on any Western Front campaign . . .' in *Haig's Command: A Reassessment*, London, Penguin, 1992, p.255 (originally published by Viking in 1991). Winter's book has itself stirred a great deal of controversy, being a sustained attack on every facet of Haig's character and conduct. Correlli Barnett in the *Times Literary Supplement* (*TLS*) published a thorough and highly critical review of the book on 19 April 1991. This was reinforced by John Hussey's criticisms in a letter to *TLS*, 10 May 1991. More damningly, Winter's claims to authority and originality through the use of archival material held in Australia were thoroughly undermined in a letter by Dr Jeffrey Grey of the University of New South Wales to *TLS* on 9 August 1991. Grey accused Winter of concocting a *mélange* of mis-identified and misquoted documents, documents run together without reference to their differing origins, and material misdated by anything up to seventeen years to achieve greater effect. He stated that Winter's 'quotations' from correspondence between the Australian and British Official Historians (C E W Bean and Sir James Edmonds) '. . . should be treated with considerable mistrust. To give but one example, on page 31 he cites Edmonds to the effect that "before 1914 the army was very feudal in its status and . . . great personages still exercised the higher patronage."' What Edmonds actually wrote to Bean, in June 1929, was: "I can't help feeling that you think the BEF of 1914 was still the feudal army it was in 1899 before the South African War . . . Efficiency, not birth, alone counted!"' It is sad to note that Bond's admirable *The First World War and British Military History* is now out of print, whereas *The Donkeys* and *Haig's Command* continue to be stocked by most high street book shops, testimony to the superior selling power of controversy over scholarship. Bond's belief that the historiography of the war has reached a point where the war may now be studied '. . . simply as history without polemic intent or apologies' has clearly yet to be fully accepted: op cit., p.12. Bond's book deals with the *historiography* of the war, a subject recently brought up to date by Ian Beckett in his 'Revisiting the Old Front Line – The Historiography of the Great War Since 1984', in *Stand To! – The Journal of the Western Front Association!*, N° 43, April 1995, pp.10–14

3 Alex Danchev cites the critical role in the production of 'Oh! What a Lovely War' undertaken by Raymond Fletcher, a journalist and military historian (and later Labour MP for Ilkeston) whose '. . . great weakness as a military historian was his inability to "get out of the trenches", as he put it . . . Very early in the play's evolution he delivered to the assembled Theatre Workshop an overview lecture designed to give the war some recognisable shape: a marathon three-hour session memorably described by the lecturer as "one part me, one part Liddell Hart, the rest Lenin!" Fletcher had another message to deliver, "a message for the sixties"'. op cit., pp.282–3

4 'Force Development is the monitoring and analysis of a broad range of trends in order to determine and articulate future military concepts, capabilities and structures to support national political objectives, and provide guidance on their implementation.' Joint Warfare Publication 0–10, pp.2–4

5 See Terraine, J, *The Right of the Line*, first published London, Hodder & Stoughton, 1985, Sceptre edition published 1988

6 See Barnett, C, *Britain and Her Army 1509–1970: A Military, Political and Social History*, Harmondsworth, Allen Lane The Penguin Press, 1970

7 The hierarchy of British Army doctrine begins with 'British Defence Doctrine', JWP 0–01, 1996 and 'British Military Doctrine', 1996. It cascades down

into 'Army Doctrine Publications' (ADPs) including 'Volume 1 – Operations' of June 1994 and 'Volume 2 – Command' of April 1995. The *ADP* series provides the link between 'the essentially timeless content of the British Military Doctrine and the tactical level Army Field Manual series, which describes how the doctrine should be put into practice.' – foreword to APD Vol 1 – Operations.

8 See, for example, Lind, W S: *The Maneuver Warfare Handbook*, Boulder and London, Westview Press, 1985 and Id., 'the Theory and Practice of Maneuver Warfare', in Richard Hooker Jnr. (ed), *Maneuver Warfare – An Anthology*, Presidion Press, 1993, pp.3–18

9 For an account of the development of German doctrine, see Martin Samuels, *Doctrine and Dogma – German and British Infantry Tactics in the First World War*, New York, Greenwood Press, 1992 and Id., *Command or Control? – Command, Training and Tactics in the British and German Armies, 1888–1918*, London, Frank Cass, 1995. Samuels is much stronger on the German side than in his considerations of British techniques and procedures. In *Command or Control?*, his selection of 1 July 1916 and 21 March 1918 as case studies for the British Army represent the Army's two worst days throughout the whole war. In his concentration on the tactical aspects of those two days, especially March 1918, Samuels ignores significant adverse factors which contributed to the events he recounts. Some of these are dealt with later in this article. Samuels shows how the German Great General Staff was able to maintain a warfighting focus through peace time, with the consequent ability to prepare efficiently for war, which the British Army has never been able to match

10 Samuels, *Doctrine and Dogma*, p.192

11 ibid., pp.18–19

12 Jackson and Bramall: *The Chiefs – The Story of the United Kingdom Chiefs of Staff*, London, Brassey's, 1992, p.51

13 Bidwell, Shelford and Graham, Dominick: *Firepower – British Army Weapons and Theories of War 1904–1945*, Boston, George Allen & Unwin, 1981, p.167, and Bond, Brian: *British Military Policy between the Two World Wars*, Oxford, Clarendon Press, 1980, p.8

14 '*BA2000 – Towards an Army of the Twenty First Century*', ECAB/P(95)6 dated 5 May 1995, paragraph 18

15 Command 2800, London, HMSO, 1995, pp.9–26. Editorial comment in *British Army Review*, N° 119, August 1998, says of the recent Strategic Defence Review that '. . . by codifying the present state of play, [it] tells us where we have got to. It tells us less of where we are going . . . the whole thrust is towards operations other than war . . . what has emerged is a very reasonable set of solutions for the problems posed by the actual operations of the 1990s.' In the long drawn out debate between proponents of Britain's 'maritime' and 'continental' strategies, whilst the Strategic Defence Review delivers its assumptions very effectively, it is those assumptions themselves that merit closer scrutiny

16 These rather misleading definitions suggest a clear-cut division of opinion, which was certainly never the case, but are used here for shorthand. Studies of the effect the debate had upon the strategic direction of the war include: Jackson, Bill, and Bramall, Edwin, op cit., Chapters 2–4 and French, David: *British Strategy and War Aims 1914–1916*, London, George Allen & Unwin, 1986. Michael Howard makes the point that the debate continued the old strategic dilemma of the '*continental*' versus the '*maritime*' element in Britain's strategic options: 'British Grand Strategy in World War 1', in Kennedy, Paul:

Grand Strategies in War and Peace, New Haven and London, Yale UP, 1991, pp.37–8

17   See French, David: *The British Way in Warfare 1688–2000*, London, Unwin Hyman, 1990, pp.xiv-xviii. Advocates of 'the British way', however, have been accused of confusing strategic grand design with necessity: French concludes that '. . . the only generalisation which is valid for the whole period is that British strategic policy was essentially adaptive', op cit., p.232. The net effect, as Correlli Barnett has pointed out, is that Britain has sought to remain distanced from the costly commitment of ground forces to continental wars and has rarely prepared, in any detail, an army in peacetime capable of fighting them: op cit., pp.147–9

18   Howard, Michael, op cit., p.31

19   Trask, David F, quoted in Gray, C S: 'History for Strategists: British Seapower as a Relevant Past', *The Journal Of Strategic Studies*, Vol. 17, N° 1, March 1994, pp.11–12

20   Terraine, John: *The Smoke and the Fire*, Chapters III-V and Table F to Chapter VIII.

21   ibid., pp.179–180 for discussion of the 'hiatus in the mobile arm' and the lack of universal communications that plagued command throughout the war. Further consideration of the communication problem and the growing experimentation with mechanisation in 1918 will be found in Bidwell and Graham, op cit., Chapter 8

22   Bailey, Brigadier J B A: 'Deep Battle 1914–1941; the Birth of the Modern Style of Warfare', *Field Artillery Journal*, Summer 1998. Brigadier Bailey, writing for an American audience, argues that the First World War witnessed a 'Revolution in Military Affairs' (RMA) that ushered in the modern style of warfare. This links in to debate in the US about the possibility of an RMA in the early 21st Century with the advent of the 'Information Age' of warfare. See also Bailey's 'The First World War and the Birth of Modern Warfare', *The Occasional, N° 22*, Strategic and Combat Studies Institute, Camberley, 1996

23   Bidwell and Graham, op cit., p.40

24   Imperial War Museum (IWM), Maxse Papers, Box 69/53/14. Letter to General Maxse dated 1 September 1918

25   Much of the BEF's wartime doctrinal development is reflected in the lengthy series of Stationery Service (SS) publications. Key publications were updated as required, hence SS135 was published initially in December 1916 as 'Instructions for the Training of Divisions for Offensive Action', and was revised and reprinted in August 1917 under the same title. It was re-published in January 1918 as 'The Training and Employment of Divisions' and then as 'The Division in Attack' in November 1918 (reprinted in January 1919). Other key SS publications referred to in the text include: SS119 'Preliminary Notes on the Tactical Lessons of Recent Operations', July 1916; SS143 'Instructions for the Training of Platoons for Offensive Action, 1917', February 1917 publication – it was revised a number of times, finally appearing as 'Platoon Training 1918–1919'; SS152 'Notes for the Training of the British Armies in France', provisionally published in June 1917 and re-issued as an authoritative instruction in January 1918; SS195 'Scouting and Patrolling', December 1917. SS publications are available within the IWM Department of Documents and copies may be purchased

26   SS135, pp.3–4

27   For a general account of Maxse's life, see Baynes, John, op cit

28   Typical of this is the comment by Russell, GOC the New Zealand Division: 'On 28 September [1917], Russell "met Lieutenant General Maxse who commanded the adjoining Corps to discuss matters, or rather to be talked to; he is full of his own ideas, which are good".': Pugsley, Christopher: 'The New Zealand Division at Passchendaele, in Liddle, Peter H: *Passchendaele in Perspective – The Third Battle of Ypres*, London, Leo Cooper, 1997, Chapter 17, p.278

29   The Directorate of Land Warfare, at Upavon, was charged in 1994 by CGS with the task of describing '. . . the capabilities likely to be required by the British Army in the first decade of the next century and the structural and doctrinal implications that result.' This was originally known as the BA2000 process but, as it becomes clear that the process needs to look further out, the aim has changed to one of establishing the lines of development to produce a capability based Future Army for 2010+, with signposts to 2020+. See Boyd, Lieutenant Colonel Steve: 'Whatever Happened to BA2000?', BAR 119, August 1998, pp.59–61

30   'Two Speculative Views of Future Warfare and Their Implications', AB/P(96)2 dated 2 May 1996 and 'British Army 2000 – The Future Army', APRC/P(97)28 dated 31 July 1997

31   Maxse, General Sir Ivor: 'Battalion Organisation', *RUSI Journal*, Vol. 56, January 1912, in IWM, Maxse Papers, Box 69/53/5, File 9/2

32   'ADP Vol 2 – Command', paragraph 0411: 'Regardless of the technical ability to communicate with every formation or unit within a span of command, studies have shown that a ratio of more than four or five subordinate points of command to one headquarters is the maximum that a commander can manage effectively.' This comment is referenced in a footnote to work by the Army Personnel Research Establishment in 1982, but reflects – almost exactly – sentiments expressed on the subject in correspondence within the Maxse Papers relating to his 'Battalion Organisation' presentation

33   Originally in Fourth Army tactical notes of May 1916, included as annexes in the *Official History* for 1916, Volume 1 and quoted in *Battle Tactics of the Western Front*, Paddy Griffith, Yale UP 1994, p.49

34   Pugsley, op cit, p.275

35   Bidwell and Graham, op cit., Chapters 8 and 14–15

36   SS135, p.23

37   Hussey, John: 'The British Divisional Reorganisation in February 1918', in *Stand To! – the Journal of the Western Front Association*, N° 45, January 1996, pp. 12–14. John Hussey has examined this reorganisation in detail, illustrating the startling fact that the government engineered a manpower shortage where none need have existed in order to '. . . compel the soldiers to reduce manpower that will reduce the waste of manpower . . .' Furthermore, it ignored Haig's preferred military solution to reorganisation, which involved the breaking up of divisions in order to reinforce the remainder to full strength in their existing orders of battle. Instead, after a near-fatal delay of some two months, the government imposed its own solution, breaking up the fourth battalion in each brigade to reinforce brigades elsewhere

38   'ADP Vol 2 – Command', paragraph 0210

39   'ADP Vol 1 – Operations', p.1A–5

40   Wake, H.: 'The Four-Company Battalion in Battle', *RUSI Journal*, Vol. 59, November 1914, in IWM, Maxse Papers, Box 9/2. This echoes Field Service Regulations 1909, Volume I, p.132, which states: 'The choice of the manner

in which the task assigned to each body of troops is to be performed, should be left to its commander'

41 IWM, Maxse Papers, Box 69/53/7, typed critique dated 6 May 1914 and signed by General Sir Douglas Haig

42 Anonymous, with a Foreword by General H S Smith-Dorrien: *A General's Letters to his Son on Obtaining his Commission*, Cassell & Company, London, 1917, pp.58–62

43 IWM, Maxse Papers, Box 59/63/4, File 6/5

44 SS135, p.5

45 Draft Future Army Force Development Concept Paper 'Recce Pull', August 1997, paragraph 5

46 Baynes, John: op cit, pp.177–180 covers some of Maxse's experimentation with wider frontages and decreased force levels at 3rd Ypres in 1917, including his comment in a letter to his wife that: 'In this last battle, I put in only two brigades on a front of 3,700 yards – that is, I put in only two brigades for my original attack. Nearly all others put in double that amount or more. I had to resist all sorts of advice (to get my own way) but as we came off on my plan I am now "a blue-eyed boy" and listened to with attention – at any rate for the time being!'. Maxse was also experimenting with infiltration tactics using small groupings of infantry and tanks in place of large, 'set-piece' operations, and with 'sham attacks' using dummies on poles (successfully – such attacks are occasionally recorded in Ludendorff's memoirs as real actions)

47 IWM, Maxse Papers, Box 69/53/13, file 53/2

48 IWM, Maxse Papers, contains all IGT's *Training Leaflets* in Box 69/53/14, File 59

49 'Tactical Memoranda circulated by GOC XIV Corps, 3rd August 1916' quoted in *The Somme 1916: Crucible of a British Army*, Michael Chappell, Windrowe & Greene, London 1995, pp.108–9

50 Whitmarsh, Andrew: 'The Development of Infantry Tactics in the British 12th (Eastern) Division, 1915–1918', in *Stand To! – The Journal of the Western Front Association!*, N° 48, January 1997, pp.28–32

51 'ADP Vol 1 – Operations', paragraph 0236

52 Defined as '. . . that aspect of the enemy's overall capability which, if attacked and eliminated, will lead either to the enemy's inevitable defeat or his wish to sue for peace through negotiations' in 'ADP Vol 1 – Operations', paragraph 0328

53 IWM, Maxse Papers, Box 69/53/7, file 17/2

54 Bidwell and Graham, op cit., p.151

55 The standard references for the development of firepower remain Bidwell and Graham's *Firepower* and Farndale, General Sir Martin: *History of the Royal Regiment of Artillery: Western Front 1914–1918*, London, Royal Artillery Institution, 1986. For a more specialised account of developments in artillery survey, see: Bragg, Sir Lawrence; Dowson, Major General A. H.; and Hemming, Lieutenant Colonel H.H.: *Artillery Survey in the First World War*, London, Field Survey Association, 1971. A more up-to-date interpretation will be found in Bailey, Brigadier J B A: 'Field Artillery and Firepower', Oxford Military Press, 1989 and Idem. 'British Artillery in the Great War', in Griffith, Paddy (Ed.), *British Fighting Methods in the Great War*, London, Frank Cass, 1996, Chapter 2

56 'ADP Vol 1 – Operations', paragraph 0352

57 Terraine, John: *The Road to Passchendaele – the Flanders Offensive of 1917: A Study in Inevitability*, London, Leo Cooper, 1977, p.336

58   Bailey, Brigadier J. B. A.: 'The Underestimation of Firepower', to be published in *Field Artillery Journal*
59   Baynes: op cit., pp.176–7
60   Holden Reid, Brian: 'War Studies at the Staff College 1890–1930', *The Occasional, N° 1*, Camberley, Strategic and Combat Studies Institute, 1992
61   Bidwell and Graham, op cit., p.40
62   See McInnes, Colin and Stone, John: 'The British Army and Military Doctrine', in: Duffy, Michael; Farrell, Theo; and Sloan, Geoffrey (eds.): *Doctrine and Military Effectiveness – Proceedings of the Conference held at the Britannia Royal Naval College, January 16th–17th, 1997*, University of Exeter, Chapter 3, and Bidwell and Graham, op cit., Chapter 13
63   Naveh, Shimon: *In Pursuit of Military Excellence – The Evolution of Operational Theory*, London, Frank Cass, 1997, particularly Chapters 5–8. Naveh's portrayal of the Soviet defeat of the *Wehrmacht* 1943–1945, after operational theory had been re-imposed in the Red Army, is overly simplistic. It ignores the wider strategic pressures on the German Army and plays down the shocking physical cost that the Soviet victory still entailed. His categorisation of the First World War as a period of 'operational ignorance' seems to be driven by the need to make history fit his theoretical framework. For a more readable account of the Soviet development of deep operations theory, shorn of the extra weight of General Systems Theory and mirrored very closely in Naveh's work, see Glantz, David M.: *Soviet Military Operational Art – In Pursuit of Deep Battle*, London, Frank Cass, 1991
64   *British Defence Doctrine*, Joint Warfare Publication 0–01, London, MOD CS(M)G, 1996, pp.4.8–4.9
65   Holden Reid, Brian: 'A Doctrinal Perspective 1988–1998', *The Occasional, N° 33*, Camberley, Strategic and Combat Studies Institute, May 1998, p. 48. For a detailed examination of Liddell Hart's historical legacy, see Mearsheimer, John J.: *Liddell Hart and the Weight of History*, London, Brassey's, 1998, especially Ch. 8. For a view that tempers Mearsheimer's 'case for the prosecution', see Bond, Brian: *Liddell Hart – A Study of his Military Thought*, and especially his preface for the Gregg Revivals edition, Aldershot, 1991 (originally published by Cassell, London, 1977)
66   Harris, J P: *Men, Ideas and Tanks*, Manchester, Manchester University Press, 1995, p. 230, footnote 16. Harris portrays Fuller as a highly strung, energetic thinker seldom constrained by reality. He concludes that Fuller's resignation of command of the prestigious 'Experimental Mechanised Force' before it had even formed was based primarily on an attack of nerves at the prospect of assuming a command appointment after twenty years in staff appointments. Fuller's claim to be the architect of the initial plan for Cambrai is discounted, with due emphasis being placed on the significance of the predicted fireplan to the initial successes and also to Haig's influence in the initial planning (pp.103–105). Harris summarises the influence of Fuller and Liddell Hart with the comment that: 'The writings of Fuller and Liddell Hart present the history of British armoured forces in the period covered by this book in terms of struggle between prescient innovators on the one hand and a very conservative, sometimes reactionary, military establishment on the other. This is misleading. The British were world leaders in the field for much of the period. Such leadership was possible only because the authorities were, for the most part, remarkably open to innovation. Fuller and Liddell Hart, moreover, failed (for obvious reasons) in their post-Second World War writings adequately to indicate the importance

of mistaken thinking by the radical tank advocates themselves. Such has been the influence of these two writers on subsequent historians that our understanding of an important topic in twentieth-century military history has been seriously distorted.' Ibid., pp. 210–217 and 319

67 Naveh, op cit., pp.108–9

68 Danchev, op cit., p.278

69 The author is grateful to Dr Brian Holden Reid for permission to use this *précis* from his accompanying notes to a lecture on the contribution of Fuller and Liddell Hart to British military theory, given to the Higher Command and Staff Course, Camberley, on 5 January, 1993

70 In his additional chapters for the re-publication of Hamley, General Sir Edward Bruce: *The Operations of War Explained and Illustrated*, Edinburgh and London, William Blackwood and Sons, 1907, pp.406–16 (originally published 1866). Hamley's original chapters contain discussion of political and military objectives and the ends, ways and means of campaign planning and the establishment of lines of operation towards the achievement of an end-state. The additional chapters provided by Kiggell for his 1907 revision are of particular interest. Kiggell distinguishes between the levels of tactics and grand tactics (the operational level of war), and notes that while tactics must develop to account for technological advances, successful tactical methods are based on enduring principles. At this level, he identifies these as: the moral factor; the character of the commander, the power of manoeuvre and combination; firepower; time on the battlefield; the use of reserves; the interdependence of the offensive and the defensive; the critical nature of surprise; and security against being surprised. In discussing these principles (with the liberal aid of quotations from Clausewitz), he sought to provide a framework for understanding war to act as a baseline for those who might wish to undertake further study. This is far from formal doctrine, but it is of note that Haig's future Chief of Staff was prepared to enter the tiltyard and consider a range of underpinning principles in a manner that stands the test of time well. Kiggell begins with a consideration of the maxim that 'the moral is to the physical as three is to one', concluding that since, among European armies, there will be '. . . but little difference . . .', it is to the other principles that we must turn to seek some comparative advantage. He stresses the importance of the character of the commander, and of combination, or the manner in which all parts of the force grasp and apply the commander's plan, using 'intelligent obedience to the directing will . . . [and] mobility that gives rapid effect to that will and permits of fleeting opportunities being taken advantage of.' He defines the importance of time on the battlefield, especially in relation to the actions of co-ordinating the activities of the fixing and striking forces. He concludes his chapter with the thought that: 'Modern war calls for an intelligent use of initiative by subordinates, and it is certain that the subordinate who grasps the broad situation most clearly will solve the local situation most intelligently.' This reiterates the earlier emphasis on the prevalence of a 'mission command' oriented approach to war even before the First World War

71 'ADP 1 – Operations', p.1A–4

72 Foch, Marshal Ferdinand: *The Principles of War* (translated by Hilaire Belloc), London, Chapman & Hall, 1918, p.292: 'To beat an adversary, it is not necessary "to sever his arms, his legs and his head, pierce his chest and burst open his belly all at once" (General Cardot). One sword thrust to the heart, or one stunning blow on the head ensures the result.'

And p.298: 'suppose, however, we should, as a result of some mental vision, discover a crack in the wall of the dam; a point of inadequate resistance . . . then the balance would be upset; the mass would rush in through the breach made, and carry the whole obstacle. Let us look for the crack, for the point of inadequate resistance . . . that is the "battle of manoeuvre."' This follows discussion at pp.296–8 of the 'inferior . . . parallel battle', a chilling foreshadowing of the Western Front stalemate 1915–17, concluding with a prescient solution to the re-establishment of manoeuvre in such circumstances anticipating the actions of 1918. Foch's work was originally published in France *circa* 1904, and consisted of his lectures to the French Staff College 1903–4. It was translated into English before the war

73 Dr Brian Holden Reid highlights the influence on the British Army of the school of Foch and Grandmaison, 'A Doctrinal Perspective 1988–98', p.15. For Foch's influence on the British Staff College before the war, and especially his close friendship with Brigadier (Later Field Marshall) Sir Henry Wilson (Commandant, 1906–10) see Aston, Major General Sir George: *The Biography of the Late Marshal Foch*, London, Hutchinson, 1929, pp.88–101

74 Foch, op cit., p.40, 282

75 ibid., pp.46–7 and 282

76 ibid., pp.285–92

77 ibid., p.298

78 ibid., pp.100–1

79 ibid., p.40

80 Quoted in Winter, Denis: op cit., p104

81 Terraine, op cit., p.55

82 From: *Notes for Corps' Commanders Lecture, XVIII Corps School, 14th May 1917*, IWM, Maxse Papers, Box 69/53/10, File 42 and Box 69/53/13, File 2. This Clausewitzian view of the enemy's Centre of Gravity being its army, or armed forces, is reiterated in Terraine's *Right of the Line*, which looks at the inter-war reaction to perceptions of the Western Front and how this translated into policy making as the next war approached: '. . . we are drawn to the inescapable conclusion that the British people collectively, leaders and led, committed between the wars the cardinal error: they "made a picture" of future war; indeed, more than one. . . . The British in the 1930s painted a picture of the German threat from which the centrepiece was strangely missing; no one, it would seem, ever asked the simple question, "what is the main element of German power?" . . . how was it possible to "miss" such an object as the German Army?' (pp.58–61). This argument is followed through into the pre-war re-armament programme, which favoured the RAF at the expense of the ability to influence events on the Continent *on land*, a point amplified by Michael Howard, op cit.: 'With hindsight, we can see that in industrial societies there is no way in which the attrition of armies can be separated from the attrition, moral as well as social, of peoples. After the [First World] war a few enterprising strategic thinkers in Britain began the quest for the philosophers' stone of a "knock-out blow". Some hoped to find it in the bomber aircraft, others in the tank. But the conventional wisdom was that another war would be much like the last, and the sensible thing therefore would be to avoid it. It was a belief that was to dominate British statecraft for the next twenty years.' (p.41). These points should be remembered when considering Harris's argument in *Men, Ideas and Tanks* that the Army between the wars did all that might reasonably be expected of it to maintain the momentum of development after the war years. That it

could not ultimately do so was due in large measure to political lack of will and the greater attraction of the RAF's 'knock-out' blow doctrine for strategic airpower. The Experimental Mechanised Force was inaugurated on Salisbury Plain in 1927, as the process of 'debunking' First World War commanders was beginning in earnest. It also followed shortly after unpopular wars in Ireland and in support of the White Army in Russia, immediately after the Army's much-resented role in the General Strike and just before the Depression. It is scarcely to be wondered at that the Army lost some of its self-belief during such a difficult period

83 Foch, op cit., pp.27–28. Foch contrasts the views of Marshal de Saxe and Napoleon on the subject: 'We again come across this "war without battle" . . . characterised in the following way by Marshal de Saxe himself, albeit a man of undeniable ability: "I am not in favour of giving battle; especially at the outset of a war. I am even convinced that a clever general can wage war his whole life without once being compelled to do so." Entering Saxony in 1806, Napoleon writes to Soult: "There is nothing I desire so much as a great battle." The one wants to avoid battle his whole life; the other demands it at the first opportunity'

84 This is particularly evident in the German Army's desire to extend the Battle of Kursk into an out-and-out battle of attrition in order to maintain the 'initiative': 'On 13 July, Field Marshals von Manstein and Kluge were summoned to East Prussia, and Hitler informed them that Citadel [Kursk] must be called off immediately . . . Manstein had not committed all his forces and was in favour of continuing the offensive as a battle of attrition; by smashing up Russian armored reserves in the Kursk salient we might forestall major offensives in other sectors. This situation should have been foreseen before Citadel was launched; we were now in the position of a man who has seized a wolf by the ears and dare not let it go.' – von Mellenthin, Major General F W: *Panzer Battles*, Oklahoma, Futura Books, 1977, p.277 (first published London, Cassell, 1955). Manstein confirms this account in *Lost Victories – The War Memoirs of Hitler's Most Brilliant General*, London, Greenhill, 1987 (first published in Germany in 1955 and translated into English for Methuen Books in 1958), pp.448–9. For a discussion of the German Army's misreading of the lessons of the First World War and their under-estimation of the role of firepower, see Bailey, Brigadier J B A: 'Trends in Procurement in the "Century of Firepower"', *Defence Procurement Analysis*, Summer 1998, pp.13–15

85 Liddell Hart, B H: *Why Don't We Learn From History?*, London, George Allen & Unwin Ltd, 1944, p.13

86 Foch, op cit., p34

87 Hamley, op cit., p.3

88 For studies of the constraints that denied such success, see Terraine's *The Road to Passchendaele* or Liddle's *Passchendaele in Perspective*

89 IWM, Maxse Papers, Box 69/53/7, file 17/2

90 SS152, revised version of January 1918, p.5

91 IWM, Maxse Papers, Box 59/63/10

92 IWM, Maxse Papers, Box 59/63/10

93 Prior and Wilson, *Command on the Western Front: the Military Career of Sir Henry Rawlinson, 1914–1918*, Blackwell, Oxford, 1992 p.305. The inference is not that Haig and Rawlinson were poor generals, who were therefore more tolerable as their capacity to influence diminished. Rather, until 1917–18, they had not been able to concentrate exclusively upon their function of

command, since the burden of raising and preparing the British Armies in France had been so utterly demanding

94 Dawnay's letter to DMO is O.B./2266 dated 8 July 1918. It was copied the next day to DASD, with the covering letter detailing the 'installation of some further machinery' to develop the work of the training sub-section at GHQ through inauguration of the post of Inspector-General of Training. With the extra resources being made available to it, Dawnay anticipated that the IGT '. . . should have a marked effect in securing progressive training, interchange of ideas, and up-to-date experience, on both sides of the Channel throughout the whole course, from the Depot in England to the front line in France.' Dawnay's original letter contains a resumé of lessons culled from both British and German experiences and details much of the tremendous improvement in tactics that had been achieved, especially: 'The vital importance of good leadership of the subordinate fighting units, and of fostering the initiative of junior commanders, especially by decentralization and avoidance of rigidity as regards the detail of plans of operation beyond the primary objective . . . [and] . . . The necessity for exploiting success wherever success can be attained; of pushing on regardless of flanks being in the air; of not wasting effort frontally against strong centres of resistance; and of trusting to the general plan of the advance elsewhere for the reduction of the latter.' IWM, Maxse Papers, Box 69/53/13, File 54

95 40/W.O./6513 of April 1918, containing an immediate assessment of the factors that had led to early reverses as well as analysis of the lessons to be learned from German tactics, including translations of three early 1918 German documents: 'Notes on the Offensive Battle'; 'Memorandum Dealing with the Tactics of the Offensive'; and 'Instructions for the Employment of Machine Guns in the Attack'

96 IWM, Maxse Papers, Box 69/53/14, File 59

KEITH GRIEVES

The Transportation Mission to GHQ, 1916

In August 1916 the Somme offensive seemed to be hampered by a shortage of sufficient gun ammunition for the artillery. Another shell crisis appeared imminent and complaints were directed at the Ministry of Munitions where officials were incredulous as shell output reached the target figure of one million per week. In France munitions officials who were investigating salvage operations near the front line noticed severe transport problems on the roads from the railheads. David Lloyd George, Minister of Munitions, drew the conclusion that the reform of transport arrangements on the Western Front required civilian intervention on a scale commensurate with the munitions crusade in May 1915. On the day that news of Lord Kitchener's death reached London, Lloyd George speculated on whether he would become Secretary of State for War and he asked Sir Eric Geddes, Deputy Director General of Munitions Supply, 'If I do go will you come and put transport right in France?'[1].

The history of the transport mission to the British armies in France in August and September 1916 and the subsequent creation of a new transport directorate at General Headquarters (GHQ) provides an insight into the organisational consequences of large-scale war and its impact on fragile civil-military relations. The membership and recommendations of the commission reflected the quest for 'experts' who might undertake specialist work on behalf of GHQ, but posed the question of how the civilian might be integrated into military decision-making hierarchies. The work of the transport directorate was distrusted by many regular army officers but Field Marshal Sir Douglas Haig, Commander-in-Chief British armies in France, was more willing to accept innovatory ideas than might be supposed. The political and military consequences of transport developments from August 1916 to March 1917 is a neglected episode in studies of the Western Front and the British government in the Great War and might usefully constitute a case study in the continuing debate on total war. In particular, the relevance of business expertise to facilitating operational activity might become as readily acknowledged in military transport as it has been in munitions supply.

The 'bottleneck' of Cape Town in 1900 brought disturbing evidence of the problems of co-ordinating traffic on railway lines during the South African war. However, railways marked an advance on the age-old dependence on 'an almost constant stream of under-horsed and overloaded wagons containing flour, powder, cannonballs, as well as clothing and reinforcements for the army'.[2] Consequently, the deployment plans of the British Expeditionary Force (BEF) in France involved the employment of thirty Railway Transport Officers and one Railway Company (Construction) and assumed that supplies would be dispersed from railheads by the horse transport of individual units.[3] Pre-war planning ignored the possibility of an intermediate zone where 70,000 motor lorries would eventually move material closer to the front line.

In 1916 the General Staff planned the opening battles on the Somme without regard for transport implications. In the post-war years the consequences of separating tactical thought and supply arrangements became a prime lesson in staff training on the 'Q' side. At Amiens eighteen miles of trains under load waited to get to the railheads and Major-General Harding-Newman concluded, 'No staff adequately educated in railway operations could have envisaged concentrating a quarter of a million men for the purposes of battle in front of such a bottle-neck'.[4] He concluded from direct experience that the key factor in the congestion on railways and roads was not the bulk of traffic but the absence of overall co-ordination. General Sir Frederick Clayton, Inspector-General of Communications (IGC), lacked influence at GHQ and had not instituted a systematic transport plan in support of military operations. In addition, the railheads were up to fifteen miles behind the front line and the density of traffic broke up the road surfaces, particularly in wet weather when horse transport left the fields and joined mechanical transport on metalled surfaces.

Ad hoc piecemeal planning to overcome the problems were evident in August 1916. The Fourth Army ordered eighteen miles of track, five locomotives and sixty wagons to relieve congestion on its roads,[5] but a larger response was needed as the volume of British military traffic which left French ports doubled in 1916. The average number of loaded wagons moved daily rose from 2,584 in January to 5,202 in December 1916.[6] On a two-day visit to GHQ in early August Geddes concluded that the operational concentration of divisions in the British sector was not matched by the adequate movement of supplies on lines of communication. In retrospect he summarised many problems:

> The organisation was bad; responsibility was divided, and no-one realised the need for Transportation until they broke the machine which was never designed to stand the strain. They blamed the Ports; they blamed shipping . . . the bottle neck was between the rail head and coast. They had no statistics, they were short of material; short of foresight; short of programmes; short of labour and imagination; and they never pushed the rail heads far forward enough.[7]

These issues were investigated in detail by the transport mission which arrived in France on 24 August 1916 and, with Haig's agreement, freely visited the rearward zone for just under one month.[8] Geddes's summary emphasised problems of control, co-ordination, resourcing, staffing and expansion, which were issues he had rectified in the supply of gun ammunition in 1916 and regularly faced as deputy general manager of the North Eastern Railway (NER) before 1914.

Geddes also had experience of the movement of troops on Indian railways to the north-west frontier during the invasion scare of 1904 before he returned to a home appointment.[9] He was a member of the Railway Executive Committee in 1913–14 which advised the War Office on mobilisation timetables, and of the Engineer and Railway Staff Corps which was a long established corps of executives of principal British railways and civil building contractors.[10] The NER employed 50,000 men in 1913 which made it one of the largest transport enterprises in Britain. Its dominant position in the industry after 1900 was maintained by investment in technical innovation, 'proactive' managerial activity and the constant review of train load efficiency by the analysis of traffic statistics and freight rates. The NER avoided compartmentalised duplication of effort, used elements of scientific management which it referred to as 'American practice', and maintained a working assumption that railways were still instruments of progress.[11] Consequently, railway managers had experience of coherent large-scale organisation and new business methods which Lloyd George 'requisitioned' to expand munitions output. After Lloyd George's departure for the War Office his successor, Edwin Montagu, vigorously complained:

When Geddes left his Ministry he took with him Nash and Beharrell, and since then I can hardly bear to look at War Office correspondence, for almost every day, if you will excuse a slight exaggeration, I receive a request for the services of some new man to be sent somewhere or other, sometimes China, sometimes France. By a curious coincidence they are nearly always North Eastern Railway men, and it looks as though we shall be left without a railway man anywhere about.[12]

Philip Nash joined Geddes's transport mission to inspect British facilities at French Channel ports. His career started at the Locomotive Department, Great Northern Railway in 1897 and he was a manager on the East Indian Railways from 1899 to 1915 when he became Director of Royal Arsenals at the Ministry of Munitions. George Beharrell's statistical expertise was used to project transport requirements of the British armies in France for 1917.[13] In 1914 he was Assistant Goods Manager and Commercial Agent at the NER before joining Geddes at the Ministry of Munitions and, subsequently, in France. They were accompanied by Colonel Mance,

Deputy Director of Movements at the War Office and Director of Railways and Armoured Trains on the Kimberley line during the South African war, and Colonel Freeland, whose Indian railways experience was known to Geddes and who was on the staff of the railways directorate at GHQ. Both officers were uncomfortable about their membership of a civilian mission which was intent on scrutinising existing procedures. Although they were energetic specialists they shared the assumption that transport in France lay firmly within the sphere of military responsibility.

However, some railway staff officers were heartened that the emerging science of statistics revealed the magnitude of the problem. Beharrell's extensive data-gathering activity identified daily discharge of cargo rates by type of article and port, the number of railway wagons available and load in tons per truck and mechanical and horse transport work rates forward of the rail head.[14] He calculated variations between existing supply movements and the 300,000 tons of traffic per week projected for offensive activity in 1917. In broad terms the mission drew attention to the projected 54% increase in total carrying capacity, which was the additional transport implication of another year of war on the Western Front.[15]

These calculations did not challenge General Staff plans for military operations in the Ypres salient in 1917 by emphasising maximum carrying loads using existing resources. Instead, *necessary* improvements were highlighted if the transport of 2,200 tons of material required per mile of front per day during offensives (of which 1,600 tons were gun ammunition and 400 tons were road metal) was to be successfully undertaken in the forward area. On advice from electric traction and light railways specialists, Geddes concluded that 1,000 miles of narrow gauge railway of $1' 11\frac{5}{8}''$ (60 cms) gauge needed to be constructed as two great transverse lines to deliver supplies from the broad gauge railheads to within three miles of the front line.[16] Priority steel allocation was obtained from the Ministry of Munitions and the light railway system, employing 25,000 men, was largely in place by June 1917.

Additionally, statistical analysis of traffic flow demanded supplementary broad-gauge railway facilities which was calculated at 1,200 miles of line, 300 new main-line locomotives and 9,000 wagons to improve ship 'turn around' times by increasing the speed of cargo discharge at ports. By June 1917 much of this large priority order was complete. In December 1917 900 main-line locomotives undertook services under British supervision and 9,000 wagons had been transferred to France. Much of the work of laying new lines was undertaken by Canadian Railway Construction troops. As a further way of increasing efficiency at ports additional berths were constructed, new cranes were sited and the control of assembling yards was integrated with wharfside time-tables. The mission also reviewed the shipment and storage of bulky commodities. It advocated the restoration of Belgian canals so that over

200 miles of navigable waterway could be more fully used for leave and ambulance train services and salvage barges.[17] Ultimately, improvements in the barge service in canal systems of north-east France and Belgium depended on the construction of new port facilities at Richborough (Kent). Its completion was delayed until March 1918 and its consumption of scarce resources became the most controversial feature of the unfolding schemes.

These recommendations mostly took solid form. The mission's refusal to compartmentalise road, rail and canal transport marked the beginning of more total management of available and projected facilities. The systematic construction and repair of roads necessitated stone quarrying in northern France to avoid the shipment of road stone from south-east England, the recruitment of the Chinese Auxiliary Corps of 15,000 men and the creation of a road construction department under the direction of Sir Henry Maybury, President of the Road Board. These wide-ranging proposals embodied the underlying principle that Britain should accept responsibility for the movement of its men and material in France and Flanders. Although the finalised plans were not submitted to Lloyd George until late October 1916, Haig was carrying out Geddes's recommendations as early as 19 September.[18]

Both Lloyd George and Haig looked to Geddes to accept the challenge of rectifying the deficiencies which were identified by the mission. On 18 September Lloyd George asked him to become Director General of Military Railways (DGMR) at the War Office. The appointment quickly drew two expressions of opposition from military members of the Army Council and led Lloyd George to give him the rank of major-general which barely defused the situation, but did give Geddes parity of status with the established hierarchy. It was a new directorate and Geddes was initially, and reluctantly, deputy to the Quarter-Master General (QMG). This role enabled Geddes to attend conferences with munition officials to press for additional resources for military transport. Geddes accepted this appointment with some misgiving on 21 September. One day later Haig informed Lloyd George that he wished Geddes to become Director-General of Transportation (DGT) at GHQ, which was effectively fourth principal staff officer, as he started to acknowledge the forgotten interrelationship of strategy and transport.[19]

A remarkable dual appointment was created. Geddes took charge of the transportation services of the British armies in France, comprising broad and narrow gauge railways, inland water transport and roads (but not ports in the first instance). He was guaranteed direct access to Haig and for over six months they met on an almost daily basis.

Typically, these Lloyd Georgian arrangements gave Geddes 'a very free hand'[20], but required him to staff the new transport directorates. Consequently, many civilian managers were temporarily invested with military rank. Brigadier-General Nash became Deputy Director General of Transportation at GHQ and Brigadier-General Sir Guy Granet, general manager of the Midland Railway, became Deputy Director General of Military Railways at the War Office. Lieutenant Colonel J G Beharrell served both directorates as a statistician. After Geddes obtained control of port facilities a key appointment as Director of Docks at GHQ was Brigadier-General R L Wedgwood, who was Chief Goods and Passenger manager at the NER in 1914. These 'pushers' provided a co-ordinating authority for transport, ended the paramountcy of pre-war Field Service Regulations in this sphere and confirmed Lord Northcliffe's conclusion 'We have brought to France a considerable portion of industrial England'.[21]

However, Lord Northcliffe, proprietor of *The Times* and self-styled experienced observer of the Western Front, strongly opposed the new transport directorate and remained (until the Battle of Cambrai) an unyielding supporter of 'capital' men on the lines of communication. He defended to the utmost the right of the army to determine the use of *its* resources. Lord Northcliffe told Sir Arthur Lee at the Ministry of Munitions:

In spite of the lack of railways, the shortage of trucks, the shortage of labour, etc. everything is being most efficiently handled. If you can get more railways, more trucks, more labour, more motor transport, better management of the shipping from England, you can get quicker transport, and of course you will require more transport as the ammunition and guns increase.[22]

This generalised and uncritical observation of the status quo found regular expression in *The Times* (and the *Morning Post*) where discussion of civil-military relations focused on the need to maintain the High Command's independence from ministerial intervention.[23]

In this context the unconventional appointment of Geddes to a senior staff post at GHQ 'fluttered the military dovecotes' in London and France. The military attache at the British Embassy in Paris pointedly informed Lloyd George:

You can never get over military prejudices. The appointment of anyone who does not belong to the military Trade Union is as welcome to soldiers, as the appointment of a bishop drawn from the ranks of stockbrokers would be to the clergy.

I heard a good deal of whispering about some mysterious contract which Geddes appears to have made with the Marconi Company. You can, no doubt, follow the line of argument, which is not likely to be favourable to you.[24]

This note to the Secretary of State for War firmly stated the exclusivity of the Regular Army officer corps, connected Geddes to the suggestion that Lloyd George had malevolent intent, and concluded that businessmen had no place in military affairs. It assumed that customary practices should remain unquestioned because the 'military Trade Union' remained the sole source of wisdom on all theatre of war activities, despite the changing nature and scale of war. For many general staff officers the innovatory developments at the BEF transport base at Monthouis or 'Geddesburg', as it quickly became known, was an unnecessary precedent.

Conversely, Haig appreciated that this particular war with its limitless supply demands could not be determined by GHQ in absolute isolation from politics and society on the home front. In his diary Haig identified the unprecedented size of the army as the prime cause of change in the balance of civil-military relations. On 27 October 1916 Haig wrote:

There is a good deal of criticism apparently being made at the appointment of a civilian like Geddes to an important post on the Headquarters of an Army in the Field. These critics seem to fail to realise the size of the Army, and the amount of work which the Army requires of a civilian nature. The working of the railways, the upkeep of the roads, even the baking of bread, and 1000 other industries go on in peace as well as in war. So with the whole nation at war, our object should be to employ men on the same work in war as they are accustomed to do in peace. Acting on this principle I have got Geddes at the head of all railways and transportation, with the best civilian and military engineers under him.[25]

This important piece of evidence distances Haig from the oft-repeated criticisms of civilian interference and draws attention to his support for specialist expertise from industry. Haig needed the transport problems to be confronted as the mobilisation of manpower and munitions had been in the first two years of the war.

He concluded that men and munitions were available but the third 'M' – movement – could not be resolved by generals and colonels who had no practical experience of large-scale transport management. Haig confounded the critics by arguing that the 'large army first' principle should not disrupt the necessary continuities of production and distribution in peace and war, and in 1916 he accepted that overlapping spheres of military and civilian activity existed. Indeed, Geddes's arrival at GHQ was a logical corollary of efficiently harnessed skills in a nation at war. These points were rehearsed in an exchange of correspondence between Haig and Lloyd George after the latter told the House of Commons on 19 November 1917 that he had pressed his advance 'on soldiers against their will in the appointment of a civilian to reorganise the railway behind the lines'.[26] Haig argued that he had first wanted Geddes's advice in January 1915 and freely sought his appointment to GHQ in September 1916. Elements of truth existed on both sides and, apart from emphasising the difficult relationship of brasshats and frocks, these exasperated attempts to reconstruct the past conveyed the success of this unconventional approach, and its high profile, as a consequence of unforeseen siege-like attritional war.

Haig valued Geddes's broad views, quick intuition of requirements and energy. Haig was impressed by the light railway system which restored his faith in the search for the *decisive* battle. He told Geddes:

As you know, I look to the Railways to do much more than supply the Armies' needs. I feel confident that at a certain moment they will give us that mobility which will enable us to out-manoeuvre the enemy, and enable me to bring a superior force of guns and men at the decisive moment to the decisive point before the enemy can take counter measures.[27]

The revival of the Clausewitzian ambition for 'breakthrough' was not facilitated by using railways to out-manoeuvre the enemy, but the growth of transport facilities forward of the rail heads was a central feature of artillery plans for the battle of Arras. It far exceeded the intensity and duration of bombardment in the opening phase of the Somme offensive. In April 1917 the decisive battle did not ensue but transportation moved forward with the armies. Geddes reported:

We had Railways on top of the Vimy Ridge, and at Fampoux – beyond Arras, and at Neuville Vitasse. We delivered all rations to the front line troops that night 'ere sunset. We had the big Naval guns on Railways mountings firing from where the enemy had been in the morning, and our own artillery – which in every battle up till then had been starved of ammunition – sent appeals to transportation to bring no more as they were tired of unloading it.[28]

Both Haig and Geddes respected professionalism, fixity of purpose and attention to detail and they found these qualities in each other, in addition to the importance of Scottish identity in their lives.[29] Geddes admired Haig's gentlemanly conduct and his loyalty was reciprocated, which enabled the opposition of General Sir Frederick Clayton, IGC, to be overcome. Haig's support for Geddes, who even Lord Esher found 'capable and tactful',[30] impressed Lord Derby, Under Secretary of State for War, who followed his recommendations with alacrity. Likewise, the opposition of Lieutenant General Sir Ronald Maxwell, QMG at GHQ, who initially tendered his resignation as a protest, was gradually defused by the growth of the vast transport base at Monthouis. Haig's support of Geddes reflected his acceptance of this 'man for the job' and his understanding of the ways in which sympathetic civilians could contribute to military efficiency in the main theatre of war.

In contrast, relations with Brigadier-General Montagu-Stuart-Wortley, Director of Movements at the War Office, was far more brittle. His compartmentalised responsibility for ports and movements in Britain, including home railways, was buttressed by the QMG, Lieutenant General Sir John Cowans and – to a lesser extent – by the arch-traditionalist King George V. In September 1916 his private secretary, Lord Stamfordham, noted that the king was glad to hear that Stuart-Wortley and Geddes were 'working in complete harmony'.[31] However, Lord Derby recorded a 'painful interview' with Stuart-Wortley and had no doubt that he had an 'intense dislike of Geddes'.[32] It was not until 8 January 1917 that the directorate of movements was brought under the authority of the DGMR.

Stuart-Wortley became a brigade commander and thus ended two years of antagonistic relations, which partly reflected the transition from a predominantly military war effort to the emergence of more total war. Cowans had rebuffed the possibility that Geddes might investigate railway conditions in France in January 1915, which took place shortly after Stuart-Wortley's unfavourable reaction to the recruitment of a pioneer battalion of NER men which was raised in York. Geddes noted that they were both Rifle Brigade officers and reflected in 1920:

> Again, it was a repetition of General Stuart-Wortley's resentment at a civilian coming in to do a technical job which the professional soldier, even a purely infantry soldier, thought he could do better.[33]

The turbulent personal relationships reflected *improvised* change at the shifting intersection of civil-military relations as the war effort constantly expanded beyond an expeditionary force focused on infantry units with horse provision for some mobility to a near stationary continental-scale commitment, which required the transport infrastructure of a large manufacturing metropolis.

There were no rules or precedents which guided the temporarily uniformed transport improvisers on the Western Front after the breakdown of August 1916. Differences of outlook were not masked by the adoption of military rank. They continued to be paid by their pre-war employers at rates far in excess of army pay, but their usefulness to the state was constantly under review as one measurable task followed another. As respect accorded to rank was only available in the most perfunctory form, improvisers depended on fickle ministerial patronage.

The most successful pushers or 'big men' staffed their own offices, which gradually took semi-permanent form. They blended varieties of expertise and working practices into hybrid organisations which were resented by officers of traditional outlook who argued that the intertwining of self-evidently military and civilian spheres could never be normalised in war. In the *History of the Great War* Geddes's appointment was presented as a short-term expedient: 'He was a specialist called in on an emergency to undertake a specialist task and given an exceptional position to enable him to perform it.'[34]

Outside the 'proper channels' the railway executives planned resource implications of enlarged traffic flow and instituted review procedures in a routinised war which lacked variable factors until 1918. They had (increasingly) limited access to Lloyd George whose wartime political aspirations were essentially derived from epitomising 'national organisations'. The rise of 'munitions Field Marshals' and their business methods were greatly lampooned in January 1918 by Brigadier-General John Charteris, Chief of Intelligence at GHQ, who noted,

> . . . the light railway will stop any of their trains whenever a body of troops appears and almost beseech them to take a lift anywhere up and down the line, so that they can record them on their graph.[35]

He noticed a great keenness on the system, as if it was a novel experience. But examples existed of plans which required more careful consideration of actual conditions near the front line. The original scheme for 1,000 miles of tactical light railways in the forward zone envisaged 800 miles of steam locomotive haulage and an electric-powered system of 200 miles which was dependent on twenty moveable power-stations. In exposed areas close to the front line electric locomotives were envisaged to reduce noise and smoke but, until the problem of maintaining and camouflaging overhead wiring near the trenches was solved, these confounded the crucial importance of invisible lines of approach.[36] Instead, the growth of tactical light railways was accompanied by the ubiquitous petrol-electric tractor. Edmonds gleefully highlighted the unsuitability of light railways in relation to the final Allied advance of 1918.[37]

In March 1917 Geddes became Inspector-General of Transportation in all theatres of war. Granet became DGMR and Nash was appointed DGT and specialist activity was extended to all theatres of war. In Mesopotamia substantial orders for barges, tugs and launches followed an investigation into inland water transport. In Salonika Sir Frances Dent, General Manager of the Chatham and South Eastern Railway and a 'specially selected expert', headed a mission to consider whether the Egyptian State Railways could supply additional railway stores.[38] Edmonds' acerbic comments reflected the growing significance of the civilian manager in this element of war: 'It seems that it should be regretted that a civilian Commander-in-Chief was not appointed when GHQ's request for more fighting men was turned down.'[39]

This remark ignored the increasing interdependency of military and civilian transport resources and the need to co-ordinate their supply and management after the emergence of a crisis on the French railways in November 1916. Britain came under pressure to extend its responsibility for the maintenance and daily operation of broad-gauge railways north-east of the line Hazelbrouck, Lille, Valenciennes and Maubeuge and particularly to relieve the shortage of rolling stock by providing 20,000 additional wagons. Geddes told Lloyd George:

I think it is no exaggeration to say that something very drastic will have to be done in England on the lines I discussed with you in order to release locomotives, rolling stock, and personnel, for use in France.[40]

As the closure of home lines and stations, reduced safety and maintenance levels, baggage restrictions and increases in ordinary fares were contemplated, the ruthless reduction of traffic on the British railways became an immediate consequence of the demand for locomotives and wagons 'never contemplated in the past'[41] as broad-gauge railways became a vital ingredient of strategic policy in 1917 and a perceptible alteration occurred in the balance of the Anglo-French war effort on the Western Front. Changes on this sensitive issue were co-operatively managed between Albert Claveille, French Minister of Public Works and a professional railwayman,[42] and Geddes. They held regular conferences which provided a starting-point for the development of inter-allied transport policies, despite the setbacks at the Calais conference in February 1917.[43] In liaison with the Railways Executive Committee, Ministry of Munitions, War Office and French military authorities, Geddes was well placed in London and at GHQ to take a broad view of the implications of improving transport facilities in France as the British war effort entered a more coherent, planned, total phase.

The significance of the transport mission to GHQ has not only been understated in histories of the Western Front and of civil society at war but also as a vital aspect of Lloyd George's rise to the premiership. It reinforced the image of dynamism which originated in his munitions crusade. In the autumn months of 1916 he undertook two 'battles' at the War Office. Apart from transport he demanded an investigation into the supply of army clothing, which was undertaken by Lord Rothermere who also used civilian expertise.[44] In addition, the rupture of relations between Lloyd George and Lord Northcliffe reflected his unorthodox short circuiting of existing procedures. The effects of his energising interventions were widely admired, and on becoming Prime Minister he was expected to transform the prospects for obtaining further men in addition to munitions and movement. Shortly before Lloyd George became Prime Minister Lord Esher noted:

> Unless Lloyd George does for the provision of men what Asquith did for munitions in appointing Lloyd George with plenary powers and what Lloyd George did in appointing Eric Geddes to grapple with military railways, we will fail to obtain the men required.[45]

Neither Lloyd George nor Geddes, nor indeed Haig, were afraid of 'thinking big' which surely was a phrase, like 'cutting red-tape', of the age and implied commitment to waging large-scale war in the quest for decisive victory. Thomas Jones noted that Geddes knew how 'to add a nought, or a couple of noughts to almost any requisition' for supplies.[46]

The work of railway managers enabled Lloyd George to appear to be as enervating an influence on the problem of transport in 1916 as on munitions supply in 1915. Managers were lent to the state and were sufficiently unhooked from their commercial transport allegiances to become disconnected as 'experts' from the railway 'interest'. Consequently, the political consequences of an 'expanding state' in wartime, such as unleashing corporatist bias or a permanent government-industry nexus, was curbed to some extent.[47] Lloyd George's assiduous cultivation of professional railway managers compensated for the insufficiently reflexive gentlemanly concept of soldiering.[48] The traditional officer corps mentality was not forcefully challenged because the hybrid organisations remained outside the confines of narrowly defined, i.e. non-technical military expertise. Consequently, 'Geddesburg' and later 'Nashville' at Monthouis, which comprised 100 transport officers – civilians and RE officers – and 30,000 railwaymen in 1918, remained an important part of Lloyd George's rhetoric that the great feats of wartime organisation were achieved by civilian experts.[49] Few military figures were accorded this accolade in his *War Memoirs* and the exceptions such as General Monash usually had civilian origins.[50]

The transport mission to GHQ in 1916 and the ensuing developments provide a salutory reminder that the enlarging scale of battle had managerial and organisational implications which the British Army found difficult to assess and solve. The arrival of businessmen at GHQ to assist its administrative functions inadvertently preserved the pre-eminence of the old officer corps. The improvement of lines of communication after August 1916 occurred in a sustained period of immobile, or stationary, warfare and the transport programme reflected the belated acknowledgement of a long war, which required substantive Anglo-French co-operation but fell short, at this stage, of trans-national management.[51]

Strategy and transport were reconnected in time for the opening battles of 1917 and the realisation grew that it was no longer enough to out-produce and out-conscript in this attritional war.[52] In 1916 confusion and congestion on railways and roads assumed crisis proportions because transport problems undermined preparations for the decisive battle. However, belatedly, the third 'M' obtained importance and the three ingredients identified by Haig of men, munitions and movement finally achieved a balance in the third year of the war.

Notes

I am grateful to participants of the BCMH conference on 'Britain and the First World War', University of Buckingham, July 1995, for their comments on an earlier draft of this paper.

1 House of Lords Record Office (hereafter HLRO) Lloyd George mss. G/252, rough notes of a conversation (between Lloyd George and Sir Eric Geddes) at the House of Commons, 10 November 1932, A J Sylvester. See also PRO WO 32/5163, Lloyd George to D Haig, 1 August 1916
2 Maj.-Gen. J C Harding-Newman *Modern Military Administration, Organization and Transportation* (Aldershot: Gale and Polden, 1933), p.6
3 HLRO Lloyd George mss. G/252, rough notes of a talk between Mr Lloyd George and Brig.-Gen.Sir Osborne Mance at Churt, 25 November 1932, A J Sylvester
4 Harding-Newman (note 2) p.16
5 W J K Davies, *Light Railways of the First World War. A History of Tactical Rail Communications on the British Fronts, 1914–18* (Newton Abbot: David and Charles, 1967), p.44
6 A M Henniker *Transportation on the Western Front. History of the Great War* (London: Imperial War Museum/The Battery Press 1992 edn (1937) p.179
7 HLRO Lloyd George mss. G/252, rough notes of a conversation [with Geddes], 10 November 1932, A J Sylvester
8 R Blake (ed.) *The Private Papers of Douglas Haig 1914–1919* (London: Eyre and Spottiswoode, 1952), p.161: PRO SUPP 12/1, E Geddes to E Montagu, 17 August 1916; Bodleian Library Oxford (hereafter BLO) Addison mss. Box 99, Diary, 21 September 1916; HLRO Lloyd George mss. E/1/1/3, Lord Derby to Lloyd George, 30 August 1916
9 K Grieves, *Sir Eric Geddes. Business and government in war and peace* (Manchester: Manchester UP, 1989), pp. 3–5; HLRO Lloyd George mss. E/2/16/2, Lloyd George to Lord Stamfordham, 4 October 1916
10 E A Pratt, *British Railways and the Great War. Organization, Efforts, Difficulties and Achievements* 2 vols. (London: Selwyn and Blount, 1921 Vol. 1), p.89
11 R J Irving, *The North-Eastern Railway Company, 1870–1914* (Leicester: Leicester UP, 1976), pp.213–66; W W Tomlinson, *North Eastern Railways. Its Rise and Development* (Newton Abbot: David and Charles, 1967), pp.726–31. The Traffic Apprenticeship scheme at the NER provided early responsibility and wide understanding of the enterprise for entrants into general management who were identified by exceptional 'personality' criteria which usually emphasised public school origins and precluded technicians. The delivery of planned experience in industry before 1914 was unusual in an age of

nepotism and after-work study. See S P Keeble, *The Ability to Manage: A Study of British Management 1890–1990* (Manchester: Manchester UP, 1992), pp.140–1, 147, 152, 159

12 HLRO Lloyd George mss. E/2/19/8 E Montagu to D Lloyd George, 11 October 1916; 'He [Lloyd George] is most indebted to you for the surrender of Geddes and Wedgwood.' BLO Addison mss. Box 37, RH Brade to C Addison, 23 October 1916

13 HLRO Lloyd George mss. G/252, notes of an interview with Sir George Beharrell at St James's House, 30 November 1932, A J Sylvester

14 Henniker (note 6) p.185

15 HLRO Lloyd George mss. E/6/1/1, Memorandum on Transport Facilities in the various theatres of war, E Geddes, 28 October 1916

16 D Lloyd George, *War Memoirs* 2 vols. (London: Odhams Press, 1938 ed.), Vol.1, p.476; Davies (note 5) p.39; PRO WO 32/5145 Outline specification and technical description of proposed 60-cm Light Railway in British War Zone, unsigned, 11 September 1916, attached to minute, E Geddes, 26 September 1916; PRO WO 158/852 History of Light Railways, for DGT GHQ, 14 January 1919, pp.2–5

17 HLRO Lloyd George mss.G/252, continuation of Interview with Sir Philip Nash, Thames House, Millbank, 28 December 1932, A J Sylvester

18 Lord Riddell, *War Diary 1914–1918* (London: Ivor Nicholson and Watson, 1933) 19 September 1916, p.211

19 Further work on transport on the Western Front might usefully modify the idea that 'paralysis at the top' at GHQ prevented change and innovation. T Travers, *The Killing Ground. The British Army, the Western Front and the emergence of modern warfare 1900–1918* (London: Unwin Hyman, 1990 ed.) p.111

20 Lloyd George (note 16) *Vol.1*, p.475

21 British Library (hereafter BL) Northcliffe Ms Add.Ms 62334, Lord Northcliffe to Sir Rennell Rodd, 7 August 1916. See also *Railway Gazette* Special military transport issue, 21 September 1920; Henniker (note 6) p.193

22 BL Northcliffe Ms Add.Ms 62334, Lord Northcliffe to Col. Sir Arthur Lee, 27 August 1916

23 On the attitude of the *Morning Post* see Riddell (note 18) p.211

24 HLRO Lloyd George mss. E/3/14/26, Col. LeRoy-Lewis to Lloyd George, 8 November 1916. For a similar comment by Hankey see S Roskill, *Hankey, Man of Secrets Vol. 1 1877–1918* (London: Collins, 1970) diary, 1 November 1916, p.312

25 Blake (note 8) 27 October 1916, pp.173–4

26 HLRO Lloyd George mss. F/14/4/78, quoted in Haig to Lord Derby, 22 November 1917; see also F/14/4/79, Lloyd George to Lord Derby, 26 November 1917

27 HLRO Lloyd George mss. G/252, rough Notes of a Conversation at the House of Commons, 10 November 1932, A J Sylvester, enclosing copy of a letter from Haig to Geddes, 13 May 1917

28 HLRO Lloyd George mss.G/252, extract from Geddes Family Tree, E Geddes, 1920. But see B H Liddell Hart, *History of the First World War* (London: Pan, 1970 ed.), p.318. The Light Railway system was at its most extensive in the Ypres sector. PRO WO 158/852 History of the Light Railways p.7

29 *British Legion Journal* March 1928, Earl Haig Memorial number, Sir Eric Geddes 'A Great Gentleman', p.263. See also J Grigg, *Lloyd George: From Peace to War 1912–16* (London: Methuen, 1985), p.367

30 P Fraser, *Lord Esher: A political biography* (London: Hart Davis, MacGibbon, 1973) journal, 8 October 1916, p.333

31 HLRO Lloyd George mss. E/2/16/3, Lord Stamfordham to Lloyd George, 5 October 1916

32 HLRO Lloyd George mss. E/1/1/6 Lord Derby to Lloyd George, 15 September 1916

33 HLRO Lloyd George mss. G/252, extract from Geddes Family Tree, E Geddes, 1920

34 Henniker (note 6) p.194

35 Brig.-Gen. J Charteris *At G.H.Q.* (London: Cassell, 1931) diary, 26 January 1918, p.283. See also p.187

36 Harding-Newman (note 2) p.9

37 J E Edmonds, Foreword, in Henniker (note 6). For discussion of the transport problems in an advance of great depth see PRO WO 158/852 History of Light Railways, p.9

38 HLRO Lloyd George mss. E/1/5/13, Granet to Lloyd George, 24 October 1916

39 J E Edmonds in A M Henniker (note 6) xxii

40 HLRO Lloyd George mss. E/1/5/16, critical position regarding French rolling stock, E Geddes and W G Granet, 24 November 1916. See also accompanying letter from Marshal Joffre to the French mission at GHQ on railway requirements with annotations by Geddes, 19 November 1916

41 Pratt (note 10), Haig to Sir Herbert Walker, Chairman of the Railways Executive Committee, 19 November 1916, p.652

42 J F Godfrey, *Capitalism at War: Industrial Policy and Bureaucracy in France, 1914–1918* (Leamington Spa: Berg, 1987), p.60

43 HLRO Lloyd George mss. G/252, continuation of Interview with Sir Philip Nash, 28 December 1932; Lloyd George mss. E/3/14/29, Col. LeRoy-Lewis to Lloyd George, 22 November 1916. See also Blake (note 8) diary, 26 February 1917, p.199; DR Woodward (ed.), *The Military Correspondence of Field-Marshal Sir William Robertson* (London: The Bodley Head/Army Records Society, 1989), Robertson to Haig, 28 February 1917, p.154

44 T Wilson (ed.), *The Political Diaries of C P Scott, 1911–1928* (London: Collins, 1970) diary, 20–22 November 1916, p.237. The same principle was also suggested for combing out men employed in sedentary work in the British armies in France

45 HLRO Lloyd George mss. F/41/5/2, Lord Esher to Lord Murray, 28 November 1916

46 T Jones, *Lloyd George* (Oxford: OUP, 1951), p.74. For example see PRO WO 32/5145, preliminary statement of personnel necessary to carry out light railway recommendations of the Commander in Chief, E Geddes, 26 September 1916

47 On the underlying role of experts in government see J Turner, 'Experts and interests. David Lloyd George and the dilemmas of the expanding state, 1906–1919' in R MacLeod (ed.), *Government and Expertise: Specialists, Administrators and Professionals 1860–1919* (Cambridge: UP, 1988), p.206

48 On the persistence of gentlemanly values in soldiering see K Simpson, 'The officers' in I F W Beckett and K Simpson (eds), *A Nation in Arms. A Social Study of the British Army in the First World War* (Manchester: Manchester UP, 1985), pp.66–8; P Kennedy 'Britain in the First World War' in A R Millett and W Murray, *Military Effectiveness Vol. 1: The First World War* (London: Unwin Hyman 1989 ed.), pp.52–3

49   Lloyd George (note 16) *Vol.1.* p.479
50   ibid. *Vol.2*, p.2016
51   PRO WO 32/5146 Guy W Granet to Lord Derby, 7 December 1917; PRO
     WO 32/5146 Lord Derby to Italian Minister of War, 21 January 1918. In
     1918 supreme control of the transportation services of the Allies remained
     an illusory ideal
52   Works used on relevant themes within the debate on total war include W
     H McNeil, *The Pursuit of Power* (Oxford: Blackwell, 1983), p.317; J Terraine,
     The Smoke and the Fire: Myths and Anti-Myths of War 1861–1945 (London: Leo
     Cooper, 1992 ed.), p.71; I Beckett 'Total War' in C McInnes and G D Sheffield,
     Warfare in the Twentieth Century: Theory and Practice (London: Unwin Hyman,
     1988), p.7. On protracted siege war see S Bidwell and D Graham, *Fire Power:
     British Army Weapons and Theories of War 1904–1945* (London, George Allen
     and Unwin, 1985 ed.), p.71. For a commendation of transport on the Western
     Front by Gough and Plumer see PRO ADM 116/1805 P A M Nash to E
     Geddes, 22 September 1917

For permission to use quotations from copyright material, I am grateful
to Lord Esher, Sir Reay Geddes, Earl Haig, and the Clerk of the Records,
House of Lords Record Office, on behalf of the Beaverbrook Foundation
Trustees.

JOHN LEE

Some Lessons of the Somme: The British Infantry in 1917

For a long time now we have been used to books extolling the virtues of the German Army in the First World War. These are frequently from the pens of American military scholars who conduct a great deal of historical research into good military practice but seem only to find such practice in the ranks of the German Army[1]. A more worrying trend is in the writing that not only praises German genius but goes on to paint a picture of a hopelessly incompetent British Army – blighted by useless commanders, wrong-headed doctrine and antediluvian tactics[2].

One could argue from a different perspective. Faced by a militarised nation with huge reserves where all adult males served in the armed forces, Britain's tiny professional Army, which had largely sacrificed itself in the desperate fighting of 1914, had to organise and oversee a massive and unprecedented expansion from a few hundred thousand to literally millions in a few months, and rapidly devise new ways of equipping and training these men for a kind of warfare which few had prepared for before 1914. Looking at this larger picture, one might be forgiven a certain admiration for the remarkable achievement of the British in creating a warfighting machine which comprehensively defeated the main enemy in 1918.

All the main combatants in the period 1914 to 1916 made many terrible mistakes, paid for with the lives of their soldiers, and were forced to learn the harsh lessons of the new siege warfare – 'trench-to-trench' fighting as it came to be known. The sustained fighting of July to November 1916 was a very important experience for the British Expeditionary Force (BEF) and was a time of intense analysis and tactical improvement which transformed its fighting power.

The BEF entered the Somme battles with tactics based on the experiences of the year 1915. In that year wholly unfamiliar trench fighting became a new routine which was punctuated by a series of offensive and defensive battles, and untried weapons systems had to be absorbed into the tactical mix under the most difficult circumstances. The initial British response was to group the specialists in the new weaponry to enable them to experiment, learn and disseminate new technical and tactical ideas[3]. Thus the skill of individual marksmen was soon recognised and each company provided snipers for a group attached to battalion headquarters. The new rifle grenades were soon the province of some five to ten specialists within each company, who often joined the hand grenade squads at battalion or brigade level. The Vickers medium machine-gun began as a battalion weapon (two guns per battalion; doubled to four by February 1915) but from October 1915, when the Machine Gun Corps came into being, it was gathered into sixteen gun companies attached to each infantry brigade. This is a much criticised development, when compared to the German deployment of machine-guns in their infantry companies, but this does not take cognisance of the fact that they were overwhelmingly committed to defensive fighting. The British were seeking ways of maximising the effect of machine-guns in offensive operations.

The Vickers guns were only withdrawn from the battalions as the new lighter Lewis guns became available. This important new weapon, never quite matched by the Germans, first appeared in June 1915 and the initial allocation of eight per battalion was doubled to sixteen by 1 July 1916. The British trench mortars were standardised by mid-1916, with each infantry brigade operating a battery of Stokes mortars, while artillery men operated medium and heavy mortars at the divisional level.

As the use of hand grenades became prevalent during 1915 (to be denounced as an obsession by 1916) most battalions produced some twenty or thirty specialists who received a lot of extra training. It was common for brigades to group all their specialists into a bombing company of some 120 men, who would operate in groups of thirty or so. These were very tough, aggressive and independently minded soldiers. During 1915 many battalions also developed a reputation as particularly aggressive trench raiders (2nd Royal Welch Fusiliers, 1st Worcesters, 1st Grenadier Guards, 6th and 7th Canadian Infantry to name but a few), which also taught many new lessons to the British infantry which were spread through the ever-growing system of battle schools in the Army.

It will come as a surprise to those who criticise the ability of the British without studying in detail their actual performance that during the fighting on the Somme in 1916 there was an intense and ongoing analysis of tactics, and that lessons learned from good practice were circulated in the form of memoranda and notes, which went towards the codification of battle drills in training pamphlets[4]. The British infantry re-invented fire and movement tactics as it carried out the hundreds of attacks that made up the larger battle. (We badly need a study of the degree to which the British borrowed tactical ideas from their French allies in this respect.) The integration of Lewis gun, rifle grenade and trench mortar fire with the advances carried out by riflemen and bombers, all blended with an increasing confidence in the gunners' ability to lay down effective creeping barrages, transformed the British battle performance. In July 1916 the main infantry formation around which the attack was organised was the company. By November it was the platoon, but now transformed into four sections of highly interdependent and effective specialists.

In February 1917 General Headquarters of the BEF published training pamphlet SS 143 'Instructions for the Training of Platoons for Offensive Action'. This is a much neglected document. (Samuels does not refer to it at all in his extensive notes and bibliography, which is a pity because he makes a fundamental error in thinking that the British platoons did not re-organise until the end of 1917. It might be dismissed as slavishly following a linear approach to tactics. In fact it provides an outline for the training of teams of specialists to overcome any resistance by the use of the most sophisticated fire and movement techniques.)

The document repays careful study, together with SS 144 'The Normal Formation for the Attack' (also issued in February 1917). It opens by explaining that GHQ now considered the platoon as the primary unit of assault. The issue of the two pamphlets together was necessitated 'partly by the shortness of time which is available for training, and partly by the lack of experience among subordinate commanders'. It is thus a brutally realistic document, but stresses almost immediately that it is an aid to the platoon commander in training and fighting his platoon, not as a 'correct line' for all situations but as a distillation of experience that should be thoroughly learnt, safe in the knowledge that it could usefully be followed in almost all circumstances. It was designed to cover both 'trench-to-trench attack' against organised defences and the 'attack in open warfare' to which the British constantly aspired to return.

The key was in the new organisation of the platoon into four specialist sections. The ideal strength of the platoon was one officer and forty other ranks (OR). It could be reinforced to forty-four; if it fell below twenty-eight men it was held to be unviable and should be merged with other units. The ideal was:

Headquarters	1 officer	4 ORs
Bombing Section	1 NCO	8 soldiers, including 2 expert throwers and 2 bayonet men
Lewis Gun Section	1 NCO	8 soldiers, including the two gunners
Rifle Section	1 NCO	8 soldiers, including picked shots, 2 scouts and bayonet fighters
Rifle Bombers Section	1 NCO	8 soldiers, four of them grenade firers

The scale of ammunition to be carried by each section in the attack was laid out. Then the characteristics of each section is discussed. The rifle (and bayonet) was still considered the primary offensive weapon – the rifle to establish a local superiority of fire; the bayonet to demoralise the enemy and dissuade him from standing his ground. The hand grenade, carried both by the specialists and all riflemen, was the secondary offensive weapon, with the main function of dealing with the enemy below ground. The rifle bomb is described as the 'howitzer' of the infantry platoon, used for dislodging the enemy from cover. The Lewis gun is the 'weapon of opportunity', highly mobile and presenting a small target on the battlefield, and especially valuable for working around the flanks of the enemy to establish enfilade fire.

In the attack the platoon went forward in a wave made up of two lines. The first line comprised the rifle section and the bombing section, each with their section commander in the centre, and with an experienced platoon sergeant going forward between the two sections. In the second line, advancing some fifteen to twenty-five yards behind, the rifle bombers followed the rifle section and the Lewis gun section followed the bombers. The platoon headquarters was located between the two sections. The bombers and Lewis gunners were always deployed on the more open of the two flanks; they were always to seek to turn any position the platoon came up against. The standard operating procedure was for another platoon to advance in the same formation some fifty to one hundred yards behind, but with the platoon headquarters leading that advance, so that the platoon commander could quickly assess how to commit his soldiers in support of the leading platoon.

If the advance was in any greater depth, or if it was in open country, subsequent platoons would advance in 'artillery formation'. The four sections moved in a diamond formation, always with the rifle section in the lead, the rifle grenade and bombing sections to the sides (with the bombers favouring the more open flank), and the Lewis gun section to the rear (from where it could deploy quickly to either side). The platoon headquarters accompanied whichever column was best suited for the purposes of command in the particular operation. The individual sections could go forward in fours, twos or single file. The platoon was widely dispersed over ground one hundred yards wide and fifty yards deep – which would minimise losses from enemy artillery and other fire (hence the description 'artillery formation').

What we have in SS143 is a battle drill based on real experience, which could be rehearsed and learnt by officers, NCOs and soldiers alike, and which was sufficiently flexible in its possible uses to meet most eventualities during the offensives conducted by the British Army during the years 1917 and 1918. The drills laid out were the basis on which the platoon training was to be organised by the platoon commander.

The tactics of the platoon in the attack are discussed. Each platoon could expect to have one task set for it, usually the capture of a 'tactical point', defined as 'a locality, the possession of which is of the first importance locally to either side'. The first principal was always to press on towards the objective and 'close with the bayonet'. This old-fashioned sounding appeal (reinforced in the training part of SS143 with quotations from the lectures on 'the spirit of the bayonet') is there to inculcate an aggressive spirit in the soldiers to assist them in the determination to complete their task regardless of the difficulties. The advice becomes more practical when it discusses what to do if held up by enemy fire. Then the rifle section is to go to ground and endeavour to find a flanking position from which to attack with rifle fire; the bombing section is to get around the enemy flank covered by fire from the rifle grenade section. The rifle bombers were to 'open a hurricane bombardment on the point of resistance from the nearest cover available'. The Lewis gun section was initially to open a traversing fire on the point of resistance to cover the deployment of the other sections, and then to work its way around one flank to bring the enemy under increasing fire on his line of retreat.

Great attention was paid to the need for careful 'mopping up' of territory won from the enemy. Behind each attacking platoon there was to be a line of 'moppers up' supplied by the following platoon for whom they were clearing the way, making sure no concealed enemies disrupted their progress to the next stage of the attack.

If the training documents are read in an open-minded way, and not in the hostile and dismissive manner of their critics, they can be seen as a thoroughly competent and useful set of basic rules to cover most eventualities. Any modern infantryman would recognise the principles expounded therein. Thus, in the section entitled 'General Rules as to Tactics', the first rule is always to aim for surprise, which is easier said than done in trench-to-trench warfare. 'See without being seen' is how the idea is encapsulated, with special emphasis on the need for care and quiet during the assembly for an attack. There should be no movement without reconaissance; that is, all advances should be by 'bounds', with scouts going forward ahead of each step. The principle of 'protection' is covered by the warning never to halt without posting sentries as lookouts.

The notes regarding the flanks are particularly interesting and give the lie to the charge that British tactics were rigid and unimaginative. After the advice always to guard one's own flank and keep in touch with neighbouring formations (usually by means of two-man patrols), the instruction is always to seek out the enemy flank and always employ enveloping tactics to dislodge him. All units were free to assist their neighbouring units, but the best way to do that was by pushing ahead forcefully and completing the task set, and then using the position won to exploit the situation. Any close study of the British offensive battles of the summer and autumn of 1917 and 1918 will yield countless examples of an intelligent and well-trained infantry doing just that.

The section of SS143 devoted to 'Training' also repays study. The first requirement of training is to foster the offensive spirit and the desire to close with the enemy as quickly as possible. 'Hostile' readers might groan and say 'I told you so!' But the very next heading concerns 'Initiative' and stresses that control on the modern battlefield was now so difficult that every platoon and section leader must be able to act without waiting for orders according to the way the battle unfolds. All men must be confident in their own skill at arms; understand the need to co-ordinate the use of weapons within the platoon and display good discipline, morale and esprit de corps. The 'true soldierly spirit' comes from confidence in one's leaders' and weapons' ability. Every section should strive to be the best in its platoon; every platoon to be the best in the company.

The training programme is given in exhaustive detail, according to the time of year and the amount of time available. But in general it was designed to impart ever greater battle skills to the men of the platoon. Thus all ranks were to be trained in steady drill (the bedrock of all disciplined and efficient armies); in physical fitness, bayonet fighting, bomb throwing and 'mopping up' (practised in pairs). The new demand in 1917 was for a return to the previous high standard of good rifle skills (which the British still quaintly called 'musketry' but which the pamphlet reminds its readers was good enough to keep the enemy out of British trenches in 1914 long before the advent of barbed wire in large quantities!), and in fire discipline. Finally, the practicalities of laying barbed wire and the construction of field works, and practice in field craft and the intelligent appreciation of ground, use of cover and the avoidance of obvious points on the map that would be covered by enemy fire gave a thoroughly realistic edge to this training programme based on years of hard won experience.

The specialists all had their own training programmes – the bombers were to be familiar with all types of enemy grenades (so that captured bombs could be used against their former owners)[5], and were enjoined to co-operate especially closely with the rifle grenadiers and the light mortars. The rifle bombing section was to practise the rapid forming of a rifle grenade barrage. The Lewis gun section was to practise coming into action and opening fire quickly. The rifle section, far from 'housing the leftovers', was to make sure that all men were skilled in the use of rifle, bayonet and hand grenade, could act as scouts and, most importantly, half were also trained as Lewis gunners and half as rifle bombers. Whatever happened, the two 'firepower' sections were to be maintained at peak efficiency.

The NCOs in charge of sections were trained in fire control, description of targets, map reading, observation and the conveying of clear information and messages. Scouts, runners and snipers received special instruction. All ranks went through night exercises, live-firing exercises and competitions to encourage pride in hard-won skills.

The platoon commander was to gain the confidence of his men through the traditional 'man management' skills of the British Army – strict discipline, setting a good example (including the ability to handle all the weapons at his disposal), recognising good effort (words of praise are more effective than constant fault-finding), demanding high standards and fostering the aggressive spirit (which SS143 picturesquely describes as being 'blood thirsty' and 'always thinking of ways to kill the enemy'!). He is enjoined to be the proudest man in the British Army – he commands the primary unit of the attack.

Since the British were always expecting to break through the enemy lines and return to a war of manoeuvre, training always included exercises in open warfare. This required a heightened use of scouts, patrols and picquets; the practice of 'encounter' actions; fighting through woods (where small columns were particularly useful) and the clearing of villages. The brief description of the latter could have come straight from a modern-day pamphlet, with its advice about always working down one side of a street, forcing entry through back doors rather than the front, etc.

The appendices of SS143 gave several diagrammatic portrayals of an 'ideal' trench-to-trench attack by a first wave platoon, the best deployment of a second wave (follow on) platoon and an attack in open warfare, together with examples of how not to do it!

The much-praised German document 'Der Angriff in Stellungskrieg' ('The Attack in Position Warfare'), which was only issued on 1 January 1918 and is held to be the 'storm trooper's manual' for the German spring offensives, tells us very little that was not covered by SS143 in February 1917. There is nothing new in its call for the use of surprise, flank attacks, high levels of training in weaponry, tactics and the maintenance of the offensive spirit, careful planning, infantry-artillery co-operation, and the swift reaction to events as they unfold. All these principles, as one would expect from an army engaged in the same war experience, are covered in the British infantry training manuals.

It is not, of course, being suggested that every British soldier was this paragon of multi-talented virtues, nor that every platoon functioned as the deadly killing machine that the training pamphlets describe. But neither need we think that every German was a model 'storm trooper' of the type that demonstrated tactics to appreciative audiences on the training grounds. Throughout 1917 and 1918 we could provide countless examples of German infantry employing disgracefully old-fashioned tactics. Nobody has ever accused the British infantry of charging in packed, shoulder-to-shoulder formations reminiscent of 1914 (or even 1870), but there are plenty of examples of the Tommies facing such tactics in 1918 and taking a bloody retribution.

A study of SS144 ('The Normal Formation for the Attack') shows that there was a major debate on tactics taking place, with two clear schools of thought in contention. The pamphlet reiterates the main points of SS143, saying again that recent experience (i.e. the fighting on the Somme) suggests the value of a standard formation familiar to the whole Army. The fact that it suggests a standard attack frontage for a battalion of just two hundred yards, together with the recommendation of wide intervals between men, lines and waves, shows that the British were already appreciating the value of a highly dispersed 'attack in depth'. The discussion of the setting of objectives (one to a platoon, two to a company, two or more to a battalion, etc.) actually advises 'plenty of depth to the attack'.

The big divide, however, is whether the first wave of attackers should be responsible for pushing through to the final objective, with follow on troops occupying and securing ('mopping up') the ground gained, or whether each unit should take and consolidate one objective and allow the next unit to 'leapfrog' on to the next objective. SS144 suggests that, where only one or two objective lines are set, the first method should be preferred, but where the artillery can provide covering barrages through the whole depth of the attack, the second method may be used.

The document is trying to absorb the two major trends in offensive doctrine developing in the Army after the Somme experience. One school (personified by Hubert Gough) feared that opportunities for exploitation would be lost if every unit was obliged to stop at a pre-determined line, dictated by the artillery plan. They could point to moments on 1 and 14 July 1916, when the attackers could have taken great advantage of early success if the leading units had been free to push ahead. This was certainly implemented by Gough when he got his big chance in the opening battles of Third Ypres, with less than happy results. Proponents of the other school (including Plumer and Rawlinson) were more concerned to conserve the lives and energy of their soldiers and place greater emphasis on the role of the artillery in conquering enemy positions of great tactical importance. They could point to tragedies overwhelming leading waves of attackers who pushed on into enemy positions, never to be seen again. (The 29th Division at Monchy-le-Preux on 14 April 1917, and the 56th Division at Polygon Wood on 16 August spring to mind.)

The basic ideas of SS143 and SS144 were reinforced by the September 1917 publication, SS185 'Assault Training'. The battle drills being taught were to become 'second nature in moments of excitement and tension', coupled with the maxim from the Field Service Regulations that 'half hearted measures never attain success in war and the lack of determination is the most fruitful source of defeat'. After the expected words of advice about improving weapons skills, there are important new sections on practising the prompt counter-attack to deal with an enemy intrusion into British positions, and the refining of fire and movement tactics by practising the advance by alternative rushes of sections under covering fire. The training was to be practical, based on common sense, and to be lively and interesting to the men. Platoon officers were to explain the purpose of it all to the men and engage their interest and commitment. There is not much in the foregoing that any German officer would disagree with. They would no doubt be bemused (or amused) by the closing section with its 'incorrigibly British' cricket analogies! You can teach a man the basics of the game and its team working, but you cannot dictate how each individual will act during each match; that is left to his personal skill and motivation to win. Once again a 'non hostile' reading of this will show that the providers of doctrine for the British Army understood that, in the tremendous turmoil of modern battle, the outcome often depended on the free will and actions of well-trained infantrymen reacting to the situation as it unfolded. One could, perhaps, criticise the British system of formal battle drills but one should also be allowed to ask which system actually evolved through the experience of battle to deliver the final crushing blows which brought the war to a victorious conclusion.

Any student of the war making a detailed study of the actual conduct of battles by the British army at this time and, perhaps more importantly, reading the 'after action reports' drawn up by the staffs of brigades, divisions and corps, will come across many examples of infantry platoons, even where they have fallen behind the protection of the creeping barrage, still capturing powerful German defensive positions by the skill of their fire and movement tactics. The local concentration of fire achieved by their rifles, Lewis guns, rifle grenades and trench mortars suppressed the enemy fire (admittedly probably rather shaky after the barrage had passed over them!), while the bombers and riflemen closed in to finish the job. The after action reports themselves show that the army was constantly looking for tactical, organisational and technical lessons to be absorbed and disseminated to improve both future training and battle performance.

Notes

1   Timothy Lupfer and Bruce Gudmundsson will be the best known of these writers. See Timothy Lupfer, *The Dynamics of Doctrine: The Changes in German Tactical Doctrine During the First World War* (Leavenworth Paper No. 4, Fort Leavenworth, Kansas 1981) and Bruce Gudmundsson, *Stormtroop Tactics: Innovation in the German Army 1914–1918* (Praeger, New York 1989)

2   See Martin Samuels, *Doctrine and Dogma: German and British Infantry Tactics in the First World War* (Greenwood Press, New York 1992) and *Command or Control? Command, Training and Tactics in the British and German Armies 1888–1918* (Frank Cass, London 1995)

3   See Tony Ashworth, *Trench Warfare: The Live and Let Live System 1914–1918* (Macmillan, London, 1980)

4   The present author thanks Captain Pat Dray, Royal Canadian Regiment, for drawing his attention to the work of 4th and 5th Army staffs in this respect. See the WO/158 files at the PRO

5   See SS126 'The Training and Employment of Bombers' and SS182 'Instructions on Bombing'

JOHN PEATY
Capital Courts-Martial during the Great War

During the Great War, 9,496,170 men enlisted in the Armed Forces of the British Empire, of whom 947,023 were killed (including Indians)[1]. Of those killed, 346 were executed (excluding Indians). In recent years an enormous amount of attention and concern has been focused on this tiny minority of men who, in the eyes of the vast majority of their contemporaries, let their country down, their comrades down and themselves down.

Interest in Great War executions was reawakened in 1974 by the publication of *The Thin Yellow Line* by William Moore. The year 1978 saw the posthumous publication of a memoir by Victor Silvester, and 1983 saw the publication of *For the Sake of Example* by Anthony Babington (the phrase was coined by Wellington, one of Britain's greatest soldiers). In 1986 the television series 'The Monocled Mutineer' by Alan Bleasdale was shown, based upon the 1978 book of that name by William Allison and John Fairley, and 1989 saw the publication of, most influentially, *Shot at Dawn* by Julian Sykes and Julian Putkowski, which was reissued in a slightly revised edition in 1992 (the phrase was coined by Horatio Bottomley, one of Britain's most corrupt politicians). The publication of *Shot at Dawn* prompted, as was openly intended by its authors, the launching of a campaign to pardon those executed; a campaign which really took off following its reissue. In support of that campaign, Babington's book was reissued in a slightly revised edition in 1993. Further support came in 1995 with the publication of *For God's Sake Shoot Straight* by Leonard Sellers. Interestingly, all these books were, with one exception, published or reissued by Leo Cooper.

The campaign for pardons has been led by Andrew Mackinlay, Labour MP for Thurrock. On 15 June 1992 Mackinlay tabled a Motion in the Commons urging the Prime Minister, John Major, to recommend a pardon for men executed during the Great War for offences other than murder or mutiny. After careful consideration, on 10 February 1993 Mackinlay's call for a pardon was rejected by the Prime Minister in a firm but fair letter. The Prime Minister wrote that that there were two main grounds on which pardons might be recommended. The first ground was 'legal impropriety or procedural error. The files record each stage of the case, up to the final decision by the Commander-in-Chief. No evidence was found to lead us, including the Judge Advocate General, to think that the convictions were unsound or that the accused were treated unfairly at the time'. The second ground was 'humanitarian'. The Prime Minister appreciated the distress of the relatives of the executed men and sympathised with them. 'I do think it is essential, however, that full account is taken of the circumstances of the time. The First World War was probably the bloodiest conflict ever [*sic* for Britain it certainly was; for many other countries it certainly was not]. At certain periods, troops from this country and those of our Allies were being killed at a rate of tens of thousands a day. Soldiers who deserted were sentenced against this background of heavy casualties amongst the vast majority of fellow soldiers who were carrying out orders. The authorities at the time took the view that deserters had to receive due punishment because of the effect of desertions on the military capacity and morale of the Allied armies. Millions of soldiers put their lives at risk and endured the most terrible sufferings. They had to be able to rely on the support of their comrades in arms'. The Prime Minister concluded: 'I have reflected long and hard but I have reached the conclusion that we cannot rewrite history by substituting our latter-day judgement for that of contemporaries, whatever we might think. With the passage of time attitudes and values change. This applies as much to past civilian trials as to military ones, in which sentences were imposed based on the values of the time. I am sure that all people, when they think of this subject now, recognise that those soldiers who deserted did so in the most appalling conditions and under terrible pressures and take that fully into account in reaching any judgement in their own mind'. Undeterred, on 19 October 1993 Mackinlay introduced in the Commons a Private Member's Bill to pardon men executed during the Great War for offences other than murder and mutiny. The Bill provided for two options: a blanket pardon (the favoured option) or a selective pardon. On 4 November 1993 the issue was debated in the Lords, when the government reiterated its opposition to pardons. Viscount Cranborne, the Parliamentary Under-Secretary of State for Defence, told the Lords that an examination of the surviving records had shown that 'the regulations at the time were not breached by the authorities'. On 18 May 1994 Mackinlay re-introduced in the Commons his Private Member's Bill. On 1 July 1994 Mackinlay presented to the Commons a petition calling for pardons. On 16 September 1995 the Office of the Leader of the Opposition announced that a future Labour government would consider the matter sympathetically. Following the election of a Labour government, on 27 May 1997, Dr John Reid, the Minister for the Armed Forces, announced a re-examination of the surviving records. On 24 July 1998, following the completion of the re-examination, Reid told the Commons that the granting of pardons was impracticable but expressed regret for the executions. Mackinlay welcomed the expression of regret but reserved his position on pardons.

Prompted by Mackinlay's campaign, a detailed and comprehensive study of the surviving courts-martial proceedings from the Great War held and open to inspection in the Public Record Office (WO71) was carried out over a period of time. In this piece I intend to outline its conclusions; then to emphasise certain points which seem to me to be of particular importance; I then intend to discuss *Shot at Dawn*; and, finally, to address the question of pardons. But first let me outline the key statistics.

It is important to note that these were compiled and published by the War Office as long ago as 1922[2]. In the period 4 August 1914 to 31 March 1920, 3,080 men were sentenced to death by courts-martial under the Army Act. Only 346 of the sentences were confirmed and carried out, that is 11.23%. In other words, 88.77% of those sentenced to death were reprieved. Of the 324 British, Dominion and Colonial soldiers executed, ninety-one (28%) were under suspended sentence for a previous offence (including nine under two suspended sentences). Of these ninety-one, forty had been previously sentenced to death (in thirty-eight cases for desertion, in one case for quitting his post and in one case for disobedience). One had been sentenced to death for desertion on two previous occasions. These figures scarcely suggest a harsh and unforgiving system of military justice. They suggest rather a system that could be tough but was usually prepared to give a man another chance.

Of the 346 men executed, the great majority (291, including three officers) were serving in Imperial (i.e. British) Forces; thirty-one were serving in Overseas (i.e. Dominion) Contingents (twenty-five Canadians, one South African and five New Zealanders); five were serving in Colonial Forces; ten were Chinese Coolies; four were Coloured Labourers; and five were Camp Followers. The great majority of those executed (322) were serving on the Western Front. The peak years for executions were 1916 and 1917.

Contrary to popular belief, very few were executed for cowardice in the face of the enemy: there were a mere eighteen executions for that offence. The great majority were executed for desertion while on active service.

Desertion was defined as the act of a man absenting himself without leave from his unit with the intention of permanently avoiding service. If a man was apprehended out of uniform and/or a considerable time after he had gone absent, this would be strong evidence of an intention never to return. It was also desertion for a man to absent himself with the intention of avoiding some important duty, such as proceeding with his unit overseas, even though he might intend eventually to return to the service. A man was declared a deserter after an absence of twenty-one days; however, if a man was apprehended within twenty-one days he could be charged with desertion just the same, if the circumstances suggested intent.

During the Great War desertion was a serious drain on manpower. Yet, remarkably, between the outbreak of war and the end of March 1920 – a period of almost sixty-eight months – only 7,361 courts-martial were held in the field[3], and only 266 men were executed, for desertion.

In addition to those executed for cowardice or desertion: thirty-seven were executed for murder; seven for quitting their posts; five for disobedience; six for striking or showing violence to superiors; three for mutiny; two for sleeping at their posts; and two for casting away their arms. After the Armistice, the only executions which took place were for murder.

Contrary to popular belief, few of those executed were callow youths. As far as can be ascertained, the great majority were, in the eyes of the law, mature adults, i.e. over 21.

Sykes and Putkowski estimate that the average age of those executed was mid-twenties. They also estimate that 40% of those executed had been in serious trouble before. They further estimate that (excluding non-combatants) 30% were regulars or reservists; 3% territorials; 40% Kitchener volunteers; 19% Irish, Canadian and New Zealand volunteers; and 9% conscripts[4]. There was of course no distinction between these groups as far as the Army Act was concerned, although the figures certainly suggest that there was a more indulgent attitude towards those who had not joined the Army, and thus submitted to its discipline, freely.

Of those executed, three were officers: 2nd Lieutenant Poole of the West Yorks; 2nd Lieutenant Paterson of the Essex Regiment; and, most notoriously, Sub Lieutenant Dyett of the Nelson Battalion, Royal Naval Division. Poole and Dyett were executed for desertion; in both their cases the death sentence was confirmed on the grounds that, if a soldier had done what they had done, he would have been executed. Paterson was executed for murdering Sergeant Harold Collison DCM MSM of the GHQ Detective Staff while a deserter.

I want now to outline the conclusions of the study of the proceedings in the Public Record Office.

(1) In every case studied the verdict and the sentence of the court-martial were confirmed by the Commander-in-Chief. Recommendations for mercy which were made in some of the cases studied were inevitably *not* acted upon, since all the cases studied resulted in execution. We do not know how many recommendations *were* acted upon because the files relating to cases where the death sentence was commuted do not survive. In the absence of the files, we do not know why the vast majority of death sentences were commuted. We do not know the relative weight attached to recommendations for mercy, points of law, medical evidence, previous conduct, etc. Not only are we without the files of those cases where the death sentence was commuted but we are also without the files of those cases where a verdict of not guilty was returned. It is therefore true to say that we have an extremely partial record of British military justice during the war.

(2) Before confirmation by the Commander-in-Chief, courts-martial verdicts were scrutinised by the Judge Advocate General at GHQ with regard to the legality of both the findings and the sentences. It follows

that in none of the surviving cases, all of which were confirmed, were material legal irregularities detected by the Judge Advocate General.

(3) A large proportion of desertions did not take place in or close to the trenches. The emotive picture of scores of men cracking up under fire is a false one: some men did lose their nerve when under attack but many absented themselves when their unit came out of the line or when it was ordered up to the front, while others did not return from leave in Britain when they should have. It is a fact that those serving on the Western Front were not continually going over the top or being shelled: they enjoyed long periods either out of the line, or in quiet sectors of the line, or at home on leave.

(4) Several of those executed for desertion were apprehended in Britain. Some men failed to return from leave. Two men (Privates Jennings and Lewis of the South Lancashire Regiment) deserted together at Waterloo Station while the draft was waiting for a train to take them to France, i.e. they were under orders to proceed overseas. They were arrested seven months later and taken to France for trial. All those who had deserted while on leave or under orders to embark and all those who had deserted in France and had managed to get back to Britain, were returned to their unit to be tried and their unit was invariably in France. No executions took place in Britain.

(5) Few men were represented during the early years of the war, although during 1916 the files increasingly record the presence of an 'accused's friend' or 'prisoner's friend' (often a barrister or solicitor in civilian life), although he did not always choose to cross-examine witnesses. Remarkably, on one occasion the friend was the accused's own CO. Even more remarkably, the accused was facing three charges of desertion and one of striking an officer.

(6) Medical opinion was called for when it was thought pertinent. Unless medical evidence existed from the time when the offence had been committed, obviously medical opinion could only relate to the man as he was at the time of his court-martial. It usually took the form of an examination by either the man's own unit MO or by a doctor at a rear medical facility. Following the examination, the MO or doctor invariably stated that the man was responsible for his actions, or knew what he was doing, or was not suffering from mental derangement.

(7) Formal medical boards were unusual. Where these were convened a record of their findings is on file.

(8) Specific reference to 'shell-shock' was very rare. However, references to loss of memory, dizziness, 'queer turns', nervousness, bad nerves, terror, etc. were common.

(9) Files for 1915–16 and for 1918 are quite full, containing not only the proceedings but also comments by superior officers up to and including the Commander-in-Chief. These were not wholly or always gratuitous,

since the unit and brigade commanders were required to provide details of the man's disciplinary record as well as a view – by, ideally, an officer who had known him for some time (not always possible given the scale of casualties) – of his personal character and his military worth. Comments by superior officers usually included the view of his CO whether the man's action was deliberate and the views of those further up the chain of command (especially at brigade and division) as to whether an example was necessary given the current state of discipline. Files for 1914 and, unaccountably, for 1917 are perfunctory, containing only the proceedings, Commander-in-Chief's confirmation, the man's conduct sheet and little else.

(10) The files of those Canadians and New Zealanders executed are not held in this country. The files of several men are listed under their assumed names. The files of Lance Corporal Price and Private Morgan (both of the Welsh Regiment and both executed for murder) are not in the Public Record Office.

(11) In all cases the courts-martial were properly constituted. Most were field general courts-martial and, as stipulated, they consisted of at least three officers, one of whom, not below the rank of captain, presided.

(12) Acts of collective indiscipline were extremely rare in the British Army, although a very small number of cases did involve more than three accused. The notorious 'mutiny' at Etaples in 1917 resulted in the execution of only one man, Corporal Short of the Northumberland Fusiliers. Nothing remotely similar to the mass mutinies in the French Army and the mass desertions in the Russian and Italian Armies occurred in the British Army, not even during the dark days of spring 1918, when only two men were executed for desertion.

(13) The overwhelming majority of the men executed were British soldiers. The next largest group was Canadian soldiers and after that Chinese coolies. The latter had an unusual propensity for murder. One of them committed suicide while awaiting execution.

(14) The overwhelming majority of executions were for offences committed with the BEF; a small minority took place in other theatres. This reflects, firstly, the great imbalance of forces between the Western Front and other theatres and, secondly, the great difference in conditions between the Western Front and other theatres.

(15) A large number of men, particularly during the last years of the war, were court-martialled for second, or even third, offences. The files relating to their previous courts-martial do not survive.

(16) Many men elected to present no defence or declined to call witnesses or make a statement; these were not limited to repeat offenders.

(17) Some of those executed pleaded guilty. One pleaded guilty to desertion: Private Byers of the Royal Scots Fusiliers. One pleaded guilty to offering violence to a superior: Private Sabongidda of the Nigeria Regiment.

(18) Almost invariably the basic facts of a man's offence were not disputed. The critical factors were the presence of intent, the man's disciplinary record (particularly whether he was a repeat offender) and the perceived need to set an example. Original conduct sheets (or certified copies) were available for the majority of the accused; some had been lost in action. Almost invariably the accused pleaded 'not guilty'. Where they elected to make a defence or plead mitigation, they invariably denied any intent. The presence of intent was therefore often based on the opinion of their officers and on evidence before the court – many deserters were not apprehended until months after they had gone absent, dressed in civilian clothes and many miles from where they had last been seen. The need to set an example was articulated by the chain of command in numerous cases, especially when discipline in the man's unit or brigade or division was thought to be bad or deteriorating.

(19) The arrival of large numbers of conscripts at the front in the period 1916 to 1918 was not reflected in a large number of conscript executions.

In a nutshell, the study found no white cases, very many black cases and a handful of grey cases. The grey cases were those of: 2nd Lieutenant Poole of the West Yorks; Private McColl of the East Yorks; Privates Johnson and McClair (real name Chapman) of the Border Regiment. All were executed for desertion. In the case of Poole, a medical board ignored evidence that he had been suffering from shell-shock. In the case of McColl, medical evidence was requested but was unavailable. In the case of Johnson and McClair, a legal ruling was sought as to their status – both men claimed that they were no longer soldiers – but there is no evidence that it was given.

I want now to emphasise certain points which seem to me to be of particular importance.

As John Terraine has pointed out, British military justice during the Great War had been designed to cater for a small regular army, drawing its recruits from 'the rougher elements of the population', and the commuting of almost nine out of ten death sentences shows that this was appreciated by those in authority. Indeed, it demonstrates 'reason and compassion' on their part[5].

Many of those executed were poorly educated, some even illiterate. However, neither poor education nor illiteracy is synonymous with an inability to distinguish right from wrong and neither is a defence under the law.

Very few men were executed for cowardice; the great majority were executed for desertion. Cowardice and desertion were distinct offences and the distinction is very important. What constituted cowardice was a subjective judgement, about which witnesses held different views. Desertion on the other hand had an objective reality: you were absent from your unit for three weeks or more. The facts spoke for themselves:

if you were arrested miles behind the lines wearing civilian clothes weeks or months after you had left your unit without permission it was pointless to argue that you were not a deserter – and hardly anyone bothered to do so. The only points at issue were the validity of any excuse and the weight of any mitigating factors. Of those who were executed for desertion, six had deserted in Britain (either on leave from France or under orders to embark for France) while eight had deserted in France and had managed to get across the Channel and reach Britain. The fact that a man deserted in or to Britain did not give him any immunity. It did however provide strong evidence of intent.

The belief that all or almost all desertions were involuntary, the result of shell-shock – that is, all or almost all desertions took place in the front line and under the impact of prolonged and numbing bombardment – is an enduring but a false one. In fact, many desertions took place away from the front line and not under the impact of bombardment. Moreover, many deserters had not served in the front line and had not been subjected to bombardment. Indeed, for several of those executed for desertion the first shot they heard fired in anger was also the last thing they heard. Take, for example, the case of Drummer Rose of the Yorkshire Regiment. Rose deserted as his unit was moving up to the line on 18 December 1914. He lived comfortably with a Frenchwoman in Hazebrouck for very nearly two years before he was informed upon, arrested, court-martialled and sentenced to death. His brigade commander wrote, with commendable restraint in the circumstances: 'I can discover no redeeming feature in this case nor any reason why the sentence should not be carried out'. Rose was executed on 4 March 1917.

The Great War was not hell for every soldier; nor was it hell all the time. Indeed, in the opinion of the noted army psychiatrist Dr Robert Ahrenfeldt, the stress experienced by British soldiers during the Second World War was 'incomparably greater' than that experienced by British soldiers during the Great War[6]. I think Ahrenfeldt goes way over the top: I quote him primarily to discredit psychiatrists, who have done much to undermine a commonsense approach to crime and punishment.

Discipline is essential to armies, for without it no army can fulfil its primary function of fighting and winning battles. Armies consist of small teams: infantry sections, gun crews, tank crews and the like. Whether the team succeeds or fails, whether its members live or die, depends on every member pulling his weight, behaving himself and not leaving the others in the lurch.

During the Great War the British Army was not a law unto itself dispensing summary justice. It was governed by the Army Act, passed annually by Parliament, which laid down what constituted an offence and how offenders were to be tried and punished. It is unjust and illogical to condemn the Army for the court-martial and execution of soldiers for desertion, cowardice, etc. when the Army was merely implementing the provisions of the Army Act. If condemnation is in order, then it should be directed at Parliament.

The fact that discipline in the Russian, Italian, French and German Armies collapsed during the Great War, whereas discipline in the British Army did not, suggests that the latter was probably about right: not too soft, not too harsh. Of the armies during the Great War, the Russian Army was undoubtedly the most brutal. In the Italian Army an iron discipline reigned: smoking on duty was punishable by death. According to Professor Brian Sullivan, of the 4,000 death sentences passed by Italian courts-martial during the war, 750 (18.75%) were carried out[7]. It would seem that the British Army inflicted the death penalty more often than the French and German Armies. It appears that during the war the French Army executed only 133 men while the German Army executed only forty-eight men. I say appears because we cannot exclude the possibility that the French and German Armies were less adept at compiling and preserving accurate statistics or deliberately falsified their statistics, excluding many summary executions. Professor Hew Strachan reminds us that in the British Army mutinies were rare and that, although discipline was dented in the spring of 1918, it did not collapse. He suggests that punishment was a larger factor in sustaining the British Army 'than the conventional wisdom allows'. He notes that the German Army's discipline was much harsher in the Second World War than it had been in the Great War (15,000 executions instead of forty-eight) and that, unlike in the Great War, in the Second World War the German Army did not collapse in a welter of desertions but fought on until the bitter end[8]. During the Great War the American Army was noted for its softness: deserters were classified and treated as stragglers[9]. It is most unlikely that this softness would have been possible if the American Army had been as heavily engaged as other armies or that it would have continued if the war had lasted. Interestingly, the American Army's softness did not extend to murder or rape and several men were executed for those offences.

Indian soldiers were tried and punished under the Indian Army Act. However, there was no appreciable difference between its disciplinary provisions and those of the British Army Act. Many Indian soldiers were executed during the war. Although the Canadian, South African and New Zealand governments were content for their soldiers to be tried and punished under the British Army Act, the Australian government was not. Australian soldiers were therefore tried and punished under the Australian Defence Act, which only allowed the death penalty for mutiny, desertion to, or treacherous dealings with, the enemy. The unco-operative and divisive attitude of the Australian government was maintained despite the appalling disciplinary record of Australian soldiers and the trenchant views of Australian senior officers. It is not surprising that junior Australian officers occasionally took the law into their own hands.

In the field offenders were tried by officers from neighbouring units and executed by soldiers from their own units. In other words, they were judged and punished by their peers: men who had faced the same dangers and who had experienced the same hardships.

A death sentence had to be unanimous: it could not be passed without the concurrence of all the officers making up the court-martial panel. A death sentence was not final: it could not be carried out without the approval of the Commander-in-Chief. The fact that almost 90% of death sentences were commuted demonstrates that a death sentence was very far from being final. Although there was no appeals procedure (not until 1951 in fact), every death sentence had to be referred up the chain of command for scrutiny and approval. The proceedings were passed to Brigade, then to Division, then to Corps, then to Army and finally to GHQ. At GHQ, after being scrutinised for legal irregularities by the Judge Advocate General, the proceedings were passed to the Commander-in-Chief. It was the Commander-in-Chief's responsibility to confirm, mitigate, remit or commute the sentence, taking into account every factor: any recommendation for mercy; any suspended sentence from a previous court-martial; evidence of the accused's character; evidence of the accused's past conduct; medical evidence; the comments of Brigade, Division, Corps and Army commanders; and the ruling of the Judge Advocate General. The surviving proceedings provide no evidence that the chain of command was circumvented or that those in the chain of command discharged their responsibilities frivolously or incompetently.

Our view of what happened is inevitably conditioned by the nature of the surviving documentary evidence. Because the files of those courts-martial where a death sentence was confirmed are the only ones that have survived, the only cases which we can study are those where mercy was not shown. If the files of those courts-martial where a death sentence was commuted had survived as well, we would be able to study every case: the vast majority of cases where mercy was shown as well as the small minority of cases where mercy was not shown. Many of the files which do survive are incomplete. However, incomplete documentation eighty years and more after the event is unsurprising and does not prove that correct procedures were not followed at the time.

At the height of anti-war and pacifist feeling between the wars, British military discipline was greatly liberalised. The death penalty was abolished for most military offences in April 1928. The death penalty for cowardice, desertion and quitting post was abolished in April 1930. Allenby, one of the finest generals of the Great War, and Plumer, one of the most humane as well as one of the finest generals of the Great War, spoke against its abolition. During the Second World War, apart from murder, the death penalty only existed for mutiny and treachery: three men were executed for mutiny, one for treachery and thirty-six for murder[10]. During the Second World War desertion was a very serious drain on manpower – very nearly 100,000 soldiers deserted[11] – and in 1942 Auchinleck, one of the most humane as well as one of the finest generals of that war, recommended the reintroduction of the death penalty to deter it. The Executive Committee of the Army Council unanimously endorsed the recommendation but it was not pursued because of political considerations. A comparison between the British Army's experience in the Great War and its experience in the Second World War tends to confirm the commonsense belief that men are less likely to misbehave in the presence of a deterrent than in the absence of a deterrent. During the Second World War prison was no deterrent. Indeed, the prospect of seeing out the war in the comparative comfort and safety of prison was not unappealing to many men, especially those at the sharp end.

I want now to discuss the most influential book about this subject: *Shot at Dawn*.

The statement at the beginning of the book that those executed 'did not receive even the rudiments of a just hearing'[12] perfectly illustrates its approach to the subject. While undeniably the product of much research, the book is not authoritative. *Shot at Dawn* has a gaping hole at its centre. Sykes and Putkowski did not consult the surviving courts-martial proceedings from the Great War – for the simple reason that they were not publicly available at the time. In fact, the surviving courts-martial proceedings from the Great War were released to the Public Record Office beginning in January 1990 and ending in January 1994. Unable to consult the proceedings, Sykes and Putkowski had to use other sources: a list of those executed (WO93), medal rolls (WO329) and war diaries (WO95) in the Public Record Office; the basic details given by Babington in his book; and memoirs of the war, most of them extremely unreliable.

Babington had been allowed to examine the surviving courts-martial proceedings and publish the basic details of many cases, providing that the identity of the men and the identity of their units were withheld. Babington adopts a scholarly approach; prefers primary to secondary evidence; and does not jump to conclusions. He concedes that senior officers did their duty as they perceived it; that courts-martial were not manipulated for improper purposes; and that the death penalty was seen by senior officers as 'indispensable to the fighting efficiency of the Army'[13]. Babington draws attention to the setting in which courts-martial took place: 'When a soldier deserted on active service he left a gap in the ranks, to the prejudice of all his more dutiful comrades. When he committed an act of cowardice in the face of the enemy he might have been jeopardising the safety of the men around him; and panic on the battlefield can spread with the speed of light, affecting even those who until then have been entirely resolute'[14].

He also draws attention to the fact that 'the weaker brethren were only an infinitesimally small proportion of the men at the front. There were hundreds of thousands of others on the battlefields . . . who overcame their fear, their misery, and their personal tribulations and carried on with resolution in the performance of their duty'[15]. However, Babington is almost as critical of British military justice during the Great War as Sykes and Putkowski. While *For the Sake of Example* is a more authoritative and balanced book than *Shot at Dawn*, it strongly reflects the fact that Babington is a judge. Inevitably, Babington judges British military justice in the Great War by the standards of British civil justice in the 1970s and 80s.

Sykes and Putkowski have the dubious honour of publishing for the first time the names of those who had been executed. The publication of the names produced considerable distress on the part of the relatives of those executed. This was both predictable and understandable. During the first part of the war relatives had usually been told the sordid truth by the authorities and had thereafter kept it a secret within the family. During the last part of the war relatives had usually been told white lies by the authorities and had thereafter lived in blissful ignorance of the sordid truth. It was undoubtedly a sin against open government, which is all the rage these days, for the authorities to have been less than frank with relatives, but it was done for the best of reasons and is to their credit I think. It is also to the credit of the authorities that the relatives of those executed received pensions; and that those executed were buried with their comrades and their graves are indistinguishable from those of their comrades.

Shot at Dawn contains many mistakes: some minor, some major. To give just two examples. Sykes and Putkowski say that Sapper Oyns of the Royal Engineers was executed for desertion[16]. He was in fact executed for the murder of CSM McCain. Sykes and Putkowski refer to the execution of five men from the Worcestershire Regiment in July 1915 as 'the biggest execution the British Army would ever experience'[17]. The treatment of the episode in *Shot at Dawn* implies that the authorities had taken leave of their senses and were in the grip of a blood lust. Perhaps we should speak of 'The Worcester Five'. The facts, however, are not as stated by Sykes and Putkowski. It is true that five men of the Worcestershire Regiment were executed in July 1915: Corporal Ives, Privates Hartells, Fellows, Robinson and Thompson. However, there was no connection between the five except that they were all in the same battalion (the 3rd): one deserted in September 1914, two in June 1915 and two in July 1915. Ives, the first to desert and the first to be tried, was shot on 22 July. The other four were shot on 26 July; they were shot separately and not together. *Shot at Dawn* insists, despite overwhelming evidence to the contrary, that all five were shot on the same day and together. There was no collusion between the five. Thompson and Robinson deserted together. Hartells and Fellows *may* have deserted together. Ives had deserted after only a month in France; he was arrested nine months later in civilian clothes.

Some of the most enlightening and informed comments on executions during the Great War are to be found in *The Redcaps* by Dr Gary Sheffield of the Royal Military Academy Sandhurst, *The British Soldier on the Somme* by Peter Liddle of Leeds University, and *On the Fringe of Hell* by Lieutenant-Colonel Christopher Pugsley. Sheffield judges that British military discipline was firm but not brutal. He emphasises that the procedure whereby courts-martial were convened and sentences referred up the chain of command for confirmation or commutation was strictly adhered to, even at the time of the Ludendorff offensive. Liddle contrasts the small number executed with the large number serving; emphasises that most of the offences were so blatant that 'scant defence could be put forward'; emphasises that soldiers knew what was expected of them and the penalties for transgression; and declares that there is 'virtually no evidence' in contemporary documents or memoirs that British soldiers considered the death penalty 'outrageous'[18]. Referring to the accounts of New Zealand executions in *Shot at Dawn*, Pugsley writes that 'each account has a number of factual errors and it is evident that both authors do not understand the procedure and levels of command at which courts-martial were confirmed and sentences reviewed and suspended'[19].

I want now, finally, to address the question of pardons.

I believe that the granting of pardons would be a great mistake. History is history. What happened, happened. We may not like our history but we rewrite it at our peril. I greatly admire *1984* – but I would prefer that it remained fiction. I believe the saying 'Strong emotion makes for bad law' to be true. I do not object to emotion: I do however believe that legislators should not let their hearts rule their heads. Have our legislators got nothing better to do than worry about the fate of convicted criminals who died before most of us were born? It is said that public opinion supports the granting of pardons (public opinion is, of course, a funny thing: it is also said that public opinion supports the restoration of the death penalty – not that our legislators have taken any notice). If true, this would not be surprising. What the average member of the public knows about the British Army during the Great War he has learnt from films and television. 'King and Country', 'Oh! What a Lovely War', 'The Monocled Mutineer' and 'Blackadder Goes Forth' are remarkable pieces of work – but nobody who has studied the subject accepts them as accurate portrayals of the British Army during the Great War.

Those who were tried, found guilty and executed during the Great War were judged and treated according to the laws, values and customs of their time. It was a time when the British Army was engaged in mortal combat with a powerful and dangerous foe. It was a time when British soldiers knew their place and did what they were told – or else. It was a time when for most people in Britain life was 'nasty, brutish and short'. It was a time when the death penalty was almost universally accepted by the British people. It was a time when most British people believed that in a national emergency the Crown had the right to put its subjects into uniform to fight its enemies – and that once in uniform, a subject's life belonged to the Crown, to dispose of as it saw fit. It was a time when most British people believed that certain things were worth dying for and worth killing for – and that the prevention of a German-dominated Europe was such a one.

The job of the historian is to try to understand the past. It is not the job of the historian to sit in judgement on the past and second guess the actions of our forebears – although, frankly, many historians do it. Much that passes as history nowadays is in fact ahistorical: it aims to judge the past in the light of the present and makes little or no attempt at understanding it. Indeed, it often wilfully misunderstands the past. I am profoundly opposed to the contemporary fashion for rewriting history in accordance with modern laws, values and customs. To modern eyes, history is full of injustices. But is it not arrogant for one age to stand in judgement on another? Are we so sure that our laws, values and customs are superior to those of the past, in this case the early twentieth century? Are we really more civilised than our grandfathers? Do we really have a greater understanding of human nature than they did? Today, we no longer inflict the death penalty, not even for cold-blooded murder. Punishment and deterrence are almost dirty words. Today, medical knowledge is much greater than it was during the Great War, especially with regard to psychiatry. Nowadays, much anti-social behaviour is excused on medical grounds. Can we – should we – impose current legal and medical practice on the past? And if we are to rewrite history, where do we start and where do we stop? I am reliably informed, for example, that Guy Fawkes was not interviewed in accordance with the PTA, let alone PACE.

Can we, eighty years after the end of the Great War, grant pardons when the Darling Committee on Courts-Martial in 1919, the Southborough Committee on Shell-Shock in 1922, the Lawson Committee on Army and Air Force Discipline in 1925 and the Oliver Committee on Army and Air Force Courts-Martial in 1938 all failed to substantiate miscarriages of justice during the Great War? All four Committees examined documents and questioned witnesses. Few of the documents and even fewer of the witnesses are still available to us.

The subject of pardons is bedevilled by the question: blanket or selective? If a blanket pardon, everyone is pardoned whether deserving or not: cold-blooded murderers and blatant deserters as well as the shell-shocked. If a selective pardon, who is to judge which men are to be pardoned and which men are to be denied a pardon (and thus recondemned) – and on what grounds? The records are very much a mixed bag: some are full and informative; some are incomplete and uninformative. Should those men whose cases cannot be properly judged because the records are incomplete and uninformative be denied a pardon for that reason or given a pardon for that reason?

The advocates of pardons cannot even agree among themselves. Babington opposes a blanket pardon and favours a selective pardon. Mackinlay favours a blanket pardon but would settle for a selective pardon; he has called for a pardon for 307 men. Sykes and Putkowski favour a blanket pardon: in 1989 they called for a pardon for 312 men; in 1992 they called for a pardon for 351 men.

The Bill proposed by Mackinlay made provision for either the granting of a general pardon or the establishment of a tribunal to review each case and to recommend pardons in those cases considered deserving. One aspect of the Bill may be noted: about a tenth of cases are excluded from consideration (although there is provision in the Bill for more, as yet unspecified, cases to be added later). The excluded cases relate to murder – although murderers were tried by court-martial and executed by firing squad just like deserters and the rest. The exclusion of cases of murder (at least initially) was intended to increase the Bill's chances: it was considered politic because of the inconvenient fact that until the 1960s murder was punishable by death under civil as well as military law. However, if Mackinlay wishes to be consistent, he cannot exclude cases of murder. Were all those executed for murder represented? Might not some have been suffering from shell-shock? Mackinlay clearly considers desertion and cowardice lesser crimes than murder. Yet during the Great War they were of equal seriousness in the eyes of the law. Indeed, in extreme circumstances desertion and cowardice could amount to mass murder.

Professor Peter Rowe of Liverpool University has highlighted the great difficulties that would face a tribunal[20]. Would the tribunal recommend a pardon where a medical problem was claimed and no medical evidence was sought? Would it recommend a pardon where there was no evidence that the accused was represented? Even if the accused *had* been medically examined and *had* been represented, it does not follow that he would have been acquitted (as several cases testify). Rowe has pointed out that a pardon goes to the conviction itself and not to the choice of sentences available to the court. A pardon would not say that the death penalty had been excessive: a pardon would say that the accused had been wrongly convicted of the crime for which he had been tried (a very different matter). He has also pointed out that the proceedings of courts-martial were subject to confirmation both as to finding and sentence; that the vast majority were not confirmed; and that bias or impropriety would have to be demonstrated on the part of the confirming officer with regard to the small minority that were confirmed. Lastly, he has pointed out that the death penalty still exists for five military offences (to do with mutiny and treachery) and that its existence has been reaffirmed regularly by Parliament. While this last point has been overtaken by events (the death penalty having recently been removed from the statute book completely – a triumph of hope over experience), the fact is that for eighty years after the Great War the gravest military offences continued to be punishable by death.

How long would the tribunal take to do its work and how much would it cost? Pardons would please the relatives of the executed men, now judged to be innocent, although it is unlikely that they would be pleased enough to forgo compensation claims. On the other hand, the relatives of those who participated in the trials and executions, now judged to be murderers, would be displeased.

Let me conclude by endorsing the plea of Ian Curteis[21]: 'All war is hideous and grotesquely unfair. Millions died unjustly on both sides in World War I and sleep now in those lines of ordered, cared-for graves – in "some corner of a foreign field that is forever England". The dust of those who died bravely and those whose deaths were shaming are irretrievably mixed. For God's sake, let them rest in peace.'

Notes

1   *Hansard*, 5 May 1921
2   *Statistics of the Military Effort of the British Empire during the Great War*, HMSO, 1922, pp.648–9
3   ibid, p.667
4   *Shot at Dawn*, Leo Cooper, 1992, pp.19–20
5   *The Right of the Line*, Hodder & Stoughton, 1985, pp.527–8
6   *Psychiatry in the British Army in the Second World War*, Routledge & Kegan Paul, 1958, p.273
7   *Time to Kill*, eds Addison and Calder, Pimlico, 1997, p.178
8   ibid, p.375
9   Cyril Falls, *The First World War*, Longman, 1959, p.335
10 *Hansard*, 20 November 1970
11 Brig. A B McPherson, *Discipline*, pp.116–7 (WO277/7)
12 *Shot at Dawn*, p.6
13 *For the Sake of Example*, Leo Cooper, 1983, p.191
14 ibid, p.57
15 ibid, p.83
16 *Shot at Dawn*, p.234
17 ibid, p.50
18 *The British Soldier on the Somme*, Strategic & Combat Studies Institute, Occ. Paper No. 23, 1996, p.22
19 *On the Fringe of Hell*, Hodder & Stoughton, 1991, p.312
20 RUSI *Journal*, August 1994, pp.61–2
21 *Daily Mail*, 12 October 1995 (Associated Newspapers)

NICK PERRY

Politics and Command: General Nugent, the Ulster Division and Relations with Ulster Unionism 1915–17

In September 1915 Brigadier General Oliver Nugent, a 55-year-old Irish regular soldier, was summoned from his brigade in France to assume command of the 36th (Ulster) Division, then undergoing training in England.[1] A tough-minded professional officer, he at once began preparing the Division for war with characteristic energy and ruthlessness.

However, his new command, raised from the Ulster Volunteer Force, had of its nature close political ties with Ulster Unionism, and Nugent's uncompromising drive for military efficiency and his disregard for domestic political sensitivities soon caused tensions both within the Division and with its supporters at home. The difficulties which resulted, and his own unease at commanding so 'political' a formation, illustrate some of the problems confronting the Army's hierarchy as it sought to mould the attitudes of its citizen soldiers and manage the expectations of their political patrons.

At first sight Nugent seemed the ideal choice to command the Ulster Division. From a Co. Cavan Protestant landowning family and the son of a general, his Unionist credentials had been established by his involvement with the Cavan UVF in 1914. Yet despite this his relationship with the Division, and with Ulster Unionism more widely, proved not always to be easy. His Irish background notwithstanding, he had been educated at Harrow and had performed nearly all his regimental soldiering in the King's Royal Rifle Corps: indeed, he had spent a large part of his life outside Ireland and was not always attuned to or wholly in sympathy with the political and religious feelings which inspired his fervently loyalist Protestant soldiers. Furthermore, although his was one of the most politically sensitive posts in the Army, he shared with many of his brother officers a general contempt for politicians (with a very few exceptions) which had its origins in the pre-war period but which intensified as the war continued. This included in his case not only Irish nationalist politicians but most Unionist ones also – 'I would like to drown or shoot all politicians or anyhow get them out here in the trenches' being a not untypical comment.[2] This obviously did not help the task of building constructive relationships with those at home.

The Ulster Division was not alone in Kitchener's New Armies in having strong political connections: the 16th (Irish) Division, formed round a nucleus of Irish National Volunteers, was closely linked to John Redmond's Nationalist Party, while the 38th (Welsh) Division owed its existence largely to Lloyd George's desire to create a Welsh Army Corps.[3] But even where formations lacked such direct political links, the Army still had to manage its relationships with local and regional political interests with care. Its territorial regimental structure and the network of local relationships it embodied provided both a justification and an opportunity for a range of groups – MPs, municipal bodies, the Territorial associations and local grandees, amongst others – to exert pressure on behalf of their 'clients' within the Army. This was reinforced by the fact that many New Army units had been raised through local rather than central initiatives. The lobbying could sometimes be very direct, as when the mayors of Belfast and several other Ulster towns wrote to Nugent in early 1918 pleading that their battalions be spared in the reorganisation of infantry then taking place.[4]

Even though senior officers, Nugent amongst them, expended much effort in their turn in lobbying their political contacts on issues of importance to the Army, attempts at 'interference' by civilians were much resented. But the high command knew that it could not afford to be wholly dismissive of interests which had influence in governmental circles or could raise their concerns in Parliament. The political pressures which Nugent faced were particular to the Ulster Division, but his experience was different in degree rather than in kind to that of other commanders.

He had had an eventful career in the years before the First World War. In the early 1890s he was involved in several minor expeditions on the North West Frontier of India; and in 1895 he served with the Chitral relief force, earning the DSO for his services. In 1898 he attended the Staff College (where one of his fellow students was Douglas Haig, with whom he did not get on) before in 1899 going to South Africa with his battalion. He was badly wounded during the first major engagement of the Boer War, at Talana Hill, and spent a year as a Boer prisoner before being invalided home. After the war he held various staff and regimental appointments, and between 1906 and 1914 commanded successively the 4th KRRC and a territorial infantry brigade before going on half-pay early in 1914 as a colonel. He returned to Ireland, by now in the throes of the Home Rule crisis, where he threw in his lot with the Ulster Unionists and was soon heavily involved in the raising and training of the Cavan UVF.

As a serving officer, albeit currently unemployed, he was a relatively unusual figure in the UVF: but his sympathy for Ulster's resistance to Home Rule was widely shared within the Army's officer corps. Over 60% of the UVF's leadership comprised former Army officers, not all of them Irish, while the stance taken by Gough's 3rd Cavalry Brigade at the Curragh received widespread support in garrisons across Ireland

and beyond.[5] Nevertheless, Nugent was not in retrospect particularly comfortable about his UVF involvement. Early in 1916 he explained his position to a strongly 'pro-Ulster' English officer:

> . . . I joined the UVF not for the purpose of rebellion or civil war because I disagreed all along on the policy which created the UVF but because I thought I should do more good in my own country by organising a force for defence in case of attack and that I would never consent to leading them in an unprovoked attack on anyone and that I said at the time that those were the conditions on which I would take part and no other. They were not popular outside of Cavan.[6]

Later he argued that he had 'always maintained that the physical force movement was a mistake and the arming of Ulster a still greater mistake. It gave the other side a lead and now neither side will disarm . . .'[7] His disillusion stemmed partly from dismay at subsequent political developments in Ireland, but also from a feeling of having been tainted by his involvement in politics and of having compromised his professional standing ('I'll never put my finger into politics again. Every man has his trade and politics is not mine'[8]). This also was a factor in his increasing antipathy towards the Division's political supporters in Ulster.

The crisis in Ireland was averted by the outbreak of war in August 1914, and Nugent was put in charge of the Hull defences. Officers with his experience were too valuable to be left in such posts, however, and in May 1915 he was given command of 41st Brigade in the 14th Division, a New Army formation. Most of his four months with the Division were spent in the Ypres Salient, an area he came to hate. The worst episode occurred at the end of July 1915 when his brigade, holding the line at Hooge, suffered heavy losses in a German dawn attack using flamethrowers, the first time these weapons had been used against the British. Better news came early in September when he learned that he was to be promoted and take command of the Ulster Division. He took up his new post in England on 16 September, and brought the Division to France the following month.

He at once set about imposing his personality on his new command. That personality was an uncompromising one. Cyril Falls, who served on Nugent's staff from 1916 to 1918 and knew him well, penned a generous tribute in the Divisional history, writing that the Division 'owed much to him, particularly to his training in the early days after its arrival in France'.[9] But Falls went further in an article he wrote many years later about his experience of commanders and staffs in the First World War, when he said: 'I have nothing to say against any of the divisional commanders whom I served, except that the first [Nugent] had a shocking temper'.[10] And there is no doubt that Nugent did have a violent temper; several times in his correspondence he admits to being so furiously angry with subordinates that he did not dare speak to them for several days for fear of what he might say. One of his COs wrote that Nugent did his shooting in the front line with weapons, on paper with an acid pen, and in the conference room with a cutting tongue and subtle wit.[11] A brother officer wrote after his death that Nugent had 'an unbending will, was self-confident in his judgements and had not the happy knack, which a few strong characters have, of subordinating his own judgement when it clashed with that of authority'.[12] In this respect neither military superiors nor political acquaintances went unscathed, which helps explain why he did not get the promotion his abilities deserved and which at one time seemed likely.

Clearly he could be very difficult, partly because of the injuries he had sustained in South Africa, from which he never fully recovered. Yet he was aware of his own failings, and had a well-developed sense of humour.

And despite his sometimes trenchant criticisms of them, he had an enormous regard for the soldiers under his command and worked constantly on their behalf. His reputation had preceded him: word in the 10th Inniskillings was that their new general was 'very soldierly but the devil of a straffer'.[13] They were soon to find out how right they were.

Nugent lost no time on assuming command in weeding out those of his subordinates whom he felt were not up to the job. Brigadier General Couchman of 107 Brigade was sacked within days of the Division arriving in France: Nugent told his wife: 'I have had to write to one of my Brigadiers and tell him he won't do, so beastly but quite unavoidable. I might have delayed it, but what good and a good man is badly wanted at once'. His GSO1, whom Nugent described as being 'the worst staff officer in the Army', had gone by the end of October, as had several battalion commanders. As Nugent put it, 'We can't afford to run risks of breakdown through people not knowing their jobs'. Brigadier General Hacket Pain of 108 Brigade went home in December, and Hickman of 109 Brigade in the spring.[14]

Nugent's ruthlessness was entirely consistent with practice throughout the BEF. The need to replace those officers who had trained the New Armies at home but who were unsuited, for reasons of age, health or aptitude, to front-line service led to a high turnover of commanders at all levels: to take just one example, in the 16th Division, which came out in December 1915, all three brigadiers had gone home by February, along with several battalion commanders.[15] But in dismissing these officers Nugent antagonised an Ulster political establishment already suspicious of him, since several of those removed had held senior appointments in the prewar UVF: for example, Couchman had commanded the Belfast UVF, Hacket Pain had been the UVF's chief of staff, and Hickman, an MP, had also been one of its leading figures. Tensions soon surfaced inside the Division, and for a period Nugent was scarcely on speaking terms with a number of subordinates, including Major Lord Leitrim and Lieutenant Colonel Pakenham;[16] these Ulster landowners were also important Unionist figures, and their disgruntlement was shared by their colleagues at home.

At the same time Nugent turned to the task of training his men for war. His briskly unceremonious approach caused ripples which were also felt in Ireland. His initial impression was that, in terms of physique, the Division was the finest he had seen, and that discipline was fairly good. He suspected, however, that it had a rather high opinion of itself, and he at once began putting it through its paces. In October 1915 he held a Divisional exercise after which, he said, 'I delivered a long criticism. There were too many mistakes and shortcomings, I am sorry to say, for a Division supposed to be ready for war'.[17] The brutality of his debrief became part of Ulster Division folklore. An officer of the 11th Irish Rifles wrote that Nugent's comments 'left an impression on the minds of those who heard them that will never fade'[18], and the second-in-command of the 10th Inniskillings was equally impressed:

> . . . few of the officers who were privileged to listen to his pow-wow after the performance will forget it. Very gravely he opened his remarks by saying how glad he was to have at last seen the famous Ulster Division going through an attack practice, but . . . how much more glad he was . . . that it was only a *practice* attack, for had it been a pukker attack . . . he would not have had the pleasure of speaking to any of the participating officers again in this world! The general went on to congratulate the officers on the excellence of their North of Ireland eyesight – he had observed that though they were all equipped with field glasses, none of them had ever found it necessary to use them . . . As a lecture it was superb . . . even though the officers felt . . . more than a little bit aggrieved, at the nature of their commander's witticisms.[19]

But it was not just the Division's tactics which Nugent sought to improve. He regarded strict discipline as essential, and made his position absolutely clear to the officers of the Division soon after his arrival:

> In all my experience of life as a soldier, I have never seen a regiment which made or maintained a reputation which had not discipline . . . It is the spirit of discipline which enables you and the men you have to lead to face losses, to go steadily to your front and to confront difficulties and dangers which would probably have frightened you into a lunatic asylum 8 months ago.[20]

Problems soon arose in one brigade in particular and Nugent was furious, telling his wife:

I am not too happy about the Ulster Division for it cannot be denied that some of them have very little discipline. The Belfast Brigade [107 Brigade] is awful. They have absolutely no discipline and their officers are awful. I am very much disturbed about them. I don't think they are fit for service and I should be very sorry to have to trust them . . . It is all due to putting a weak man in command of the Brigade to start with and giving commissions to men of the wrong class.[21]

Nugent decided to tell 107 Brigade, which contained a number of units that had been the pride of the pre-war UVF, what he thought of them and an officer of the 9th Irish Rifles, Frank Crozier, recalled:

General Nugent . . . assembles all the officers of our brigade in a village schoolroom where he delivers a strafe, not wholly deserved but very good for us, which I shall always treasure in my mind as the complete example of what can be said by the powerful to the powerless in the shortest space of time possible, consistent with the regulation of words and space for breathing, in the most offensive, sarcastic and uncompromising manner possible.[22]

The problems went beyond simply rebuking the officers, however. Only four men of the Ulster Division were executed during the First World War; but it is no coincidence that three of them, all from 107 Brigade, were shot in the first few weeks of 1916, all for desertion. (107 Brigade was actually transferred out of the Ulster Division for a period in the winter of 1915–16 as part of an experiment in which a regular brigade was exchanged for a New Army one in each New Army division: Crozier thought that Nugent had deliberately selected it for transfer as a punishment but in fact Nugent had opposed the move from the outset and 107 Brigade returned to the Division early in 1916.)[23]

There were other issues, generally stemming from inexperience, to be addressed. Early in November Nugent complained: 'I regret to say these Irishmen are horribly dirty in their habits. They don't seem to have learned much in that way since they enlisted'.[24] He cracked down on standards across the board, being hugely pleased when in January 1916 Lord Cavan, his corps commander and a Guardsman, praised the Division's turnout. On being told by his wife some time later that he had been described at home as a 'pukka tiger' he commented wryly '. . . it probably refers to my ferocious strafing of slackness and to a general and salutary fear of me which the Division has'.[25] No aspect of the Division escaped his notice, including disputes between his chaplains: 'My parsons give me some annoyance. The Presbyterian and the Church of Ireland chaplains will not coalesce as they ought. I had to talk to them so I hope to see an improvement'.[26]

This experience of occasionally uncomfortable adjustment to operational conditions was common to all New Army divisions. But there was an additional dimension to Nugent's attempts to impose himself on the Division which was as much political and cultural as military. Ultimately he was an Irish rather than an Ulster unionist. His home was on the periphery of Ulster, and as he explained to his English wife:

> We are not really a N of Ireland family and as a matter of fact, the Nugents fought for James and against William in the days when the north was founding itself. All our family associations lie in the midlands of Ireland and it is merely a geographical accident that we live inside Ulster.[27]

On another occasion he elaborated (contrasting the Nugents with other landed Cavan families): 'We are Irish because we have intermarried with the Irish who owned the country before us . . . the excitement that [Nugent's involvement with the UVF] caused is really proof of how much the country people look upon the Nugents as their natural leaders'.[28]

It followed that he sometimes felt an outsider in a formation that was very tightly bonded by political and religious belief, and he found the more extreme versions of Ulster loyalism uncongenial. Nugent used his letters home to his wife to let off steam, and in July 1916 his frustration showed:

> Do you find the women of the North very difficult? You can't find them more difficult than I find the men. They are the most self-centred people I have ever met. If you are not Ulster and if you don't subscribe to every Ulster prejudice and if you are not as intolerant as they are, they will have nothing to do with you. They simply won't accept you. I have found that for 10 months and I feel today no nearer them and no more in touch with them than when I came. I'm merely the Divisional Commander, a person who has to be obliged and who can be very disagreeable if he isn't, but I'm merely an incident and anyone who followed me would be merely an incident. They are magnificent soldiers but very hard to know.[29]

Within the Division he tried hard to discourage both sectarianism and too overt displays of 'party' political affiliation. Despite his personal antipathy towards Roman Catholicism he issued instructions that Catholic churches were to be treated with respect, an edict which earned him a papal medal, much to his amusement.[30] He insisted to visitors 'that neither politics nor religious differences were ever discussed out here'.[31] In August 1916 the King visited the Ulster Division, and Nugent wrote:

> [The King] would talk . . . of the Ulster Division as the Irish Division

and I had finally to explain that we were the Ulster Divn and that there was an Irish Division so he said he thought it was a pity we were not called the Irish Divn too as he thought 'Ulster' savoured of politics. I firmly and gently put him right and said there were no politics in the Ulster Division.[32]

This was inevitably difficult to enforce, given the Division's origins and the presence of several MPs and other Unionist activists in its ranks, and from time to time Nugent's exasperation could not be contained:

D-n their politics. I wish I had refused to have anything to do with them. I always feel just the same with this Division that they would really rather have someone else. I know they are always writing home about everything I do or say and can't stand anything but praise. They had too much butter given them while at home.[33]

One of his most capable staff officers, W B Spender, an Englishman but an ardent Unionist, left on promotion in July 1916. Nugent, despite recognising his abilities, was glad to see him go: 'He is too much mixed up with the politicals in Belfast and talks and writes too much to them'.[34]

Nugent, unsurprisingly, regarded his own intense personal belief in King, country and empire, and his absolute support for the war effort, as a commitment to values which stood above party politics. But he seems to have been oblivious to the contradiction between his rejection of 'politics' in the Division and his own strong and frequently expressed conservatism, and his undisguised hostility towards the Liberals – especially Asquith – Irish nationalism and, increasingly, Ulster Unionism.

Inevitably he was never able to rid the Division entirely of its Ulster loyalist dimension, which was viewed with suspicion by some regular officers, not least those serving in the regular Irish battalions. (For example, an officer of the 2nd Irish Rifles, which was transferred to the 36th Division in the autumn of 1917, noted that the battalion's southern Irish officers resented their move to the 'poisonously loyal' Ulster Division, while an officer of the 1st Irish Rifles, which followed suit in February 1918, confided to his diary 'Definitely settled that the Battalion will leave that fine Division the 8th and go to the 36th – the political division as we know it'.)[35] Its more strident manifestations did, however, reduce over time through a combination of Nugent's badgering, the disciplines and preoccupations of operational service and the gradual dilution of the original ethos of the Division through casualties and distance from home.

Letters written in anger or frustration give a misleading impression of his attitude towards his men, for whom he had genuine respect and affection. In his calmer moments he was able to take a more objective view (even if sometimes rather a cynical one – he commented after visiting a bombing class 'These Ulstermen are first rate at it. I can fancy how they would enjoy throwing bombs amongst the Nationalists in a street row in Belfast')[36]. He was always concerned for his soldiers' welfare, and his correspondence is full of references to the privations they were enduring in the front line. He made a point of visiting his units five or six days a week, often in the forward trenches, and he had a number of narrow escapes from artillery, machine-gun fire and enemy aircraft while doing so. He was deeply proud of his soldiers' achievements: on 2 July 1916 he wrote to his wife: 'I cannot describe to you how I feel about them. I did not believe men were made who could do such gallant work under conditions of modern war.'[37] He was at pains to stress the duty of his officers to their soldiers, telling them that they must work 'on the principle that there is nothing too small to worry over if it tends to the comfort, health or fighting efficiency of your men . . . It is what you are in the position of an officer or NCO to do'.[38]

He succeeded in moulding the Division, through intensive training, tireless attention to detail and insistence on initiative and aggression at every level, into one of the best of the New Army formations. Its spectacular success on 1 July 1916 was due in large part to the thoroughness with which Nugent had prepared it and the care with which he planned the assault (including, crucially, his decision to deploy his leading waves into no man's land before zero hour).[39] The same strong grip was evident in all the Division's subsequent battles – Messines, Cambrai, the March 1918 German offensive – with the exception of Langemarck (August 1917), fought in appalling conditions under a commander, Gough, whom Nugent did not admire. By contrast, he thought the world of Plumer, a regard that was reciprocated (Plumer's chief of staff told Nugent after the war that 'yours was the best run division in our old Second Army', while Plumer, who contributed the Foreword to the Divisional history, wrote warmly of Nugent and his contribution).[40] The officers and men under his command too held Nugent in great respect, if not always affection, and appreciated his concern for their welfare and his determination not to waste their lives needlessly: an officer of the Division said of him that 'every man knew exactly where he was, and that the objectives would be taken with as little loss as possible'.[41] By the middle of 1916 leader and led had largely settled down with each other.

Nugent's relations with politicians at home, on the other hand, deteriorated steadily as the war went on. His instinctive distrust of them was reinforced by his landowner's disdain for the Belfast-based leadership of Ulster Unionism. The gulf became unbridgeable when, in June 1916, the Ulster Unionists decided to pursue a partitionist settlement which excluded three Ulster counties, including Cavan. Lord Farnham, Nugent's ADC and leader of the Cavan Unionists, returned home to argue against the proposal, but Nugent was under no illusions:

113

. . . the Belfast people won't hesitate to chuck us over. I see Arthur [Farnham] spoke against excluding Cavan but what is the use of talking about it? It won't stop it if the Belfast people want us to be handed over in order to save themselves. The only thing that is certain is that it will not satisfy the nationalists.[42]

The decision dented Nugent's faith in the one Irish politician he did admire, Sir Edward Carson. But the issue above all else which became the touchstone for his frustration and contempt for politicians was Irish recruitment. The lack of depth in the manpower available to Irish units was already clear by late 1915, as recruitment rates in Ireland, already proportionately lower than in Britain, began to fall away further. Both Nugent and the Unionist leadership were well aware of the difficulties the Irish divisions would face once they began to sustain heavy casualties, a point James Craig made in the House of Commons in January 1916 when calling for Irish conscription.[43]

Nugent like many other senior officers, was a strong supporter of compulsory service in Ireland, and lobbied Carson and other politicians constantly on the subject. In April 1916 he told Carson:

. . . this Division cannot exist unless we do [have conscription] and that it would be so bad for the future if there were 2 parties in the north of Ireland, those who gave their sons or husbands and the cowards who lurked at home, that if we must suffer, do let us all suffer together and so have a common bond of union.[44]

His anger over what he regarded as the lukewarm support he received ('I do not particularly trust the Ulster members in this matter any more than the Nationalists', he complained)[45] was soon greatly exacerbated by the news of the proposed exclusion of Cavan. His dislike focused particularly on Craig, and in June 1916 he fumed: 'I hear James Craig told Colonel Ricardo that he had no time to talk about recruiting, that the H[ome] R[ule] question must be settled first. He ought to be shot if that is true'.[46]

In much of his criticism Nugent was unfair. Ulster in fact provided around half of Irish enlistments during the war, with Belfast alone contributing more than a third of the overall total. Irish Protestants, most of whom lived in Ulster, provided an estimated 45% of Irish wartime enlistments despite representing only 25% of the island's population, while within the province of Ulster itself the Protestant section of the community, 53% of the total, provided 73% of the recruits.[47] But the initial recruiting surge could not be sustained, even in Unionist areas, in the absence of conscription. Nugent was only too aware that his Division needed men to survive, and that there was a pool of manpower in Ireland, including Ulster, which had not yet been fully tapped. Furthermore, like others inside and outside the Army he believed – however unrealistically – that conscription, if implemented with determination, would unite the different political strands in Ireland. He was scathing about those whom he believed did not share his commitment: in August 1916 he got a letter from the Grand Master of Belfast Orangemen congratulating the Division and saying that their hearts went out to it, to which Nugent replied sharply that if their bodies accompanied their hearts ('none of them are enlisting') it would be much more to the point: 'I think it is sheer impertinence to write flapdoodle of that kind at the present time'.[48]

The anticipated manpower crisis finally arrived in the autumn of 1916, precipitated by the heavy casualties suffered by the 16th and 36th Divisions on the Somme. Neither formation could be recommitted to full-scale action until they were brought up to strength, but not enough Irish replacements were available to do so. By September 1916 Irish infantry units were some 17,000 men under strength, with the shortfall growing daily. Radical solutions were considered, including the amalgamation of the two Irish divisions serving on the western front.[49]

Both Redmond and Carson were horrified by this prospect (the latter's preference, if the Ulster Division had to disappear, being that it be merged with the Highland Division).[50] Nugent, by contrast, favoured the idea: 'I am most desirous, if the two Divisions have to disappear as separate units, that they should be merged in each other'.[51] But he also pressed hard yet again for conscription, for political as well as military reasons: he told Carson that 'compulsory service now would be the moral regeneration of the country',[52] and expressed to his wife the hope that conscription 'might kill politics for all time in Ireland, and what a blessing that would be'.[53]

In the event the decision was taken at political level to preserve the two Irish formations by a combination of drafting in non-Irish soldiers, breaking up Irish units to provide replacements and transferring regular Irish battalions to the Irish divisions. Nugent, while disappointed that there was to be no Irish conscription, was content with the new arrangement, noting that 'the "Ulster" designation, or "Irish", as the case may be, will be taken away as soon as the Irish Divisions have more than 50% of men from Great Britain in their ranks. This is reasonable. Anything which gives us men is better than the state of suspended animation in which we have lived for the last four months'.[54]

By the turn of the year, however, the Division was still under strength and when in December 1916 a Belfast newspaper asked for a Christmas message to the people of Ulster Nugent leapt at the opportunity. 'I am giving them beans and no mistake', he remarked happily, 'laying it on with scorpions'.[55] His message duly appeared:

A message to the people of Ulster from the Ulster Division must contain, besides greetings and good wishes, some hard truths . . . the

Ulster Division is growing stronger day by day, but its ranks are being filled up by Englishmen and Scotchmen: men who have not shirked duty, and who have done for Ulster what she has, as yet, failed to do for herself.[56]

He sent the press cutting to his wife a few days later:

I enclose the Belfast News Letter with my message to the Ulster loafers . . . Don't you think it a rather good message, just some plain speaking. I have had 2 letters of protest already which shows that it left a sting.[57]

In fact it caused deep offence, made worse when nationalist demonstrators in Dublin reproduced it on placards as evidence that Unionist criticisms of the nationalist contribution to the war effort were hypocritical.[58] Ulster Unionism generally was outraged (its leaders were reported to be still furious the following May), there were calls in the Belfast press for his dismissal, and it was rumoured that James Craig had refused to have anything to do with the Ulster Division while Nugent was in command.[59]

In terms of encouraging recruitment the episode was wholly counter-productive, and by fatally damaging Nugent's relations with the Ulster leadership it reduced his influence still further. Yet if his rather clumsy attempts to stimulate Irish recruitment achieved little, he was not totally unmindful of the fact that he would eventually have to return to Ireland to live amongst those he was castigating. At the same time he felt himself under increasing pressure from his own superiors, who were themselves both frustrated by Ireland's perceived failure to 'do her bit' and conscious of resentment in Britain that Irish units were being bailed out by English recruits.[60] This came to a head in the spring of 1917 over the question of the Division's title.

Large-scale drafts of English replacements had begun reaching the Division in January 1917 and by April it was back up to strength. The proportion of Irishmen in the infantry battalions, though reduced, still stood at around 60%, but when supporting arms were taken into account (the Divisional artillery was not recruited in Ireland) the overall proportion of Irishmen in the Division had fallen to around 50%. At the end of April Nugent received an unwelcome message from a visiting GHQ staff officer:

The gist of it is that the C in C out here [Haig] won't use us for any purpose but holding the line so long as we call ourselves the Ulster Division, because he considers that it is unfair to Englishmen who have compulsory service that they should be sent to fill up a Division supposed to be composed of volunteers from Ulster, but who won't volunteer, that if we want to be called Ulster we must fill up our own ranks, but that if we are prepared to drop the title of Ulster we shall be treated as any other Division, get men and be used in something more glorious then trench drudges.[61]

Nugent was appalled, less by the thought of losing the title than by a well-founded fear that he was being used:

Now the whole difficulty is this, that GHQ won't put this in writing, but they want me to start the correspondence by offering on behalf of the Division to drop the title of Ulster. What would happen? The politicians at home would at once kick up a row, call it an insult to Ulster and so on. The War Office would then say 'we never suggested it. The GOC the Ulster Divn suggested it of his own initiative.' Can't you imagine the outcry amongst the cats round Lady Carson's com[mi]ttee table and the stayathomes of Belfast. They would never rest till they got me hounded out and we have to live in Ireland after the war. I would do it all the same tomorrow if it is the only way, but it is so unfair to try and throw the onus of taking the first step upon me that I am trying to get GHQ to say it in writing. Why should I be made the scapegoat for the wrath of the dirty politicians of the Craig type.

Nugent also vented his frustration at his Division's inability to play its full part in the fighting:

Not that I have a word to say against the men out here. They are always good, but I wish I had never seen a political Division and the people who thought they were going to run it can never forgive me because I would not allow any politics in it.

He sought Plumer's advice, who much to Nugent's relief at once offered to raise the issue himself.[62] Nugent in turn consulted his commanding officers, telling them that the loss of the title would be a blow and he much wished to retain it, but that the Division had too much self-respect to wish to cling to a title to which it had no claim or which would offend non-Irish soldiers serving in its ranks; that higher authority should decide; and that the main objective was to keep the Division in being as a fighting formation irrespective of its name.[63] At a conference on 16 May the COs unanimously supported Nugent's view, asking that the title be retained, emphasising that their attachment to it was 'from association and sentiment and in no way political', but accepting that the chain of command's decision should be loyally supported. Nugent warned them 'that they must remember they were soldiers and must not start work behind the backs of higher authority by writing to their political friends'.[64] He then formally reported to his corps commander that in the opinion of his officers and himself the title was highly valued not just by Ulstermen but by a majority of the Englishmen serving with the Division, that its loss would be deeply felt, and that they wished to keep it; but that the decision rested with the higher command.[65] Faced with this GHQ dropped the proposal: but the Ulster Division received no further large-scale drafts of English troops while Nugent was in command and had to depend increasingly on the cannibalisation of its own units to provide replacements. Nor did Nugent do himself any favours with Haig, who was widely believed to have blocked the award of his knighthood at the end of the war.[66]

Here the position rested to the end of Nugent's period in command. It was in fact a situation with which he was relatively comfortable. He had failed to get Irish conscription, and his relations with the Ulster Unionist leadership (other than Carson) had effectively broken down: but the immediate question of obtaining replacements had been resolved, and the Division had successfully retained its identity, in terms of title and composition, in a manner which amounted to an explicit rejection of the 'political' identity which he so disliked.

Nugent continued to have strong opinions on Irish politics. He came increasingly to the view that Ulster should be forced to accept a compromise solution in exchange for full nationalist participation in the war effort. But from now on his preoccupation was with commanding his division in a series of fiercely fought engagements, and he had neither the inclination nor the opportunity to dwell overmuch on Irish politics. In May 1918 he was replaced in line with the Army's policy of bringing in younger officers as divisional commanders. The news was greeted with genuine regret in the Division. He went on to command a division in India during the Third Afghan War and eventually retired from the Army in 1920.

Militarily Nugent was a highly capable officer, and the Ulster Division earned an enviable reputation under him. He was only partially successful, however, in his attempts to 'depoliticise' it and his efforts to do so caused friction both with some subordinates and with their political supporters in Ireland. This in itself would not have led to the rift with the Ulster Unionist leadership that occurred in 1916–17: that was caused by the larger issue of Irish recruitment, which also put pressure on Nugent's relations with his military superiors, and was exacerbated by his difficult personality and his anger over the exclusion of Cavan. Only Hickie of the 16th Division faced comparable pressures, which he seems to have been better able to manage (though in the absence of his private papers it is impossible to know what strains there were under the surface).

Nugent died in Co. Cavan in 1926 and was commemorated at a memorial service in St Anne's Cathedral in Belfast. Reflecting the political difficulties he wrestled with, no senior member of the Northern Ireland government came. But in recognition of his qualities and abilities as a soldier, several thousand former members of the Ulster Division did.

Notes

1 This article draws heavily on Nugent's extensive correspondence, mainly to his wife but also to a range of political and military figures, contained in the Public Record Office of Northern Ireland's important Farren Connell collection. I am indebted to the Deputy Keeper of the Records of Northern Ireland for permission to consult, and quote from, these papers
2 Oliver Nugent [ON] to his wife, Catherine ('Kitty') [CN], 15 October 1916, Farren Connell Papers, Public Record Office of Northern Ireland [FCP], MIC/571/2
3 Terence Denman, *Ireland's Unknown Soldiers* (Dublin, 1992), pp.25–37; Colin Hughes, *Mametz* (King's Lynn, 1990, 2nd edn), pp.15–34
4 See, for example, the correspondence in Nugent's papers for January-February 1918 (FCP, MIC/571/7/11)
5 Hew Strachan, *The Politics of the British Army* (Oxford, 1997), p.112; Ian Beckett, *The Army and the Curragh Incident, 1914* (London, 1986), pp.22–4
6 ON to CN, 5 February 1916. The officer with whom Nugent was corresponding was the future General Sir Edward Hutton
7 ON to CN, 6 June 1916
8 ON to CN, 18 October 1916
9 Cyril Falls, *The History of the 36th (Ulster) Division* (Belfast, 1922), p.244
10 idem, 'Contact with Troops: Commanders and Staff in the First World War', *Army Quarterly* 88/2 (1964), p.178
11 F P Crozier, *The Men I Killed* (London, 1937), p.67
12 *The King's Royal Rifle Corps Chronicle* (1926), pp.241–4
13 Account by Lt Col. F Macrory, 10th Inniskillings War Diary (PRO Kew, WO95/2510)
14 ON to CN, 10 and 31 October 1915
15 Denman, *Ireland's Unknown Soldiers, p.62*
16 ON to CN, 8 December 1915
17 ON to CN, 16 October 1915
18 Captain A P I Samuels, *With the Ulster Division in France* (not dated), p.16
19 Macrory, op. cit.
20 Talk to Officers and NCOs of the Division, September 1915 (MIC/571/7/3A)
21 ON to CN, 26 October 1915
22 F P Crozier, *A Brass Hat in No Man's Land* (London, 1930), p.77
23 ibid, p.78
24 ON to CN, 6 November 1915
25 ON to CN, 22 March 1917
26 ON to CN, 1 June 1916
27 ON to CN, 18 February 1916
28 ON to CN, 10 August 1917
29 ON to CN, 16 July 1916
30 ON to CN, 19 January 1916
31 ON to CN, 23 January 1916
32 ON to CN, 14 August 1916
33 ON to CN, 18 February 1916
34 ON to CN, 20 July 1916

35 J Lucy, *There's a Devil in the Drum* (London, 1938; reprinted 1992), p.345; Captain Whitfeld Diary, 2 February 1918 (Imperial War Museum)
36 ON to CN, 24 November 1915
37 ON to CN, 2 July 1916
38 Talk to Officers and NCOs of the Division (op. cit.)
39 Falls, *Ulster Division*, pp.51–2
40 Harington to Nugent, 8 January 1922 (FCP, MIC/571/13/1); Falls, *Ulster Division*, p.x
41 F P Crozier, *Impressions and Reflections* (London, 1930), p.172
42 ON to CN, 9 June 1916
43 *House of Commons Parliamentary Debates 1916*, 82, col. 81
44 ON to CN, 14 April 1916
45 ON to CN, 10 May 1916
46 ON to CN, 6 June 1916
47 P Callan, 'Recruiting for the British Army in Ireland during the First World War', in *The Irish Sword*, 66 (Summer 1987), pp.42–56
48 ON to CN, 10 August 1916
49 Minutes of the Proceedings of, and Precis prepared for, the Army Council for the years 1915 and 1916, 55 (WO163/21, PRO)
50 Carson to Nugent, 10 October 1916 (FCP)
51 Nugent to Carson, not dated, but October 1916 (FCP)
52 ibid.
53 ON to CN, 8 October 1916
54 Nugent to Brigadier General Hacket Pain, 5 November 1916 (FCP)
55 ON to CN, 19 December 1916
56 Nugent to the Editor of the *Newsletter*, 19 December 1916
57 ON to CN, 30 December 1916
58 ON to CN, 3 March 1917
59 ON to CN, 21 March and 26 May 1917
60 For example, in March 1917 questions were being asked in Parliament about the number of Irish battalions receiving non-Irish drafts (*House of Commons Parliamentary Debates 1917*, 91, col. 376)
61 ON to CN, 29 April 1917
62 ON to CN, 2 May 1917; Plumer to AG GHQ, 3 May 1917; ON to CN, 6 May 1917
63 ON to CN, 26 May 1917
64 ON to CN, 17 May 1917
65 Nugent to IX Corps, 16 May 1917
66 Whether for this or for some other reason Nugent did not receive his knighthood until 1922, after Haig's retirement. In congratulating him, Plumer wrote: 'It should have been given you long ago'; Harington that 'it was monstrous, as I have so often said, that you had not received it years ago'; Major General Hickie, formerly GOC of the 16th (Irish) Division, that 'I have always felt your bad treatment just as keenly as if it had been my own'; Colonel Ricardo that 'I have always deplored the dirty work that kept you out of a reward that everyone recognised was your due'; and Hutchinson Rai, another former subordinate, that 'You should have had it long ago, if – as I have always understood – Haig is responsible for the omission it doesn't enhance his reputation for fair play.' (MIC/571/13/1/1)

WILLIAM PHILPOTT
Britain, France and the Belgian Army

Recent historiography of the Great War has begun to address the coalition nature of the war, in particular the high political decision making which lay behind alliance military policy, although much work remains to be done in this area and an overall synthesis of individual case studies is a long way off.[1] Military cooperation in the field is as yet an almost unexplored avenue of research. This study makes a first tentative step to fill this gap by examining the relations of the three national armies which shared the trials of the western front, at the operational level of command.

Historians of the western front have tended to concentrate on the policies and actions of the two principal protagonists in that campaign, Great Britain and France. If not overlooked, then it is at least considered insignificant that the trials of four years of trench warfare were shared by a third allied army; the six Belgian divisions encamped behind the inundations on the river Yser for four years from November 1914 to October 1918.[2] In purely military terms perhaps this neglect is justifiable, since the Belgian army made a negligible military contribution compared to that of Britain and France, and the defensive strategy adopted by the Belgians from the end of 1914 does not make for exciting or controversial history like the Somme or Passchendaele. Nevertheless, in overlooking the Belgians, as their British and French allies were apt to do at the time, historians have neglected an interesting and illuminating aspect of the western campaign. Looking beyond the military contribution of the Belgian army to victory on the western front, to its moral and political importance to the allied campaign, considerable light is thrown upon a number of important aspects of the development of the coalition campaign on the western front; command relationships between the allies' military leaders; coalition strategic policy on the western front; Anglo-French relations and Entente diplomacy.

Before addressing these themes, it is useful to outline Belgium's position and role on the western front, in order to understand how Belgian military policy was developed. Belgium was a reluctant member of the allied coalition; indeed in deference to her neutrality she never formally declared war on Germany, but simply claimed to be defending her territory against foreign aggression as an associate power of the Entente. Since, in consequence, Belgium did not sign the September 1914 Pact of London committing the allied nations not to make a separate peace, she remained a weak link in military line on the western front as well as the political solidarity of the alliance.[3] While not the subject of this essay, it is significant to note in passing that this position was reflected in Belgium's wartime diplomacy, which in seeking a compromise peace with Germany and the evacuation of Belgium was out of synchronisation with that of Britain and France. Luckily for the allies Germany never offered acceptable terms.[4]

Belgium's unique political position parallelled her singular military position. When war broke out the Belgian army was militarily important; more so than the British Expeditionary Force (BEF) in terms of size (six infantry divisions to the BEF's initial four in France) and strategic importance, acting in its self-appointed role as the advance guard and army of observation of the allied armies in the early battles on the frontiers.[5] Of course the poorly trained and ill coordinated Belgian field army could not hope to stand up to the might of the German army unsupported,[6] and by the end of August 1914 had retreated into the national refuge of Antwerp, where it remained until driven out during the siege of early October. Pursued by the Germans along the North Sea coast, it eventually found sanctuary behind the inundations of the river Yser in the last unoccupied corner of Belgium, where it was to sit, as secure as any force along the western front, for the next four years.[7] Of necessity the strategy the Belgians then adopted was strictly defensive; better to husband the army, the last symbol of a free Belgium, to give Belgium a voice at the peace conference, than to squander it in indecisive attritional attacks like those of the British and French.[8] This was certainly the view of the army's commander, King Albert I, whose personality and thoughts on strategy and policy need elaboration for they are central to an understanding of the allied military relationship.

King Albert's resolution and determination in command of the Belgian army have never been in question. However, his rigid defence of Belgian integrity and interests – 'guaranteeing the maintenance of the independence and integrity of Belgium in the future' as he put it in his appeal to the guaranteeing powers in August 1914[9] – were to bring him into conflict with both his allies and his own government. The king himself was firm in the defence of his own prerogative, virtuously equating his own fixed ideas with the interests of his nation.[10] Forced by events into the arms of the Entente, by temperament and experience Albert himself had more sympathy with the forceful autocratic methods, if not the objectives, of the Central Powers. Constant struggles with his own ministers over the right direction for Belgian policy, as well as with allied representatives over the coordination of Belgian policy with that of the Entente, only served to strengthen his belief that authority and might would always have the advantage over abstract liberal principles.[11]

King Albert's views on the Entente's policy and strategy are to be found in his own correspondence and war diaries, and those of his aide de camp, Commandant Galet.[12] King Albert was disillusioned with the French early on, a consequence of the authoritarian demeanour of the French commander-in-chief, General Joffre, and his refusal to respond to Belgian calls for support during the war of movement.[13] The king was initially more enthusiastic for the British, who had done as much as their limited military resources would allow to bring succour to the Belgian army trapped in Antwerp.[14] However, by the end of 1915 Britain's persistence with a futile offensive strategy at the behest of the French had earned them equal contempt.[15] Indeed the French had supplanted the British in King Albert's affections by the middle of 1916, a consequence of GHQ's desire to conduct an offensive from Ypres across Belgian soil.[16] By the end of 1915 Belgium had, through the king's political and military intransigence, become isolated from her allies. She had no say in alliance strategic decision making – General Wielemans, who represented Belgium, took no part in discussions at the Chantilly conference which met in early December to determine strategy for the coming year[17] – and not having signed the Pact of London was not formally represented at allied political conferences.[18] Although efforts were made to bring the Belgians into line with the allies,[19] they proved abortive,[20] and the king continued to pursue a separate diplomatic and military policy through 1916 and 1917, as his disillusionment with allied strategic policy and despair at ultimate allied victory increased.[21] This delicate political and military situation was further complicated by Belgium's reliance on her allies for military equipment and financial and humanitarian aid.[22]

The longer the trench stalemate went on, the more the king came to regard the offensive strategy of Joffre, Sir John French and Sir Douglas Haig, the successive British commanders-in-chief, as costly and futile. Not only was he not prepared to sacrifice Belgian lives in the pursuit of that strategy, but he was also strongly opposed to any offensive on the northern flank of the allied line. He was happy to let his allies attempt to restore Belgian independence by indirect means; indeed he advocated an offensive as far away from Flanders as possible, which would save occupied Belgium from the devastation that would result from operations on Belgian soil.[23] His preferred method of solving Belgium's problems was diplomatic, not military – a compromise peace.

Although out of synchronisation with the strategic and political objectives of the allied high commands and his own government, King Albert's views could not be ignored because of his position and status. On the political level he was sovereign of an allied nation. On the military level he was supreme commander (in fact as well as title) of an allied army. The problems this unique dual responsibility caused are well illustrated by the king's frequently stormy relations with Belgium's Prime Minister and Minister of War, Comte Charles de Broqueville, which unfortunately it is impossible to examine in detail here.[24] De Broqueville and the Belgian coalition ministry were strongly opposed to the king's policy of peace without annexations and a strict defensive posture until it was gained. Nevertheless, they could not challenge the king's constitutional position as supreme commander, nor his royal prerogative to direct Belgium's foreign policy, and had to acquiesce, if not without a struggle, in the face of royal intransigence.[25] Examination of the king's diaries and correspondence suggests that Albert felt that his rivals behind the lines were at least as formidable and dangerous as his enemies across the Yser. Indeed an examination of Belgium's military relations with her British and French allies tends to bear this out.

Both the British and French governments and high commands had to deal with an important but obstreperous ally in a coalition campaign. Of course not only King Albert was at fault. Joffre in particular, but French and Haig as well, were not the most sympathetic of characters when it came to dealing with their allies,[26] and King Albert's petulance is to some degree understandable when faced with imperious and demanding allies. Indeed with hindsight it might be conceded that Albert came to have a more realistic view of the military stalemate on the western front than the allied commanders-in-chief who persisted in driving their troops mercilessly against the enemy's entrenchments.[27] But at the time the king's refusal to fall in with the military policy of his more powerful allies must be judged a weakening factor in the military alliance on the western front, for it prevented a concerted offensive policy, particularly in the Flanders sector where British military effort was concentrated.

From the outset Joffre's assumption of the supreme authority of a 'generalissimo', while justified because of France's predominant military contribution to the alliance in the early months of the war, was to cause problems with both Sir John French and King Albert. Both were fiercely independent in spirit, and this demeanour was backed by constitutional prerogatives preventing the subordination of their respective armies to foreign authority, and reinforced by disillusionment with French military leadership after the disastrous opening battles on the frontiers.[28] Consequently Joffre could never command his allies, only recommend that they follow his directives. To his credit he recognised before battle was joined that military coordination would prove a problem for the alliance, but his methods and actions when dealing with his allies proved inimical to building the 'mutual confidence' upon which military collaboration would instead have to be based.[29]

Joffre had hoped to extend his authority to the Belgian army by an exchange of staff officers.[30] However, the appointment of Colonel Aldebert to command the French military mission at Belgian headquarters was to prove counter-productive. Aldebert saw his task to be to ensure that the

Belgians conformed to Joffre's operational plan; that is, to persuade King Albert to bring the Belgian army into line on the left of the allied armies opposing the German army's advance through southern Belgium. It is well known that Joffre's operational plan, 'plan XVII', discounted the possibility of a major German violation of Belgian territory north of the river Meuse.[31] The Belgians, in their role of advance guard to the allied armies, were soon aware of the extent of the German turning movement through northern Belgium, intelligence which they passed to the French military mission. It got no further.[32] Instead of modifying his plan to meet the changed circumstances of battle, Joffre persisted with his speculative counter-offensive in southern Belgium with consequences which are only too familiar.[33] The Belgians, who had been pressing futilely for French support on a line from Antwerp to Namur to check the German advance and save much of Belgium, consequently found themselves unsupported. They were forced, in the face of overwhelming odds, to retire into Antwerp shortly before the Anglo-French armies began their lengthy retirement to the Marne.[34]

These first few weeks of coalition war brought home to the Belgians the unreliability of their major ally, as well as Joffre's authoritarian manner. One casualty of the retreat to Antwerp was Aldebert, who resigned in protest at the Belgians' refusal to conform to French operational strategy.[35] Aldebert's narrow-minded subservience to Joffre's authority – what Galet termed the French military mission's pretensions to command the Belgian army[36] – pushed the Belgians along the path to complete military independence, out of an instinct of self-preservation as much as hubris.[37] The outcome of this fiasco was that the Belgian army was to remain cut off from the main allied armies until the end of September, by which time the military position on the northern flank had taken a turn for the worse and Antwerp was under siege.

The Belgians had higher expectations of their British allies, not least because it was the War Office which had approached the Belgian staff before the war with a view to coordinating military action in the event of a violation of Belgian neutrality.[38] However, when war broke out Britain found her freedom of action constrained by her pre-war military talks with the French general staff. Although direct assistance to the Belgians was discussed at the War Council which met on 5 August 1914 to determine Britain's military strategy,[39] it was only possible to answer Belgium's appeal for military assistance in the most ambiguous of terms; the BEF was to 'act in concert with the French army for the assistance of Belgium'.[40] After early defeats carried the BEF south and east of Paris, Britain's leaders had cause to regret their action. They had the will, but not the means, to bring assistance to Belgium. It is indicative of the desperation of Britain's military leaders that Winston Churchill, the First Lord of the Admiralty, conceived his famous but far-fetched proposal to transport Russian troops 'with snow on their boots' from Archangel to Ostend to succour the Belgian army and defend the Channel ports. The inability of Britain to act alone in support of the Belgian army was exposed only too clearly in early October when, lacking unequivocal French support, Lord Kitchener, the Secretary of State for War, was unable to raise enough troops to relieve the siege of Antwerp.[41]

The Belgians' retirement from Antwerp was at least covered by British and French troops gathered to relieve the fortress. This brought the Belgian army for the first time into direct cooperation with the Anglo-French armies trying to outflank the German line in the 'race to the sea'. It was clear that differences still existed between the French and Belgian commands. Joffre wanted the Belgians to retire southwards to support the Anglo-French offensive against the German army in the vicinity of Lille.[42] King Albert was not to be convinced and, like Sir John French after the retreat from Mons, insisted on withdrawing his shattered army from the allied line to rest.[43] Joffre hit upon a novel and effective way to bring some order to the chaos on the allied left wing. General Foch was appointed to coordinate the operations of the British, French and Belgian forces in that area. However, the presence of the sovereign King of the Belgians prevented a formal allied submission to French authority and it was only possible to extend the informal, and clearly inadequate, arrangements for cooperation existing between Sir John French and Joffre to the Belgian army.[44] Although Foch's appointment allowed closer supervision of France's allies, both King Albert and Sir John French maintained the same independent demeanour as hitherto, and so military operations remained subject to the vagaries of divided command, exacerbated by Joffre's overbearing authority. Foch was at least successful in persuading the Belgians to turn and fight before they had left Belgian soil. Closely supported on both flanks by French troops, they held the line of the river Yser until the German advance along the coast was checked by inundating the ground in front of their position.[45]

Once the military position had settled down after the first battle of Ypres, Joffre could think about putting the allied military forces on the northern flank in better order. While Foch's appointment had served the purpose in the short term, Joffre felt it necessary to strengthen his own authority over the allied forces in Flanders. His effort to subordinate the Belgian army was motivated in part by a desire to keep all allied operations under his own control, which had proved difficult when dealing with two independently minded allied commanders-in-chief; was partly a response to what he considered the poor military performance of the Belgian army in the first few months of the war; and also, although it is rarely explicitly stated in French documents, was partly due to a fear that the British would come to exercise too great an influence over the Belgian army at French expense.

By the end of 1914 the Belgian army had become a pawn in the military politics of Belgium's two powerful allies. Sir John French for example complained to Churchill after Foch was appointed;

> 'I tried hard to retain a hold on the Belgians and *with them* to operate alone on the northern flank: but the French smelt a rat and sent *Foch* and a *mission* to take charge of the Belgians. I feel sure it was a political move. They were afraid of our developing a separate kind of campaign and they are determined to keep everything under their own control.'[46]

Indeed the last months of 1914 witnessed a covert struggle between the British and French commands to extend their influence over the Belgian army, stubbornly resisted by King Albert who saw the maintenance of complete Belgian independence and impartiality as the only way to secure Belgium a voice at the peace conference after most of her territory had been occupied.[47] At best the actions of Joffre and Sir John French might be justified as an attempt to improve military efficiency and security in the coastal region. At worst, they must be judged a cavalier attempt to extend further their personal power and influence at the expense of their allies; in Joffre's case to secure undisputed supreme command of all allied forces on the western front; in French's case to increase the strength of the British army in preparation for an independent offensive along the Belgian coast to capture Zeebrugge.[48]

In October Joffre had suggested that the king should give up the command of his army to one of his generals, who might then be formally subordinated to French authority, which would remove the complication of placing an independent sovereign under an allied general, and allow more effective coordination of the allied forces on the northern flank.[49] Predictably the king was not amenable.[50] Indeed close cooperation between the Belgian and French armies during the battle of the Yser only occasioned further friction as reinforcements promised by Foch were slow to arrive, and in King Albert's opinion inadequate.[51] The French were equally dissatisfied with the Belgian army's performance on the Yser. Consequently, after the military position had settled down in November, Joffre's next suggestion was that the Belgian army be broken up and incorporated into the French army by brigades, to remove a weak military link in the allied line and a weak political link in the chain of command. Naturally this *amalgame* proposal was rejected,[52] as was the alternative suggestion of appointing a French chief of staff to the Belgian army.[53] Such schemes only served to increase King Albert's suspicion of the French.[54]

King Albert had been more sympathetic to the British, despite their equal inability to furnish the Belgians with effective military support during the battle of the Yser.[55] Yet at the end of the year Sir John French too came up with an *amalgame* plan for the British and Belgian armies, in order to strengthen the BEF for the Zeebrugge offensive. Inevitably this was also rejected and Albert's enthusiasm for his British allies cooled.[56] Albert did his best to meet allied criticisms of Belgian military effectiveness as far as this was practicable without compromising Belgian independence. The king at least agreed to support French's coastal offensive with artillery,[57] to reorganise the army's high command and formations on British lines, to extend the Belgian line if necessary, and even to create an armoured car squadron for the Russian front.[58]

By the end of 1914 the situation and role of the Belgian army for the rest of the war was effectively determined. They had no voice in the strategic direction of the campaign, and gave only the most reluctant support to their allies' offensive operations.[59] It was a policy very much associated with King Albert, who did his best to maintain the Belgian army's freedom of action during the lengthy war of attrition on the western front. The continued existence of an independent Belgian army was to prove a potential source of weakness in the allied military effort, both offensive and defensive,[60] as well as a bone of contention between the Anglo-French commands, and friction continued intermittently over these issues throughout the war.

In these circumstances French authority could only be exercised by indirect means. Firstly, the French acted as paymaster and munitioner to the Belgian army, a responsibility which France increasingly assumed from Great Britain in order, as the Postmaster-General Charles Hobhouse surmised, 'to get the Belgians in her pocket'.[61] Secondly, the French employed a policy of *encadrement*;[62] that is, ensuring that the Belgian army remained supported by French troops on both flanks, which would seem to confirm Hobhouse's assumption, as far as it was possible to get King Albert into a pocket. It seems that the French high command's policy of *encadrement* was motivated as much by a desire to prevent undue British influence over the Belgian army, as from a need to render the defensive line in the north secure. Sir John French's plan for an *amalgame* of the Belgian and British armies in January 1915 might be seen to justify this policy. Indeed some Frenchmen feared that Britain sought territorial compensation on the north European coast as their price for entering the war.[63] Although this was not the case, this fear added a political element to any consideration of the distribution of the defensive line in the north.[64]

This anxiety was to play a part in complicating military policy on the northern flank. The position of the passive Belgian army, 'l'armée neutre' as the French staff contemptuously called it,[65] and the British army's ambitions had to be taken into account when reviewing the defensive security of the line in Flanders and in preparations for an offensive against the Belgian coast. Although the Belgians preferred to work with the British army rather than the dictatorial French, it was only with great reluctance that Joffre consented in principle in January 1915 to the extension of the British line northwards to link up with the Belgians, and to the British and Belgian armies working together to prepare a joint offensive against the coast.[66] In fact this union was never allowed, for French, and indeed Belgian, suspicions of British ambitions persisted.[67] Consequently a *Détachement du Groupe des Armées du Nord*, albeit of decreasing size as the war progressed, continued to hold the Boesinghe sector of the front between the Belgian right and the British left, while a second detachment held the Nieuport sector between the Belgian left and the sea. Joffre maintained that this *encadrement* was for strategic reasons; the northern detachments gave direct support to the unreliable Belgian army, allowed Joffre rapidly to reinforce the northern sector in the event of a German offensive against Dunkirk or Calais, and enabled him to maintain control over operations in Flanders which would not have been possible if the whole northern sector was in British hands. Although at the time British suspicions on the point were never substantiated, it is clear from French sources that these detachments were also retained for the political object of ensuring that their ally did not come to exercise too great an influence over the Belgian army at French expense.[68] 'The intense hatred entertained by the Belgians for the French', reported to Sir John French by Tom Bridges, GHQ's liaison officer with the Belgian army, in April 1915, suggests that there was some justification for French fears.[69]

Subsequently King Albert came to be as suspicious of the growing power and influence of his British allies, particularly as Haig developed plans for a large scale offensive from Ypres against the Belgian coast. When Haig and Lord Curzon met King Albert on 7 February 1916 to discuss Belgian participation in a coastal offensive, Haig 'was quite astonished that [the king] should have taken such a purely selfish view of the case',[70] for at the same time de Broqueville was actively pressing Haig to supply the Belgian army with heavy guns to enable them to take the offensive.[71] Albert feared that close cooperation with the British army in this operation would compromise Belgian military independence. He had no great desire simply to substitute the Belgian army's *encadrement* by the French with that of the British. By now he clearly favoured liberating Belgian territory by indirect means – an attack against the German lines of communication behind the French front rather than a destructive offensive through Belgium.[72]

Haig's revived proposal of a northern flank offensive in the summer of 1917 again met Belgian hostility. When Haig visited Belgian headquarters on 25 May to outline his intentions, King Albert stressed the tactical difficulties of attacking on the Belgian front, and only consented to attack when he judged that Anglo-French operations farther south had sufficiently weakened German opposition on the Belgian front.[73] A further difficulty encountered by Haig in planning this offensive was *Grand*

Quartier Général's (GQG) continued reluctance to allow the British to work closely with the Belgian army. Haig had first raised the question of taking over the Boesinghe sector for future offensive operations in May 1916, but at that time French objections had obliged him to drop the matter.[74] Although this sector was handed over to the British in December 1916,[75] when offensive operations were mounted in Flanders in 1917 General Pétain insisted that a French army cooperate between the British and Belgian armies at Boesinghe, introducing the usual delays and difficulties associated with the conduct of joint offensive operations. Although the Nieuport sector was handed over to the British for the Flanders offensive in July 1917, this was conditional on its return to the French army after the operation.[76]

The Belgian army's military and political importance was highlighted in the final year of the war. In preparation for the coming campaign the French commander-in-chief hoped that the Belgians could be persuaded to put their armed forces in better order, by decreasing the number of battalions and increasing the number of divisions and artillery units, so that the Belgian army would be capable of offensive action.[77] In fact the first crisis faced by the allied armies in Flanders was defensive, following the German offensive in March 1918. It had long been recognised that the presence of French detachments in the north weakened the defences of the coastal region,[78] and both the Belgians and British became anxious about what would happen if the Germans broke the allied line and threatened the Channel ports.[79] At least by this time Foch had been appointed 'generalissimo' to coordinate the operations of the allied armies on the western front, although as might be expected, the 26 March and 3 April Doullens and Beauvais agreements over joint command were never extended formally to the Belgian army.[80] Although Foch's appointment could not remove the long-standing differences between the allies, it at least furnished an effective organ for reconciling or bypassing them. When the Germans struck in Flanders in April, directly threatening the Channel ports, Foch put in hand measures for the joint defence of the Flanders front.[81] But the British government insisted on a declaration of strategic priorities on the western front. Foch declared that of the two principal strategic objectives, unity of the Anglo-French front and the defence of the Channel ports, the former should be the allies' priority.[82] The British and Belgians could not accept this decision with equanimity. When the diversion of reserves southwards in June threatened the defensive security of the ports,[83] GHQ had in mind forming a bridgehead with the American and Belgian armies to cover the Channel ports in the event of a French collapse, 'absolutely counter to the accepted policy of not losing touch with the French'.[84] As Foch adhered to his earlier declaration of strategic principles it was apparent that responsibility for the safety of the allied line in Flanders now rested with the generalissimo. Haig's instructions were modified accordingly.[85] Even King Albert proved more amenable to Foch's authority, even if it was never formally acknowledged by the Belgian army.[86]

Therefore this tale of allied rivalry and confusion can at least end on a positive note. A new spirit of allied cooperation is clearly evident in the September 1918 Flanders offensive. King Albert, supervised by a French chief of staff, commanded an allied army group composed of the Belgian, British second and French sixth armies, supported by the Royal Navy, in an operation to break out of the Ypres salient and turn the flank of the German position at Lille. The offensive was an unprecedented triumph for allied cooperation, the Belgian army entering Ostend on 17 October and Zeebrugge on 19 October, and the British army Lille on 17 October.[87] There had been a remarkable turn around in the king's attitude. By late 1918 the Anglo-French armies were sweeping the Germans before them and the time had come for a victorious offensive to liberate the homeland, and for Belgium to take her place amongst the victors. Indeed, with no experience of offensive operations, the king even went so far as to request that a French chief of staff be assigned to his headquarters to coordinate the allied operation.[88] It was one thing for the Belgian army to be subsumed by her more powerful allies and forced to follow a costly offensive policy which promised no tangible reward; quite another for the King of the Belgians to be asked to command allied forces in a well organised march to victory. But perhaps as remarkable as the change in the king's attitude was the change in that of his allies, following Foch's appointment to the supreme command.

Although the ovation the Belgians received after the war was not perhaps justified by the indifferent cameo performance which their army played in the military campaign in 1914 and 1918,[89] their participation was central to the drama of the western theatre. The Belgians' continued resistance was politically if not militarily significant, while the role of King Albert in the coalition cannot be ignored. The Belgians' independent stance must be seen as one more source of friction in a military alliance bedevilled by confusion, misunderstanding and suspicion.[90] The Belgian army's passive stance was a continued source of defensive weakness, and undermined attempts to pursue a more offensive policy on the northern flank, causing frustration and consternation at allied headquarters. Moreover, King Albert's active pursuit of a compromise peace undermined the political unanimity of the alliance. Yet King Albert, almost driven from his national soil and dependent upon his allies for military and economic aid, had a difficult hand to play during the war years. His single-minded pursuit of Belgian independence and integrity must be recognised as a justifiable course of action, if trying for himself, his ministers and his allies. His determination and obduracy at least paid off. The king was perhaps more successful in the pursuit of his military and political objective vis-à-vis his allies than they were in relation to the Belgians. The Belgian army not only survived four years of attritional warfare, but was indeed the only army which grew rather than shrank in size in 1918. Belgium was saved from excessive physical damage outside the area of the Ypres salient, and the king was able to liberate occupied Belgium at the head of the army he had husbanded so long in anticipation of that moment.

Notes

1 For recent work see 'L'alliance Franco-Britannique Pendant la Grande Guerre', *Guerres Mondiales et Conflits Contemporains*, 180 (October 1995), pp. 3–63, especially R A Prete, 'Présentation', pp.3–5

2 For example, in K Robbins, *The First World War* (Oxford: Oxford University Press, 1993 edn), p. 34, after settling down on 'a not invariably solid line confronting the Germans' in October 1914 the Belgian army receives no further mention

3 M-R Thielemans (ed.), *Albert Ier: Carnets et Correspondance de Guerre, 1914–1918* (Paris & Louvain la Neuve: Editions Duculot, 1991), pp.36, 47, 53 & 58

4 ibid., pp.51–62 & 85–106 *passim*

5 'Journaux de Campagne de Commandant Galet', in *collection des papiers* Lesaffre (collection 161), *Archives Générales du Royaume*, Brussels, files 12, 17 & 18; Lt.–Gen. E J Galet, *Albert King of the Belgians in the Great War* (trans. Maj.-Gen. Sir E Swinton, London: Putnam, 1931), p.148

6 Galet, *Albert*, pp.74–5

7 Galet, *op. cit.*, is the fullest account of Belgian operations in 1914

8 Thielemans, *Carnets*, p.46

9 Galet, *op. cit.*, p.62

10 See for example the king's address to the nation on the outbreak of hostilities, ibid., p.62

11 King Albert diary (15 January 1916), Thielemans, *Carnets*, pp.61 & 243

12 See notes 3, 5 and 16

13 W J Philpott, *Anglo-French Relations and Strategy on the Western Front, 1914–1918* (London: Macmillan, 1996), pp.19–21

14 Thielemans, *Carnets*, p.40

15 Curzon to King Albert (21 November 1915), Curzon papers, India Office Library, London, MSS EUR F 112/382

16 M-R Thielemans & E Vandewoude (eds), *Le Roi Albert au Travers de Ses Lettres Inédités, 1882–1916* (Brussels: Office International de Librairie, 1982), pp.121–2

17 'General Staff Conference at Chantilly' (6 December 1915), War Office: Directorate of Military Operations and Intelligence, Public Record Office (PRO), Kew (WO 106): WO 106/1454

18 De Fleuriau to Curzon (2 January 1916), Curzon papers, MSS EUR F 112/116, fols 81–2

19 Curzon to King Albert (21 November & 21 December 1915), Curzon papers, MSS EUR F 112/582

20 The April 1916 Declaration of Sainte-Adresse, in which the Entente powers pledged themselves to fight until Belgian independence had been restored,

did not satisfy King Albert, who still feared for Belgium's post-war integrity: Thielemans, *Carnets*, pp.61–2

21 See for example ibid., p.102; Curzon to King Albert (1 January 1917), Curzon papers, MSS EUR F 112/582

22 Thielemans & Vandewoude, *Lettres Inédités*, p.574

23 Thielemans, *Carnets*, pp.77–84 & King Albert's diary (7 February 1916 & 3 February 1917), ibid., pp.248–9 & 298–9; Philpott, *Anglo-French Relations*, pp.119–20 & 139

24 See Thielemans, *Carnets* & Thielemans & Vandewoude, *Lettres Inédités*

25 Thielemans, *Carnets*, pp.44–50, 75–6, 99 & 106

26 W J Philpott, 'Britain and France go to War: Anglo-French Relations on the Western Front, 1914–1918', *War in History*, 2/1 (January 1995), pp.43–64 *passim*

27 Albert to Curzon (8 December 1915), Thielemans & Vandewoude, *Lettres Inédités*, pp.625–31; Albert diary (30 September 1916), Thielemans, *Carnets*, p.287

28 Philpott, *Anglo-French Relations*, pp.15–30 *passim*

29 Marshal J Joffre, *The Memoirs of Marshal Joffre* (trans. T. Bentley Mott, 2 vols, London: Geoffrey Bles, 1932), *i*, p.161

30 Galet, *Albert*, p.96

31 Joffre, *Memoirs*, *i*, pp.1–112; S R Williamson, *The Politics of Grand Strategy: Britain and France Prepare for War, 1904–1914* (Cambridge, Mass: Harvard University Press, 1969), pp.205–6

32 Galet, *Albert*, pp.88 & 148–51: Galet Journal, file 18

33 Joffre, *Memoirs*, *i*, pp.163–7

34 Galet, *Albert*, pp.92–122; Philpott, *Anglo-French Relations*, pp.19–21

35 Galet, *Albert*, pp.122–5; Galet journal, file 21

36 'La mission française pretendait s'[?] dans le commandement de notre armée', Galet journal, file 17

37 ibid., files 18–21

38 Philpott, *Anglo-French Relations*, p.6

39 'Secretary's Notes of a War Council Held at 10 Downing Street, 5 August 1914', Cabinet Office: Cabinet Papers, 1915–16, PRO (CAB 42): CAB 42/1/2; Philpott, *op. cit.*, pp.6–12

40 'Secretary's Notes of a War Council Held at 10 Downing Street, 6 August 1914', CAB 42/1/3

41 Philpott, *op. cit.*, pp.31–46

42 'Mesures prises pour sauver l'armée' (9 October 1914), Thielemans, *Carnets*, pp.174–5

43 'Mesures prises dans les journées du 10 et du 11 octobre pour reposer l'armée et en faire un instrument de combat', ibid., pp.175–6

44 Millerand to GQG (telegram, 9 October 1914) and Joffre to Millerand (telegram, 11 October 1914), *Cabinet du Ministre de la Guerre, Service Historique de l'Armée de Terre*, Vincennes, 5N18; Joffre, *Memoirs*, *i*, p.309; Thielemans, *op. cit.*, p.42

45 'Mesures prises pour mettre l'armée en état de résister' (12–16 October 1914), Thielemans, *op. cit.*, pp. 177–9 & p. 43; Marshal F Foch, *The Memoirs of Marshal Foch* (trans. T. Bentley Mott, London: Heinemann, 1931), pp. 125–52 *passim*

46 French to Churchill (25 October 1914, French's italics), in M. Gilbert, *Winston S. Churchill: Vol. III, 1914–1916: Companion* (2 vols, London: Heinemann, 1972), *i*, pp.218–9

47 Thielemans & Vandewoude, *Lettres Inédités*, p.105; Thielemans, *Carnets*, p.44

48 Philpott, *Anglo-French Relations*, pp.54–66 *passim*
49 Galet, *Albert*, pp.251–2
50 Thielemans, *Carnets*, p.42
51 'Mesures prises pour mettre l'armée en état de résister' (16 October 1914), Thielemans, *Carnets*, p.179; Thielemans & Vandewoude, *Lettres Inédités*, pp.534–6
52 King Albert to Foch (24 November 1914), Thielemans & Vandewoude, *Lettres Inédités*, p.544; Thielemans, *Carnets*, p.46
53 'Report by Colonel Bridges on Belgian Action on the Yser, 16 October to 25 November 1914', Cabinet Office: Cabinet Papers, 1880–1914, PRO (CAB 37): CAB 37/122/172. At roughly the same time the French were trying to have the independently minded British Chief of Staff, General Murray, replaced by the more francophile General Wilson. Foch to Joffre (9 November 1914), Joffre papers, *Service Historique de l'Armée de Terre*, Vincennes, 1K268/2/9
54 Thielemans & Vandewoude, *Lettres Inédités*, p.549
55 ibid., pp.535–6; French diary (9 December 1914), French papers, Imperial War Museum, London, 75/46/2
56 French diary (7, 27 & 29 December 1914), French papers; King Albert to French (1 January 1915), Thielemans & Vandewoude, *op. cit.*, pp.551–2
57 French diary (4 January 1915), French papers; French to Churchill (9 January 1915), Gilbert, *Churchill Companion, i*, pp.398–9
58 Thielemans & Vandewoude, *op. cit.*, pp.105 & 552
59 Génie to Joffre (1 June 1915), Joffre papers, 1K268/3/1; 'Campagnes Belges du 1915, 1916, 1917 et 1918 d'après les carnets de campagne du E M Galet', especially *titre* 2, 'Campagne de 1915', pp.1–3, typescript, Lesaffre papers, file 37
60 See for example, 'Note ayant servi de base à l'entretien du Roi avec le général Foch' (25 May 1915) & 'Note relative à nos organisations défensives', by Galet (August 1915), Thielemans & Vandewoude, *op. cit.*, pp.113, 575–6 & 596–9
61 E David (ed.), *Inside Asquith's Cabinet: From the Diaries of Charles Hobhouse* (London: John Murray, 1977), pp.183, 193 & 209
62 Joffre to Millerand (15 January 1915), *Cabinet du Ministre de la Guerre*, 5N132
63 'Report on visit to France and Belgium', by Wedgewood (October 1915), Mottistone papers, Nuffield College, Oxford, file 3, fol. 17; Rawlinson diary (30 March 1916), Rawlinson papers, Churchill College, Cambridge, RWLN 1/5; E L Spears, *Liaison, 1914: A Narrative of the Great Retreat* (London: Heinemann, 1930), p.84
64 See for example French to Kitchener (8 April 1915), Personal Collections: Kitchener papers, PRO (PRO 30/57): PRO 30/57/50/80; Bertie to French (13 January 1915), French papers, 75/46/11; Joffre to Millerand (13 March 1915), *Cabinet du Ministre de la Guerre*, 5N132
65 Baird to Curzon (8 November 1915), Curzon papers, MS EUR F 112/581
66 French diary (9 & 27 December 1914, 21 & 23 January 1915), French papers; '*Procès-Verbal* of a meeting between Sir John French and Joffre at Chantilly' (21 January 1915), War Office: GHQ Correspondence and Papers, PRO (WO 158): WO 158/13/3; French to Kitchener (28 December 1914), Kitchener papers, PRO 30/57/49/60; Joffre to Foch (19 December 1914) & GQG study of the front north of Ypres (21 December 1914), *Fonds* Joffre-Foch, *Service Historique de l'Armée de Terre*, Vincennes, 14N16
67 Joffre to Millerand (13 March 1915), *Cabinet du Ministre de la Guerre*, 5N132
68 'Il y a lieu de ne pas laisser les Anglais mettre en poche le roi ALBERT': Observations on English appreciation of German forces, by 3rd bureau,

GQG (7 January 1915), *fonds* Joffre-Foch, 14N16; Asquith to Venetia Stanley (20 December 1914), in M & E Brock (eds), *H.H.Asquith: Letters to Venetia Stanley* (Oxford: Oxford University Press, 1982), p.331; 'Retention by the French of the Outlying Section of the Allies' Line between Dixmude and Ypres', memorandum by Lord Lansdowne (20 June 1915), Kitchener (Creedy) papers, PRO (WO 159): WO 159/7/13; 'Views of Joffre on extension of British line and retention by French of portion of line between British and Belgian armies', 'very secret and confidential' memorandum (29 June 1915), Kitchener papers, PRO 30/57/57/26; *Procès-verbal* of a meeting at St Omer (11 July 1915), WO 158/13/20

69 French diary (2 April 1915, French's italics), French papers

70 Haig diary (7 February 1916), Haig papers, National Library of Scotland, Edinburgh (accession 3155)

71 See correspondence between de Broqueville and Asquith in the Asquith papers, Bodleian Library, Oxford, box 28

72 Haig diary (7 February 1916); King Albert diary (7 February 1916 & 3 February 1917), Thielemans, *Carnets*, pp.59, 77–9, 248–9 & 298–9; Thielemans & Vandewoude, *Lettres Inédités*, pp.121–2 & 647

73 Haig diary (25 May 1917)

74 Haig diary (21 May 1916); Haig to Joffre (22 May 1916) & Joffre to Haig (25 May 1916), WO 158/14/114 & 115; Butler to Des Vallières (28 May 1916), Haig papers, file 106

75 Haig diary (12 October 1916); Joffre to Haig (10 & 19 November 1916) & Haig to Joffre (13 November 1916), WO 158/15/158, 159 & 164

76 'Note on British and French Reliefs and Frontages' by Davidson (2 May 1917), Haig papers, file 113; Haig diary (5 & 10 May & 7 June 1917); 'Record of Amiens Conference' (18 May 1917), WO 158/48/8; Philpott, *Anglo-French Relations*, pp. 108, 138 & 147

77 Pétain to *Ministre de la Guerre* (30 November 1917), *Les Armées Françaises dans la Grande Guerre* (11 vols, Paris: Imprimerie Nationale, 1929–37), vol. VI/1, annexes I/133, pp.227–8

78 'Retention by the French of the Outlying Section of the Allies' Line' (note 68); Haig to Joffre (22 May 1916), WO 158/14/114

79 Haig diary (13 January 1918)

80 Foch, *Memoirs*, pp.315–6; Philpott, *Anglo-French Relations*, pp.154–6

81 Foch, *op. cit.*, pp.335–6

82 Haig diary (27 April & 2 May 1918)

83 Gordon to Curzon (6 June 1918) & Curzon to King Albert (7 June 1918), Curzon papers, MS EUR F 112/581

84 Maj.-Gen. Sidney Clive diary (5 June 1918), Cabinet Office: Correspondence used in the Compilation of the Official History, PRO (CAB 45): CAB 45/201

85 Haig diary (7 June 1918); 'Instructions of the Secretary of State for War to the Field-Marshal Commanding-in-Chief, British Armies in France' (21 June 1918), in Brig.-Gen. Sir J Edmonds (ed.), *Official History of the Great War: Military Operations, France and Belgium* (14 vols, London: Macmillan for HMSO, 1922–48), *1918, iii*, appendix ix, pp.351–2

86 Foch, *Memoirs*, p.317

87 *Official History, 1918, v*, pp.57–92 & 269–93; 'Campagne Belge du 1918', Lesaffre papers, file 37, part 5; Philpott, *Anglo-French Relations*, p.159

88 Foch, *Memoirs*, pp.470–1

89 See for example ibid., pp.196 & 209–10

90 Philpott, *op cit, passim*

GARY SHEFFIELD

'A very good type of Londoner and a very good type of colonial': Officer-Man Relations and Discipline in the 22nd Royal Fusiliers, 1914–18

The importance of the officer-man relationship in the alleviation of battle-field stress and the maintenance of morale has often been noted. Many of the witnesses before the British 'Shellshock Committee' of 1922 stressed the primary importance of officer-man relations in the maintenance of morale, as have many recent writers on the subject. The weight of evidence thus clearly indicates that the relation between the leader and the led is of great importance in holding an army together and making it fight efficiently.[1] This paper will argue that the leadership of the 22nd (Service) Battalion Royal Fusiliers (Kensington) [22/RF], when faced with the challenge of commanding a unit containing a large number of middle-class soldiers, evolved a disciplinary regime that was very different to that of the Regular Army, being characterised by an informal inter-rank relationship and a minimum of externally imposed discipline and 'bullshit'. As a result the 22/RF came to resemble a prewar Territorial or even a wartime Dominion unit, rather than a Regular battalion of its parent regiment.

The 22/RF was one of 557 battalions of the New Armies raised between August 1914 and June 1916. It was formed from the amalgamation of two companies raised by William H Davison, the Mayor of the London Borough of Kensington, and 600 men recruited to serve in the 'Colonial Light Infantry'. Neither unit was able to recruit up to strength, so the colonials became A and B Companies, the Kensingtons C and D. The resulting unit was described by the historian of the Royal Fusiliers as 'combining a very good type of Londoner and a very good type of colonial, and the two amalgamated very successfully'.[2]

The type of man that made up the bulk of the 22/RF was very different from the unskilled workers and unemployed who filled a good proportion of the ranks of the pre-war Army. The colonial companies had their origin in a newspaper advertisement of 12 September 1914 that appealed for men with 'any association with the OVERSEAS DOMINIONS and COLONIES'. Some 'colonials' connections with the Empire were somewhat tenuous, and a steady stream of colonials left the battalion from an early date and were replaced by ordinary British recruits. Much anecdotal evidence suggests that many of the colonials were of relatively high social standing. A resident of Horsham (where the 22/RF were trained in 1915) contrasted the shabby appearance of some of the London recruits with that of the men from 'Kimberley and Jo'burg' [sic]. Although it is unsafe to assume that all 'colonials' were prosperous, there is no evidence of poverty among the overseas contingent.[3]

C and D companies lacked the initial social homogeneity of the colonial companies. Davison had originally intended to be selective in his recruiting, drawing his men from local business houses, which would have excluded the working classes. The severe competition for recruits put paid to this idea, and Davison was forced to widen his search and accept men of lower social status. From the very beginning, Davison decided to work on the 'pals' principle that friends and workmates could serve in the same company.[4] Thus a group of men who belonged to the same rugby football club joined C company and a small clique of friends from a department store enlisted in 13 platoon. This policy produced platoons that had the social homogeneity that the battalion as a whole lacked. For example, 12 platoon consisted almost entirely of working-class men. By contrast, 13 platoon was recruited from 'solicitors, bank clerks, press men, [and] business men'[5]. There seems to have been some attempt to place men who joined the 22/RF as individuals in platoons where they would mix with men of a similar type. In general, it appears that the majority of 22/RF's personnel in 1914–15 were of middle-class origin, with a strong leavening of workmen. The original 22/RF seems to have contained only a small proportion of men actually resident in Kensington, although it did have a local character of sorts, in that perhaps one third of its men were drawn from West London and other men may have worked in Kensington but lived outside the area.[6]

To a great extent, military life made social distinctions meaningless. The same process was used to turn both stevedores and solicitors into soldiers, and all men had to take their share of boring and unpleasant duties, regardless of their social position in civilian life. However, the attitudes, life style and even speech of the stevedore were alien to the solicitor. In other battalions, some (but by no means all) middle-class men had unhappy experiences while serving in platoons consisting of working-class men. To the inevitable rigours of army life, which came as a shock to some men used to a sedentary existence, was added the loneliness of service amongst men with whom they had little in common, and whose language frequently consisted of a litany of obscenities. In the 22/RF social segregation by platoon ensured that the clerk or shop assistant could avoid contact with their social and educational inferiors. A similar result was achieved by elitist 'pals' units and Territorial 'class corps' which charged entrance fees, which effectively excluded the working classes from enlistment. Paradoxically, such segregation did not produce division within the 22/RF. To be allocated companions of a similar background to oneself was a very different matter from being plunged into the company of men with whom one had little in common. The practical application of the 'pals' concept in this way made military life palatable for the middle classes, almost by accident. All platoons were united in loyalty to their officers and to the good name of the 22/RF. This had two major consequences. First, it provided ideal conditions for the development of 'primary' or 'buddy' groups within the unit. Second, the solidarity that resulted formed an excellent basis for the development of a disciplinary system based on 'self-', rather than 'imposed' discipline. Such a system would have been impossible to operate in a disunited battalion that lacked morale and cohesion, no matter how educated the soldiers of the battalion might have been.

In September 1914 a Regular officer, Lieutenant Colonel J A Innes was appointed Commanding Officer (CO) of the 22/RF. Innes's second-in-command, Major Randle Barnett-Barker, seems to have stamped his authority on the 22/RF from the very beginning, and 'BB' commanded the battalion on the Western Front from November 1915 until December 1917.[7] Barnett-Barker was also a Regular, who had served with the Royal Welsh Fusiliers before retiring in 1906.[8] In many ways, Barnett-Barker's approach to man-management bore a resemblance to the pre-war ethic of *noblesse oblige* which had characterised pre-war officer-man relations. The author has written on this topic elsewhere,[9] and here it will suffice to say that most pre-war officers had recognised that it was their duty, on both philanthropic and pragmatic grounds, to ensure that their men were well cared for. Barnett-Barker clearly recognised that fighting men were more efficient if physical discomfort was minimised. Where Barnett-Barker differed from the majority of his brother Regular officers was in his modification of the basic tenet of the social code of the pre-war Army, the rigid separation of the ranks. There are many comments in Barnett-Barker's letters that reveal his genuine affection for his men.[10] As commanding officer of the 22/RF, Barnett-Barker was able to make life more bearable for his men, and as another officer of the battalion commented, the Colonel was 'always devising schemes for making this or that man happier'.[11] Barnett-Barker established informal, friendly relationships with his men, anticipating the populist generals of 1939–45 by moving among his troops, chatting informally and distributing cigarettes.[12] Barnett-Barker thus combined the attributes of the typical officer and gentlemen, whose eccentricities and bearing lower-class soldiers are reputed to admire, with those of a Patton or a Montgomery.

Barnett-Barker was shrewd enough to recognise that the better educated citizen soldier required something more than the odd word of praise or packet of cigarettes to sustain his morale. He sought to bridge the gulf between officer and man, to give a human face to the Army, and he largely succeeded. Barnett-Barker was popular with educated and articulate Other Ranks such as the French-Canadian Destrube brothers, and with men such as 'Olly' Berrycloath, a working-class private with a far from unsullied disciplinary record. When he was interviewed in 1984, Berrycloath, unprompted, produced a battered photograph of his old Colonel and announced that 'a finer officer and gentleman you could not care to meet'. It was a measure of Barnett-Barker's flexibility and originality of mind that his Kitchener Army subalterns – mere civilians in khaki – felt that this Regular officer was spiritually one of their number, not an officer of the old school.[13]

Most officers of the 22/RF followed Barnett-Barker's example, in establishing paternal, but friendly and informal relationships with the Other Ranks. Captain R E Banbury, Lieutenant C J Fowler and Captain Roscoe were just three officers who were admired, even loved by their men; in 1984, for instance, an Other Rank testified to his sense of personal loss at Roscoe's death.[14] Similar evidence could be offered concerning many other officers,[15] but such evidence should not be accepted without qualification. Obituaries, letters written to mourning parents and reminiscences published in OCA magazines might be thought to be prone to exaggerate the positive and minimise or ignore the negative qualities of the individual under discussion. However, even after such qualifications are accepted, it is clear that such men as Fowler were regarded as good officers by the men they commanded, who, in return for paternal care and effective leadership, offered loyalty and obedience.

Soldiers sometimes idealise superior officers as father figures and use them as a focus of loyalty to the group.[16] Many men of the 22/RF seem to have extended their trust to officers much more senior than their platoon and company commanders. Not only Barnett-Barker, but Major Christopher Stone and Lieutenant Colonel W J P T Phythian-Adams (respectively the Battalion's last second-in-command and commander) were well regarded, as was the commander of 99th Brigade from 1915 to 1917, Brigadier General R O Kellett. Kellett complemented the paternal care for the 22/RF demonstrated by almost all the battalion's officers, from Barnett-Barker downwards, and helped to give the upper echelons of the Army a human face. The soldiers of the 22/RF knew that there was at least one man in the hierarchy who had their best interests at heart and who, in Stone's words, was 'keeping a fatherly eye on "the boys"'. Kellett was a frequent visitor to the trenches, and thus sealed the relationship by showing willingness to share a little of the frontline soldiers' danger and discomfort. At its first general meeting after the war, the 22/RF's OCA voted to send Kellett 'a grateful message to our beloved General' – a remarkable tribute to a senior officer who was bound by informal but very real mutual ties of loyalty and affection to a fighting unit.[17] The commanders of 2nd Division, Major-Generals Walker and Pereira, were remoter figures than Kellett but also enjoyed a measure of popularity within the 22/RF. The latter greatly endeared himself to the 22/RF OCA after the war by attending children's

Christmas parties, at which he introduced himself as 'Uncle General Pereira'.[18]

Clearly many inter-rank relationships in the 22/RF moved beyond the usual position of leader and led, and close personal relationships developed. I have argued elsewhere that the conditions on the Western Front were exceptionally favourable for the establishment of good officer-man relations[19], but there are some specific reasons why this should be so in 22/RF. The ages of the original officers of the 22/RF were an important factor in the promotion of good officer-man relations. Many were, by military standards, relatively elderly; about half of all officers, and one third of all subalterns were aged 31 or over. In many cases these men had fifteen years of experience in a civilian profession, and brought to the Army their own ideas, an experience which did not necessarily accord with traditional Army methods of doing business. Some had experience of teaching at public schools, and the age of others encouraged the officer to take a literally paternal attitude towards their men. 2nd Lieutenant 'Pussy' Woods recalled that Major Boardman acted 'as father and mother to me and the company' when he joined the battalion as a 'grinning boy of 19'.[20] Other officers had only recently left school. Many of the 'men' commanded by these boy subalterns were also very young, and it is perhaps unsurprising that boys of similar ages made friends across the rank and class divide. Of very great importance is the fact that the original officer corps of the 22/RF were almost all educated at a public school. The public schools produced ideal officers who were disciplined, dutiful, loyal to the corporate body, resourceful but conformist, paternal, with a keen sense of military virtues.

Relatively few of the original officers of the 22/RF had any military experience beyond a little drill in a school Officer Training Corps (OTC), and 65% of those who had seen military service had served in a non-Regular unit.[21] Devoid of the prejudices and preconceptions of the Regular subaltern, the temporary officers of the 22/RF would have been far more amenable to Barnett-Barker's concept of leadership than if they had been products of Sandhurst or Woolwich. In sharp contrast to the state of affairs in the pre-war Army, it was relatively easy for Other Ranks to obtain commissions. The 22/RF began to receive officers promoted from their own ranks – men such as E C Rossell, commissioned from B company in July 1915, and F W Palmer, who was commissioned within the battalion in 1917 after winning the VC at Miraumont in February of that year. It appears that these ranker-officers continued to enjoy friendly relations with their erstwhile comrades. Sergeant Roland Whipp, for example, served in the same section as Palmer in 1914 and remained on good terms with him after his elevation to commissioned rank. As the war went on, the officers of the 22/RF were increasingly drawn from the lower middle and even the working classes. In May 1916 Stone commented that 'The old 22nd is being infused with a new element of bourgeoisie', and in September

1917 the battalion's padre lamented the decline in the social standing of the battalion's officers.[22] One veteran suggested that officer-man relations were actually enhanced by this further reduction of the gulf between the ranks. This opinion is in sharp contrast to the widespread dislike of ranker-officers that one often comes across among soldiers of the Great War. Private C Mizen of the 23/RF, for example, thought that promoted NCOs, far from having a sympathetic view of the rank and file, found it necessary to assert themselves with officious behaviour.[23]

All the evidence suggests that the 22/RF, unlike many other 'pals' battalions, retained its original character, particularly in terms of officer-man relations, discipline and *esprit de corps*, throughout the war. The primary reason for this lies in the continuity of command. Barnett-Barker remained at the helm for all but three months of the 22/RF's active service. He was succeeded as commander by Phythian-Adams, who had joined the battalion as a subaltern in 1914 and had, as was described in Barnett-Barker's valedictory address, been 'born and bred a 22nd man'. Christopher Stone, who had joined the battalion in early 1915, was appointed second-in-command. By contrast, the 22nd's sister unit, 17/RF, was commanded by four colonels in the same period, all appointed from outside the battalion. Phythian-Adams and Stone were firmly in the Barnett-Barker mould and enjoyed the latter's full confidence. Indeed, Barnett-Barker had been afraid that one day an officer would be appointed to command who had no respect for the 22/RF's idiosyncrasies. In early 1918, shortly after the battalion was disbanded in the reorganisation of the British Expeditionary Force, he wrote:

> On calmly considering things, I am not so sad as I was. If anything had happened to ---- or ---- the dear old Regiment would have drifted into strange hands and anything might have happened to them.[24]

There was also a certain amount of continuity of personnel among the rank and file. If 13 Platoon is typical of the battalion as a whole, approximately 18% or 200 of the original members of the 22/RF would still have been serving with the battalion in September 1917.[25] This figure is almost certainly too high, but clearly there was a hard core of survivors who passed on the body of traditions of the unit to new drafts and thus ensured the survival of spirit and character of the original 22/RF.

Tony Ashworth has suggested that some (although not all) infantry battalions 'evolved into communities and became the core of the soldiers' formal military experience and their socio-emotional lives'. The 22/RF was one of these battalions, and it is likely that the state of officer-man relations within the unit was instrumental in helping the 22/RF to develop into a community. Many officers and men also testified to the family spirit of the battalion, and the 22/RF endured as a community into the post-war period, through the establishment of an OCA, which survived until 1977.[26] The distinctive quality of officer-man relations in the 22/RF lay in the destruction of social barriers that had prevented intimacy between diverse social groups in the pre-war Regular Army. Some officers and men, particularly in the colonial companies in the early period of the war, were on first name terms, while others observed the formalities of title but otherwise dispensed with the niceties of military etiquette. Captain Grant, for example, was always called 'Sir' by his servant, Private Beale, but the two men enjoyed a friendly relationship that even survived the occasion when Grant discovered Beale sleeping in the former's bed, wearing Grant's pyjamas. Many other such friendships could be described.[27]

The importance of the officer-man relationship in the evolution of the 22/RF into a community is demonstrated by the reaction of both soldiers and officers to officers who were unwilling to accept the egalitarian nature of the 22/RF or who failed to live up to the standard expected of leaders. Major J B Scott, who joined the 22/RF in 1917, was regarded as an unpredictable and irascible man who was inclined to assert his authority in an officious manner, and both officers and men invented humorous and uncomplimentary songs and verse about him. Another officer, C E Raven, who served as padre in 1917–18, had somewhat elitist attitudes and failed to adjust to life in the 22/RF. As a result Raven was condemned to lead a lonely life and, unlike his predecessor, Padre E P St John, he failed to be 'accepted' by the officers and men of the 22/RF.[28]

In an altogether different category was another officer found cowering in a trench at the beginning of an attack. His platoon sergeant swore at him and physically bundled him over the parapet. It is possible that this same officer was the one whom Barnett-Barker had transferred with the recommendation that he be court-martialled for cowardice, because of his detrimental effect on Battalion morale. A loss of confidence in their officers by soldiers is damaging to any military unit. In the 22/RF, where morale was enhanced by the fact that the Battalion formed a community in which the ties of friendship and loyalty cut across the formal structure of rank, such a loss of confidence would have been disastrous and Barnett-Barker ruthlessly extirpated inefficient officers. Generally, inter-rank friendships were not allowed to interfere with the operation of discipline, although in 1915, when a colonial sergeant got up a petition that sought to overturn Barnett-Barker's decision (taken on operational grounds) not to allow an officer to go overseas, Barnett-Barker had the sergeant arrested.[29]

The presence of a sizeable number of colonials in the 22/RF presented a challenge to traditional notions of military discipline. The original recruits had enlisted in a specifically 'colonial' battalion – on the understanding that they would be paid at the colonial rate, which was higher than that of the British soldier – and some resented amalgamation with a British unit. Some may have feared the imposition of Regular discipline. In October 1914 one newly joined subaltern described the difficult task the battalion leadership faced in commanding the colonials. They had an egalitarian outlook, and refused automatically to accept the right of a young officer to be their commander. He foresaw problems in teaching them to respect commissioned officers, and believed that the battalion would be unmanageable unless things changed. In the event, the colonial problem was much less traumatic than it appeared in October 1914. The colonials did learn the importance of formal military discipline, but the enlightened regime employed in the 22/RF ensured that they were not alienated by an attempt to squeeze them into the Regular mould.[30]

Although many officers conceived an affection for their men, the adoption of a radically different social code in a New Army unit was relatively unusual. Christopher Stone described Barnett-Barker as possessing 'the card player's brain – keen, calculating and decisive, looking far ahead and far behind'. Barnett-Barker therefore 'nursed and trained' the battalion 'on his own lines, with very definite ideas as to the means of extracting the best from the material'. He adapted his methods 'with real liberality of thought to the new conditions of warfare and the new types of soldiers'. Barnett-Barker's approach was possible because the highly motivated and enthusiastic volunteers of 1914 possessed a rather different mentality to that of the average pre-war Regular soldier. While Barnett-Barker grasped this essential fact, Innes did not adapt as easily. He issued battalion Standing Orders in 1915 which attempted to impose pre-war social relations on the 22/RF. One paragraph commands that 'No Sergeant Corporal or Lance Corporal is ever to associate or drink with a Private Soldier'. This instruction was widely, perhaps universally, ignored. When the 22/RF was formed, the natural leaders that emerged were often legitimised retrospectively. There was little attempt to enforce the segregation of NCOs from men. Instead, privates and NCOs (and, indeed, officers) fraternised quite happily without any apparent detriment to discipline.[31]

However, informal relations were by no means universal in Kitchener units. Many Regular soldiers believed that spit and polish in the field inculcated pride and enhanced morale. Many temporary soldiers took the opposite view, that it was yet another pointless demand made on them by the Army, and Barnett-Barker seems to have leaned towards the latter idea. Although Barnett-Barker himself was invariably impeccably turned out, he tolerated considerable informality and eccentricity in the dress of his officers and men on active service. Before the Battalion embarked for active service, he solemnly announced that 'anyone who cleaned his buttons out there would be shot at dawn'. Similarly, Barnett-Barker was quite capable of disregarding the niceties of military discipline. During the Somme fighting in 1916 he dismissed a case brought against a group of men charged with a minor offence because 'The Lewis Gunners did splendidly in Delville Wood'. One man who was involved in this case testified to the positive effect that Barnett-Barker's action had on his morale. Other examples suggest that other officers followed Barnett-Barker's example in applying humanity and common sense to discipline.[32] The soldier of the 22/RF was aware that he was not totally impotent and friendless in the face of an impersonal and arbitrary coercive authority. Rather, his officers could usually be relied upon to treat him in a humane and sensible fashion. By contrast, militarily inefficient men did not fare so well, and were transferred out of the unit. One private, described as 'unreliable and useless' was executed for desertion, but it is important to note that he had been under observation for some time, and he was not shot for a momentary lapse.[33] The ultimate test of morale is combat effectiveness, and the 22/RF had a good combat record from their first action in May 1916 to their last in December 1917. While good relations between officers and men were the rule rather than the exception in many infantry battalions of the First World War, relatively few units seem to have adopted an enlightened disciplinary approach. The 22/RF was indeed fortunate in possessing in Barnett-Barker a commanding officer who encouraged the creation and maintenance of a relatively liberal disciplinary regime.

Notes

This chapter is based on G D Sheffield, 'The Effect of War Service on the 22nd Battalion Royal Fusiliers (Kensington) 1914–18, With Special Reference to Morale, Discipline and the Officer-Man Relationship' (MA thesis, University of Leeds, 1984)

All interviews were conducted by the author in 1983–5 with veterans of the Great War. Some material was made available and some interviews granted, on the understanding that the precise source was not revealed in print. All such material is referred to as 'Private source' in the footnotes.

1   Parliamentary Papers [PP], *Report of the Committee of Enquiry into Shellshock*, 1922, XII Cmd. 1734, 759. pp.14, 16, 17, 20; R Holmes, *Firing Line* (London, Jonathan Cape, 1985), p.259
2   H C O'Neill, *The Royal Fusiliers in the Great War* (London, Heinemann, 1922), p.17. See also C Stone (ed), *A History of the 22nd (Service) Battalion Royal Fusiliers (Kensington)* (London, privately published, 1923), pp.7–9
3   *Evening Standard*, 12 September 1914, p.4; W[est] S[ussex] C[ounty] T[imes], 12 December 1914, p.8; *Mufti* [journal of 22/RF Old Comrades Association], Xmas 1937, p.4.; R Whipp, *Interview*, *Mufti*, Summer 1963, pp.15–16
4   Stone, *History* p.9; Kensington Library, Local History section, Broughshane Cuttings Books, Second Series [BCB] Vol 2, 1914, p.61
5   W Clark, H Berrycloath, *Interviews, 22nd Royal Fusiliers Fortnightly Gazette* [22/RF FG], 19 July 1915, p.131; *Mufti*, Summer 1961, p.6, *Mufti*, Summer 1945, p.4
6   *Mufti*, Xmas 1965, p.10; Sheffield, 'Effect' p.28, table 7
7   For example Davison in Stone, *History* p.15, Stone, *BB* (Oxford, Blackwell, 1919), p.16; B N W William-Powlett, Diary, 6–8 February 1915, I[mperial] W[ar] M[useum]
8   BCB Second Series, Vol II 1914, p.74; *Abergavenny Chronicle and Monmouthshire Advertiser*, 5 April 1918, p.3; Stone, *BB* pp.26–7

9   G D Sheffield, 'The Effect of the Great War on Class Relations in Britain: The Career of Major Christopher Stone DSO MC', *War and Society*, Vol.7, No. 1, (May 1989), pp.88–9; G D Sheffield and G I S Inglis (eds), *From Vimy Ridge to the Rhine: The Great War Letters of Christopher Stone DSO MC* (Ramsbury, Crowood, 1989) [hereafter Stone, *Vimy*], pp.15–16

10   Barnett-Barker Papers [BB Mss] 6, 13, 17 December 1915, 1 January 1916. All letters in this collection are from Barnett-Barker to his wife. I am indebited to the late J P C Sankey-Barker for giving me access to his father's papers

11   Stone, *BB* p.25

12   BB Mss, 17 December 1915, *Mufti*, June 1954, p.2; H Berrycloath, *Interview*

13   Kensington Mss 8534, P Destrube letters, 30 January 1917; H Berrycloath, *Interview*; Stone, *BB* p.26

14   *Mufti*, June 1958, p.9. Christopher Stone Papers [Stone Mss], 1 June 1916. IWM [all letters in this collection are from Stone to his wife]; Correspondence relating to the writing of the history of the 22nd Royal Fusiliers (71563 Stone, C, 316,322) [IWM Stone], Mrs E Fowler to C R Stone ND (*c*.1922), IWM, Department of Printed Books; *Mufti*, Summer 1928, p.2; G Challis, Interview, *Mufti*, January 1920, p.1

15   See Sheffield, 'Effect', Chapter 4

16   S A Stouffer et al, *The American Soldier*, Vol.II (Princeton, 1949), p.123

17   Stone, *History* p.56; G Challis, *Interview*; H E Harvey, *Battle Line Narratives 1915–1918* (London, Brentano's, 1928), p.89; C E Jacomb, *Torment* (1920), pp.271–2; *Mufti* December 1919, p.3

18   *Mufti*, Spring 1937, p.12; see also *Mufti*, June 1954, p.iii and Autumn 1933, p.4

19   See G D Sheffield, 'Officer-Man Relations, Morale and Discipline in the British Army, 1902–22', PhD, University of London, 1994 (currently being prepared for publication by Macmillan) and 'Officer-Man Relations, Discipline and Morale in the British Army of the Great War' in H Cecil and P Liddle (eds.), *Facing Armageddon: The First World War Experienced* (London, Leo Cooper, 1996)

20   See Sheffield, 'Effect' p.24a, Table 5; D Winter, *Death's Men* (Harmondsworth, Penguin, 1979), p.65; *Mufti*, Xmas 1923, p.12

21   Sheffield, 'Effect' p.27 Table 6

22   R Whipp, *Interview*; Stone, *Vimy*, p.51 Raven to Burgess, 29 September 1917, C E Raven papers, L[iddle] C[ollection], University of Leeds

23   Private source; C Mizen, *Interview*

24   Stone, *History*, pp.55, 61

25   *Mufti*, Xmas 1945, p.5

26   T Ashworth, *Trench Warfare* (London, Macmillan, 1980), p.8; *Mufti*, Xmas 1962, p.11; C J Hancock to Stone, nd, IWM Stone; *Mufti*, June 1955, p.5

27   H Berrycloath, *Interview*; *Mufti*, June 1948, pp.3–; *Mufti*, Autumn 1939, p.11

28   G Challis, *Interview*, *Mufti*, December 1951, pp.3, 12; Raven Mss, 21 May 1917, 29 September 1917, 31 January 1918, LC

29   Private source; *Mufti*, Xmas 1943, p.6; June 1950, p.3

30   W J T P Phythian-Adams letter of 10 October 1914. I am indebited to Mr Henry Phythian-Adams for allowing me access to his father's papers

31   Stone, *BB*, pp.25–6; *The Standing Orders of the 22nd Royal Fusiliers* (Horsham, 1915); *West Sussex Gazette* 4 February 1915, p.11, 15 April 1915, p.10; Harvey, *Battleline Narratives* pp.129–30, 164–5

32   Stone, *History*, p.25; *Mufti*, August-September 1920, p.6; *Mufti*, Summer 1973, p.3

33   WO93/49, Public Record Office

PETER SIMKINS

Somme Reprise: Reflections on the Fighting for Albert and Bapaume, August 1918

In August 1918, just over two years after the disastrous opening of the 1916 Somme offensive, the BEF found itself fighting yet another series of offensive operations over the same battleground between the Somme and the Scarpe. Much of the ground won at such painful cost in 1916 had been lost to the Germans in the spring of 1918 and now had to be taken again. Many of the divisions which had participated in the 1916 battle returned to the area as part of Byng's Third Army or Rawlinson's Fourth Army. Indeed, some formations – such as the 38th (Welsh) Division at Mametz or the 18th (Eastern) Division at Trones Wood – had once more to fight for the very objectives they had first captured in 1916. Yet, in sharp contrast to the events of 1916, the Third and Fourth Armies – in less than a fortnight between 21 August and 3 September 1918 – not only re-took Albert but also secured Bapaume and Péronne, the latter objectives having remained beyond the grasp of the Allies two years earlier and having been occupied only when the Germans had withdrawn to the Hindenburg Line in the spring of 1917.

The story of the fighting around Albert, Bapaume and Péronne during the last 'Hundred Days' was not one of undiluted success for the Third and Fourth Armies. As in most major battles, the friction of war inevitably produced command mistakes, failures of cooperation, variations in unit performance and examples of sheer bad luck. But, overall, there were significant differences in what had been achieved in over four-and-a-half months in 1916 and in under two weeks in August-September 1918. These differences were not merely indicated by ground gained or the rate at which it was won; they also lay in the nature and style of the operations themselves.

It must be acknowledged, at the outset, that the German defences were not of the same type as they had been in 1916. Although much of the area fought over in 1918 was criss-crossed with old trench lines and there were recognised main defensive positions such as the Albert-Arras railway, the Germans no longer depended principally upon a linear system – at any rate, *not* west of the Drocourt-Quéant and Hindenburg Lines – but, instead, held the ground by fire and in depth, with machine-guns and artillery providing the core of their resistance.[1] As on 24 August, the German machine-guns were often sited in well-camouflaged nests up to

147

150 yards in front of the main points of resistance and, unless hit by the British barrage, could and did prove troublesome for hours on end.[2] In the case of artillery, Henry Karslake, GSO1 of the Tank Corps, noted the special problems posed in the opening phase of the operations between 21 and 23 August by the German outpost zone which was some 3,000 yards deep. 'In conjunction with this system', he wrote, 'the enemy keeps the majority of his guns about 5,000 yards back from their front line. This is just too far for effective counter-battery work against all the batteries and too far for the initial surprise to let the tanks reach the guns before they recover from the first shock'.[3] When the Germans withdrew from a particular location – as they *were* doing repeatedly during this period – they normally did so with great skill and in good order, covered by rearguards who fought on ground carefully selected to give the maximum possible advantage to defending machine-gunners supported by field artillery. The successive fall-back positions were frequently far enough behind one another to stop attacking troops who had carried a first objective from immediately overrunning a second. Machine-gun posts had fields of fire of up to 1,500 yards and were so placed that there was little or no cover for attackers approaching from the front or flanks. According to the historian of the New Zealand Division: 'Unoccupied intervals were left merely as traps. Moreover, each centre of resistance was sited for all-round defence. The destruction or capitulation of one did not materially facilitate the task of our units on either side, for, while neighbouring centres held out, further progress into the gap was, in daylight at least, extremely arduous'.[4]

British and New Zealand accounts of the fighting in late August are generous in their tributes to their opponents, especially the German rearguards. Solly-Flood, who commanded the 42nd (East Lancashire) Division, later described the performance of the German rearguards as 'magnificent', and the historian of the 63rd (Royal Naval) Division relates that they fought 'hard and scientifically, and would not retreat until we had so manoeuvred as to threaten their line of retreat'.[5] When withdrawing artillery, the Germans would often open an intensive bombardment, both to hold off the attackers and to use up ammunition that would otherwise have been abandoned; they also sometimes left artillery sections or even single guns in woods to cover the retirement of their infantry, then used trench mortars to maintain covering fire while the isolated field guns were themselves pulled back. The rolling country north of the River Somme, with its ridges, spurs and woods, unquestionably suited such methods.[6] Nevertheless, for all the skill displayed in these operations, not all German units fought with equal determination. Several sources record how, at Riencourt on 30 August, twenty or so Germans were persuaded to surrender by a stretcher-bearer of the 1/10th Manchesters who was armed with nothing more lethal than an empty bottle.[7] Andrew Thorne, of the 3rd Grenadier Guards, recalled that on 23 August, the Germans near Gomiecourt and Hamelincourt – having failed to make headway in counter-attacks the previous day – 'showed very little signs of fight and prisoners were easily rounded up'. P G Yorke, the Brigade Major to the CRA of the Guards Division, remarked that a large proportion of the soldiers in the reinforcing German units appeared, at this stage, to be very young, raw and inexperienced.[8] The 'steady persistent resistance of the old battle days of the Somme and the Arras front' was now lacking, observed the historian of the British 17th Division.[9] By 3 September, in the view of the commander of the 188th Brigade, many of the Germans now facing the Royal Naval Division were 'demoralised and put up no fight. They were much worse at fighting in the open than our people were'.[10]

It is worth noting, in this context, that as the operations around Albert and Bapaume progressed, the German defenders actually enjoyed a numerical superiority in terms of divisions involved. As the official historian points out, nineteen additional German divisions were thrown in against the Fourth Army and seventeen more against the Third Army and the Canadian Corps on the right of the British First Army. Including the German divisions originally in the line on 21 August – many admittedly 'of poor quality' – the Fourth Army 'gained its success with sixteen divisions against thirty-three, and the Third Army and Canadian Corps with eighteen against at least another thirty-three'. On some occasions the Germans also had a clear local superiority, as, for instance, in the Thilloy-Bapaume sector on 26 August, when three tired divisions of the British IV Corps attacked nine German divisions, 'four of which were comparatively, and three quite, fresh', though another was so battered that it had to be withdrawn that night.[11]

Whereas Haig had been deluded about the true fighting state of the German Army in earlier years, GHQ was more accurate in its assessment of the extent of German demoralisation in August 1918 – underestimating it, if anything. Historians are generally familiar with Haig's telegram to his Army commanders on 22 August in which he predicted that the Germans had neither the means to deliver large-scale counter-attacks nor the numbers to hold a continuous position against the BEF's advance. 'Risks which a month ago would have been criminal to incur, ought now to be incurred as a duty', he declared.[12] Denis Winter, however, cites the less well-known instructions of the following day in which Haig conceded that, because the German defences were organised in depth, 'a sudden break can only be expected under very exceptional circumstances'. Winter interprets this statement as an example of dithering on Haig's part and as a demonstration of the Commander-in-Chief's deception in producing one set of orders for public consumption and posterity and another for the officers who had to overcome the enemy. In fact, Winter's highly selective quotation distorts the real purpose of the orders of 23 August.

What Haig goes on to advocate is that advanced guards should be used to discover the precise location of the German centres of resistance and machine-gun posts, adding that, when these positions were ascertained, 'tanks and the usual enveloping tactics can be employed', though the tanks should be held back until the preliminary reconnaissance was completed. Once the main German battle positions had been broken, Haig urged, it was 'essential that the advance should then be conducted with rapidity and every advantage taken of the enemy's disorganisation'. Subordinate commanders must use their initiative and the power of manoeuvre 'and should not be cramped by the habit of moving in continuous lines'. The condition of the German troops, he concluded, 'is such that bold and resolute measures are required. Reserves must be pushed quickly in where success has been gained so that by manoeuvre and exploitation the advance of neighbouring units and formations may be facilitated'.[13] Given the operational situation that day, Haig's orders of 23 August – far from being indecisive or deceitful – may be regarded as embodying a sound mixture of justified optimism, encouragement and tactical common sense.

One can similarly argue that, insofar as they helped to shape the course of the battle, Haig, GHQ and the Army commanders showed more imagination than in most previous offensives. Striking successive blows against the Germans at different parts of the front, the BEF's first attack in this phase was by the Third Army on 21 August, with the Fourth Army extending the offensive on the right over the next two days and the First Army joining in on the left on 26 August. This time the main direction of the Third and First Army thrusts was south-east, and the leverage they were able to apply by 26 August compelled the Germans to begin withdrawing behind the Somme Canal south of Péronne and along the high ground through Le Transloy, abandoning Bapaume. Rawlinson wisely endorsed Monash's daring plan for the capture of Mont St Quentin and Péronne by the Australian Corps between 31 August and 2 September while, farther north, the Canadian Corps simultaneously broke through the Drocourt-Quéant Line. The Germans were now forced to fall back to the Canal du Nord and Sensée as well as to the Hindenburg Line itself – in effect giving up all the ground they had won in March. As Gregory Blaxland has neatly put it, the Australian and Canadian Corps 'had gored the German line like the horns of a bull, while the various British divisions, and one New Zealand, gave plenty of weight to the thrust of the forehead'.[14]

Although they issued the directives which determined the weight and objectives of most attacks in August and September, the senior commanders – from Haig down to corps level – exercised much less control over the daily conduct of the battle than in previous years. Recent studies suggest that there had been a noticeable swing towards tactical decentralisation in the BEF by the 'Hundred Days'.[15] In the semi-open warfare of August-September 1918, each objective, to some extent, posed its own set of problems which required individual solutions. There was no longer a simple tactical formula appropriate to the majority of attacks, and greater flexibility was needed at divisional and brigade level. As Robin Prior and Trevor Wilson have remarked: 'Actions were continuous and small in scale. Plans were improvised by divisional generals or brigadiers as the situation demanded. Often there was no time to refer these plans to corps commanders, let alone to the Army commander'.[16]

An example of the tactical devolution that had taken place is the fact that, on 27 August, in the attack towards Morval, no single start time was fixed by Shute's V Corps headquarters and each of its three attacking divisions began to move at different times between 0100 and 0900. The same corps again allowed variable zero hours for its divisions five days later, on 1 September.[17] Quite apart from the able commanders of the Dominion formations, the BEF was fortunate that, in the changed conditions of August 1918, the quality of its *British* divisional commanders in the Third and Fourth Armies was also, on the whole, higher than that of their counterparts in 1916. They included H W Higginson, one of the 18th Division's most gifted brigade commanders in 1916 and 1917 and now leading the 12th Division; the Sapper, Richard Lee, who took over the 18th Division from Ivor Maxse and was seen at his best in the more fluid battle of late August and early September 1918; the innovative Solly-Flood, who had served with the 12th Division and then as Director of Training at GHQ before assuming command of the 42nd Division in October 1917; David 'Soarer' Campbell, of the 21st Division, whose nickname derived from the name of the horse which, as a subaltern, he rode to victory in the 1896 Grand National; and a future CIGS, Cyril Deverell, of the 3rd Division. Among the brigade commanders who distinguished themselves in the August-September operations were Edmund Ironside (99th Brigade, 2nd Division), another future CIGS; Hanway Cumming (110th Brigade, 21st Division), described by David Campbell as 'a magnificent leader of men' and 'a soldier of the very highest class'[18]; and A J McCulloch (64th Brigade, 21st Division), whose handling of a difficult night advance on 23–24 August displayed outstanding skill and enterprise. An officer in the 2nd Division was particularly impressed with Ironside's command style on 23 August, when the latter gave him, first, verbal orders on the ground and then written confirmation in only a few brief paragraphs, 'thus avoiding the mass of written orders which had become so fashionable at this period of the war'.[19]

Good leadership and initiative were not only demonstrated at divisional and brigade levels. Henry Aubrey-Fletcher, GSO2 of the Guards Division, wrote that it was wonderful to see 'company commanders having a chance to command their companies instead of being told what to do by the Corps Commander'.[20] Though the official historian is occasionally critical of the performance of British battalion officers, comparing them unfavourably with their Dominion counterparts, there were sufficient instances, in the operations under review, of outflanking and envelopment manoeuvres by individual battalions and brigades to indicate that the conclusions drawn by Edmonds are a trifle unfair.[21] If the general standard of junior leadership in the Third Army, for example, was as inadequate as Edmonds sometimes implies, it is hard to explain how, in the event, many units adapted themselves, within a fortnight, to more fluid conditions of warfare and achieved most, if not all, of their objectives. On the first day of the offensive, platoon and company officers of both the 3rd and 63rd (Royal Naval) Divisions earned plaudits for the way in which they maintained direction in thick mist.[22] Even Norman Cliff, who became a pacifist after serving in the ranks of the 1st Grenadier Guards, acknowledged the crucial role played by his battalion commander, Major the Hon. W A Bailey, in the attack of 24 August: 'His careful planning and fearless leadership drew out of us the best that we could give and the whole exercise went as slickly as a parade'.[23] Bailey was not unique. The 13th Royal Fusiliers (37th Division), who took part in the capture of the village and railway cutting at Achiet le Grand on 23 August, were commanded by Lieutenant Colonel R A Smith. In the words of his divisional commander, Major General H Bruce-Williams, he was 'a bank clerk by profession, a born soldier (and heavy drinker!) and he led (not followed) his men. They would follow him anywhere'.[24] The same day, with the situation at Irles uncertain, Lieutenant Colonel H A Colt, CO of the 12th Gloucestershires (5th Division), organised a second attack in the evening on his own initiative, taking the village.[25]

On the other hand, the transition from trench warfare and set-piece assaults to more open fighting exposed the weaknesses of some officers and it is relatively easy to find evidence of bad command decisions, poor staff work and insufficient liaison and co-ordination in the operations around Albert and Bapaume. For example, the commander of the Guards Division, Geoffrey Feilding, was 'not on particularly good terms' with VI Corps headquarters, according to the GSO1, Edward Grigg, while the GSO2, Henry Aubrey-Fletcher, accustomed to the 'carefully organised and synchronised attacks' of 1916 and 1917, was uncomfortable in the conditions of August 1918, when he felt that attacks were launched 'haphazard, with no co-ordination, no preparation, and very little artillery support'.[26]

On 25 August, following a misunderstanding about the zero hour that had been agreed, the 3rd Guards Brigade, under Brigadier General Follett, went forward at 0430 instead of 0930 and, not surprisingly, had no support on either flank.[27] Another formation with senior command and staff problems in this period was the 63rd (Royal Naval) Division.

Relations between the divisional headquarters and IV Corps were strained – 'a miniature Gunner v. Sapper war' was how one brigade commander described it – and the recent appointment of a new GSO1 did not help matters. This officer was thought to be partly responsible for the lack of control and liaison in the division's unsuccessful attacks on Thilloy.[28] Bruce-Williams, commander of the 37th Division (also in IV Corps), thought that the 63rd Division's commander, C E Lawrie (a Gunner), was 'quite out of touch with actualities' and 'had a poor G.S. staff'.[29] All these problems seemed to come to a head on 24 August when, in response to instructions from Lieutenant General Harper (IV Corps), Lawrie ordered the 188th and 189th Brigades, assisted by eight tanks, to advance in echelon at 1930 and attack Le Barque and Thilloy. Traffic congestion behind the front, German gas shelling, and attacks by low-flying aircraft on the Hawke and Hood Battalions delayed the 189th Brigade's assembly; several of the battalion headquarters had no maps of the objectives; the tanks did not arrive in time; and when Brigadier General H D De Pree (189th Brigade) rode forward to reconnoitre, he was met by heavy fire from beyond Loupart Wood. Despite the fact that the 188th Brigade, and the New Zealand Division on the left, were already on the move, De Pree – the senior officer on the spot – called off the attack around 1915 'to the accompaniment of foul language with great difficulty', as the commander of the 188th Brigade recalled. Lawrie at once relieved De Pree of his command but, after an enquiry, was himself replaced by Major General C A Blacklock on 30 August. Although De Pree was thus officially exonerated and given another brigade, the cancellation of the attack caused a good deal of unfavourable comment. Even twenty years later, both the former commander of the Drake Battalion, D M W Beak – who won the VC in the August fighting – and of the 188th Brigade, Sir John Coleridge, believed that a great opportunity had been missed on 24 August. 'It was a fine conception in the mind of the Corps Commander (Uncle Harper) this attack on Thilloy', wrote Coleridge, 'and had it come off, as it ought to have done, a wedge would have been driven into the enemy line and many of his troops and guns about Bapaume might well have been cut off . . .'[30] Notwithstanding its problems in late August, the division went on to perform well in subsequent operations, especially in the Quéant-Inchy area on 2 September.

Historians such as Prior and Wilson have been right to stress the key role played by artillery in paving the way for ultimate Allied victory in 1918.[31] The creeping barrage, which had been experimental two years earlier, was now a standard tactic and could usually be relied upon to lead the green $18\frac{1}{2}$–$19\frac{1}{2}$-year-old conscripts, of which many of the BEF's infantry battalions were now largely composed, onto their initial objectives. Smoke shells were often included in the barrage to help guide the infantry.[32] The scale of such barrages varied but a fairly representative example was that fired by seven brigades of field artillery for the 2nd Division's night attack on Sapignies and Béhagnies on 25 August. The composition of creeping barrages also varied and they might consist, for instance, of 10 per cent smoke, 45 per cent high explosive and 45 per cent shrapnel, as in the case of the attack by the 32nd Division and 1st Australian Division on 23 August, or 84 per cent shrapnel and 16 per cent smoke, as provided for the Guards and 56th Divisions in the VI Corps operations the same day.[33] Heavy artillery brigades were most frequently used for counter-battery work or for neutralising centres of resistance such as villages. As Edmonds underlines, the nature of the German defence system, with ground held by fire and in depth, meant that, except in the case of defended localities, the British artillery could not always support the infantry as quickly as before. In a more fluid battle, the rapid transmission of information back to the guns could not be guaranteed; the battle line was often ill-defined, telephone links absent and the precise location of German positions unknown. Hence the extreme range of the opening barrage sometimes dictated the limit of the initial infantry advance.[34] Moreover, the use of the creeping barrage did not necessarily ensure immediate or automatic success. On some occasions, as for the 37th Division's early evening attack near Bihucourt on 23 August, the barrage was put down too far in front of the infantry; on others, such as the 62nd Brigade's attack towards Eaucourt l'Abbaye on 25 August, machine-gun fire checked the infantry, causing them to lose the barrage; or, in yet another case – that of the 2nd Division's attack on Sapignies and Béhagnies on 23 August – the pace of the barrage was calculated to suit the Whippet tanks which preceded the infantry but, in practice, it proved too slow for the former and too fast for the latter.[35]

It would also be a mistake to assume that the creeping barrage was either used as a matter of course or invariably in a straightforward manner. The BEF's tactics of August 1918 were, in fact, more flexible and decentralised than that, with corps and divisions often choosing their own methods to overcome particular obstacles. Thus, for VI Corps on 21 August, the field artillery did not fire a continuous creeping barrage, except through the villages of Moyenneville and Courcelles, but instead laid down three standing barrages in succession. The New Zealand Division dispensed with a barrage for its attack at 0630 on 26 August, placing its faith, in this operation, on close support artillery – a field battery being allotted to each assaulting battalion – while *converging* creeping barrages were fired in a combined attack on Sailly Saillisel by the 38th and 18th Divisions, of the Third and Fourth Armies respectively, on the evening of 1 September.[36]

For the barrage fired to support the convergent attacks by divisions of V Corps near Thiepval at 0100 on 24 August, 144 field guns and sixty heavy guns were available – a small number for a front of over 8,000 yards but, as Edmonds remarks, 'sufficient to satisfy the infantry at this stage of the war'.[37] It should be noted, in addition, that, in a fair proportion of the attacks which took place under the changed conditions of August 1918, it was not so much the nature and composition of the barrage, or the weight of covering fire, but rather the availability of *close* artillery support that counted most. The speed with which sections, batteries or even whole brigades of field artillery were able to move forward after firing the opening barrage – or as the artillery component of an advanced guard – was often a vital factor in maintaining the momentum of attacks or in determining their outcome.

A case in point was the close support provided by two 18-pounders of the 82nd Brigade RFA for the 18th Division's attack at Trones Wood on 27 August. Firing some 200 rounds in the first ten minutes from a position near Montauban, they enabled the 10th Essex and a company of the 8th Royal Berkshires to overcome troops of the German 2nd Guard Division and capture the wood.[38] Close support by the artillery in a defensive role could be equally important. On the late afternoon of 24 August, a single 18-pounder which had been brought forward helped to repel two counter-attacks against the 17th Division at Pozières, and, on 27 August 122nd Brigade RFA, galloping by sections through a German heavy artillery barrage, came up in close support and enabled the 38th Division to beat off a counter-attack in the Longueval-Delville Wood area.[39] A major problem in such circumstances was that of ammunition supply. Gunners could no longer draw freely on nearby dumps, as in the days of trench warfare, and, in the V Corps sector, guns and ammunition had to be moved forward, under fire, over improvised bridges and narrow causeways across the Ancre.[40] Nor, in a moving battle, was it easy for artillery officers to keep control of their batteries and sections, 'due to the constant redistribution and plans for successive attacks at short notice'. Officers commanding ad hoc artillery groups in close support or advanced guards frequently had to do so from an infantry headquarters with insufficient staff support and inadequate telephone and signals resources.[41] Yet, more often than not, the difficulties were surmounted. The capture of Miraumont by the 42nd Division on 24 August was a good example of artillery-infantry co-operation at its best: heavy guns pumped shells into the centre of the village; field guns smothered the outer circumference with shrapnel to keep down the enemy machine-gun fire, while the infantry brigades worked round outside. When the two columns met on the farther side the guns ceased fire, and at noon infantry patrols entered from all sides and 'mopped up'.[42]

Tanks certainly constituted a useful component of the all-arms 'weapons system' which the BEF had developed and assembled by August 1918, but one should not exaggerate their influence. In a sample of 198 individual divisional attacks which took place in the operational sectors of IV, V and VI Corps (Third Army) between 21 August and 3 September 1918, and which are mentioned in the official history, tanks are positively identified by Edmonds as a valuable, or even marginally helpful, factor in only twenty-six cases (13.13%). Referring to the opening of the Third Army offensive on 21 August, Tim Travers states that 'where the infantry was properly trained in tank-infantry co-operation, as in VI Corps, and when tanks had proper protection, all went well, but where the corps commander, Harper, of IV Corps, was ignorant of the tanks, and where tanks had little protection, the attack had problems'.[43] However, the implication here that Haldane's VI Corps – apparently seen by Travers as a formation which understood mechanical warfare – would therefore inevitably do better than the less progressive IV Corps is not really supported by the facts. Again taking the same sample of 198 divisional attacks mentioned by Edmonds, one finds that the divisions of IV Corps were wholly or partly successful in thirty-three out of fifty-nine *opposed* attacks (56%) while divisions of VI Corps were wholly or partly successful in twenty-six out of fifty-four (48%). In addition, one should bear in mind that the terrain in the IV Corps sector, especially on the right near Miraumont, presented greater difficulties for tanks than the flatter ground to the north in much of the VI Corps area, and also that IV Corps subsequently faced some particularly tricky tactical situations, such as that around Thilloy. In this light it seems doubly dangerous for Travers to suggest that not only was Haldane necessarily more successful than Harper but also that this could be ascribed to a proper understanding and employment of tanks. Travers concedes that, even within VI Corps, the 3rd Division had little previous experience of training or working with tanks and that its commander, Deverell (an infantryman), was generally negative in his comments upon them, though, according to the Tank Corps HQ, Deverell did give them credit for their part in the capture of Gomiecourt on 23 August.[44] Deverell was not alone in VI Corps in having reservations about tanks. Brigadier General Osborn, the GOC 5th Brigade (2nd Division), related how the 'Tank merchants . . . would not hear of anything to the detriment of the new weapon but we who had to fight with it realised certain shortcomings much accentuated by the lack of liaison'.[45]

Apart from their contribution to the assaults on 21 and 23 August, tanks were probably most useful thereafter – at least in the operations under review – in assisting the infantry to overcome German strongpoints and machine-gun nests, examples of this being the support provided by two tanks for the 8th Somerset Light Infantry (37th Division) at Biefvillers on 24 August; the help rendered by eight Mark Vs in the 2nd New Zealand Brigade's action at Monument Wood, near Bapaume, on 25 August; and the part played by Mark IVs in the taking of Vaulx Wood by the 62nd Division on 2 September.[46] It is unrealistic of Edmonds and, more recently, Travers to criticise GHQ for not organising more mass tank attacks after Amiens.[47] In the tactical conditions of late August, when the divisional objectives were often individual villages or woods, mass tank attacks would have been rather like using a steamhammer to crack a series of small, if tough, nuts. Besides, as Paul Harris has recently observed, Allied offensive operations after Amiens were characterised by the rapid mounting of successive blows at different parts of the front, thus giving the Germans no respite: 'To have deliberately reduced the tempo in order to allow most British tanks to be concentrated for action in one place would have been ridiculous. Their concentration would not have conferred sufficient advantage to have offset the loss of momentum'.[48]

The use of tanks for supply purposes should not be overlooked. A Whippet brought up ammunition for a section of the 2nd Battalion, Machine Gun Corps (2nd Division), during the fighting around Mory Copse on 24 August; and a supply tank delivered small arms ammunition and water to troops of the 42nd Division in the assault on Villers au Flos on 2 September.[49] Air supply of rifle and Lewis gun ammunition by parachute was not unusual in the 'Hundred Days', the New Zealand Division being supported in this way on 26 August.[50] Other weapons – including low-flying aircraft in a ground-attack role – helped to maintain the impetus of the advance. At Villers au Flos, light carriages were improvised for 6-inch mortars, which were then manhandled across rough ground and went into action in forward positions, with some Stokes mortars, in close support of the infantry.[51] Earlier, on 25 August, two light trench mortars had been instrumental in crushing machine-guns which were holding up the 62nd Division's progress near Le Sars, enabling the 2nd Lincolnshires to turn the enemy's flank north of the village.[52] Machine-gun barrages fired during the fortnight in question included those supporting the attack of the 113th Brigade (38th Division) at Usna Hill and of the 5th Division south and south-west of Achiet le Petit on 23 August.[53] Two days later the 5th Division employed direct, enfilade and overhead machine-gun fire in its successful assault on Beugnâtre. And, in the 12th Division's attack on Méaulte on 22 August, Royal Engineers projected fifty drums of burning oil into a trench to neutralise German fire until the divisional barrage arrived.[54]

However much help was furnished by tanks, aircraft, machine-guns and trench mortars, it still fell to the infantry, on most occasions, to take and clear the successive objectives. As I have written elsewhere, the standard of performance of the infantry – especially in view of the large proportion of young conscripts – as well as the degree of sophistication of small-unit tactics, were much higher by the 'Hundred Days' than has perhaps been previously supposed.[55] There is ample evidence that the divisions of the Third and Fourth Armies in late August and early September frequently employed encirclement tactics and outflanking manoeuvres, while night attacks became more common.[56] Having been held up in front of Ovillers in the early hours of 24 August, the 38th Division attacked again in the evening, applying encirclement tactics to pinch out the village, and also pushing forward on the flanks of stubborn resistance. On 26 and 29 August the Division used similar tactics at High Wood and Delville Wood respectively. Its successes in all three of these attacks were in marked contrast to the repeated and bloody assaults which had proved necessary before these objectives had fallen to the BEF in the summer of 1916.[57]

Greater operational flexibility at divisional and brigade level, with a corresponding willingness to alter tactics to meet local circumstances, was also apparent in the variety of attack formations adopted. Lieutenant Colonel R G Smithard, CO of the 7th King's Shropshire Light Infantry (3rd Division), wrote that, during this period, his unit generally advanced in sections in 'worm' or 'blob' formation.[58] On 23 August the two leading battalions of the 5th Brigade (2nd Division) – both with an average bayonet strength of only 400 – advanced in 'Company column of platoons', each on a front of 200 yards and a depth of 500 yards with an interval of 100 yards between them.[59] Farther south, the 13th Brigade of the 5th Division attacked with all three battalions abreast.[60] Where possible, the momentum of the advance by the Third and Fourth Armies was maintained by the 'leap-frogging' of one unit through another and by the creation of all-arms brigade groups or advanced guards. All-arms co-operation was sometimes found wanting but, in the better-balanced BEF of August 1918, any one component, or group of components, of the 'weapons system' was often able to compensate for the failure of another. When it worked well, inter-arm co-operation could be brilliantly effective, as is shown by the following account of the 42nd Division's action at Villers au Flos on 2 September:

> An aviator, seeing that the infantry were in difficulties, flew over the German posts and attacked them with machine-gun fire, and at the same time a battery of 18-pounders was withdrawn from the barrage and switched on the machine-gun nests, while trench mortars, machine-guns and neighbouring infantry, on their own initiative, brought their full available volume of fire to bear. This proved too much for the Germans, a number of whom surrendered, and the 5th and 7th Manchesters went forward.[61]

Edmonds criticises the BEF for its failure to exploit successes vigorously and make more use of the tactics of penetration, describing the operations around Albert and Bapaume as 'a gigantic drive in line'.[62] However, this complaint seems to ignore the fact that narrow-front attacks had often courted, and resulted in, disaster in previous years and that, in the days after 21 August, the divisions of the Third Army, in particular, were only just beginning to adjust to attacking in semi-open conditions. It is also important to remember that the Germans had not lost their ability to make timely counter-attacks. Some divisions, like the 47th (London) and 63rd (Royal Naval), had to deal with five or six counter-attacks during this period, many being aimed precisely at the vulnerable junctions between formations.[63] A haphazard advance, without adequate flank protection, would therefore have had its own dangers. Furthermore, Edmonds himself records how, as a result of the BEF's rolling series of blows across a fairly wide front, the Germans were kept off-balance, with their divisions 'hopelessly intermixed' and with reinforcements 'thrown piecemeal into the fight'.[64] Admittedly, the BEF's successes were costly. The Third Army and the Canadian Corps of the First Army suffered 55,716 casualties up to 3 September, and the Fourth Army 33,730 in this phase of the fighting.[65] Even so, it is debatable how far losses could have been reduced, and the advance still maintained, when artillery often had difficulties in moving forward rapidly and tanks broke down, arrived late or were knocked out by direct hits. The 'mechanical solution' was not necessarily an ever-present option in a moving battle and front-line commanders often had to use what was actually to hand rather than wait for what was desirable. In the final analysis, the divisions of the BEF can be said to have adapted remarkably quickly to the new conditions and to have demonstrated a fair amount of flexibility and improvisational skill without inviting major setbacks. In these respects, for all its continuing mistakes, failures and minor tragedies, Haig's Army had come a long way tactically, if not geographically, since 1 July 1916.

Notes

1 Brigadier General Sir James Edmonds, *Military Operations, France and Belgium, 1918, Volume IV* HMSO, London, 1947 (hereafter *OH, 1918, IV*), p.184
2 *OH, 1918, IV*, p.258
3 Lieutenant Colonel Henry Karslake (GSO1, Tank Corps), 'Notes from the battle, 21st/23rd August 1918', 23 August 1918, PRO WO 95/94
4 Colonel H Stewart, *The New Zealand Division, 1916–1919: A Popular History Based on Official Records*, Whitcombe and Tombs, Auckland, 1921, p.458
5 Major General A Solly-Flood (GOC, 42nd Division) to Brigadier General Sir James Edmonds, 15 November 1937, PRO CAB 45/185; Douglas Jerrold, *The Royal Naval Division*, Hutchinson, London, 1923, p.309
6 *OH, 1918, IV*, p.314
7 See, for example, Frederick R Gibbon, *The 42nd (East Lancashire) Division, 1914–1918*, Newnes, London, 1920, p.164; Solly-Flood to Edmonds, 15 November 1937, PRO CAB 45/185; Captain F Howarth (Adjutant, 1/10th Manchesters) to Edmonds, 4 November 1937, including notes by Colonel J A Chisholm Taylor (1/10th Manchesters), PRO CAB 45/187
8 Lieutenant Colonel A F A N Thorne (CO, 3rd Grenadier Guards) to Edmonds,

16 May 1938, PRO CAB 45/187; Brigadier P G Yorke (Brigade Major to CRA, Guards Division) to Edmonds, 6 and 19 September 1938, PRO CAB 45/187

9   A Hilliard Atteridge, *History of the 17th (Northern) Division*, Glasgow University Press, 1929, p.385

10   General Sir John Coleridge (GOC, 188th Brigade) to Edmonds, 15 April 1938, PRO CAB 45/184

11   *OH, 1918, IV*, pp.301, 422

12   Haig to Army Commanders and the GOC Cavalry Corps (OAD 911), 22 August 1918. The full text is reproduced in Appendix XX of *OH, 1918, IV*, pp.587–8. See also p.265 for an assessment of the extent of German disorganisation and demoralisation by 25–26 August

13   Denis Winter, *Haig's Command: A Reassessment*, Viking, London, 1991, p.204; Haig to Army Commanders, the MGRA, and the commanders of the RAF and Tank Corps (OAD 912), 23 August 1918. A copy of this document can be found in the papers of Major General G P Dawnay at the Imperial War Museum, IWM 69/21/6

14   *OH, 1918, IV*, pp.166–70, 179–83, 193–4, 211–12, 237–8, 297–9, 310–13, 356–7, 366–83, 389–423; Robin Prior and Trevor Wilson, *Command on the Western Front: The Military Career of Sir Henry Rawlinson, 1914–18*, Blackwell, Oxford, 1992, p.342; Gregory Blaxland, *Amiens: 1918*, Muller, London, 1968, p.214

15   Prior and Wilson, *Command on the Western Front*, pp.300, 305, 339, 342; Tim Travers, *How the War was Won: Command and Technology in the British Army on the Western Front, 1917–1918*, Routledge, London, 1992, pp.109, 145–51; Paddy Griffith, *Battle Tactics of the Western Front: The British Army's Art of Attack, 1916–1918*, Yale University Press, New Haven and London, 1994, pp.22–3, 27; see also Peter Simkins, 'Co-Stars or Supporting Cast?: British Divisions in the "Hundred Days", 1918', in Paddy Griffith (ed.), *British Fighting Methods in the Great War*, Frank Cass, London, 1996, pp.50–69

16   Prior and Wilson, op.cit., p.342

17   *OH, 1918, IV*, pp.323, 378

18   Introduction by Major General David Campbell in Hanway R Cumming, *A Brigadier in France*, Cape, London, 1922, pp.9–14. It should be pointed out that Godley, who temporarily replaced the exhausted Butler in command of III Corps, told Haig on 17 August that he was 'not quite satisfied' with Lee, although his comments were made after the 18th Division had experienced problems at Amiens and *before* its run of successes in late August and early September. Similarly, Shute of V Corps – 'a very hard man to satisfy', according to David Campbell – told Haig on 25 August that Campbell 'had not shown up very well; he was always raising objections and difficulties'. Haig observed: 'No doubt he [Campbell] is tired, having been fighting since the very beginning'. Given that elements of Campbell's 21st Division had, on 23–24 August, carried out an exceptional night advance, Shute's remarks may have been prompted more by Campbell's argumentativeness than by any perceived shortcomings in the division's command and performance. A month later, Shute acknowledged that the division had 'done splendidly': Haig diary, 17 August, 25 August and 25 September 1918, PRO WO 246/35 and 256/36

19   Lieutenant Colonel C A Howard (CO, 1st King's Royal Rifle Corps) to Edmonds, 23 June 1938, PRO CAB 45/185

20   Major H L Aubrey-Fletcher (GSO2, Guards Division) to Edmonds, 15 July 1938, PRO CAB 45/187

21   See, for instance, *OH, 1918, IV*, pp.183–4, 292–3, 515

22 Lieutenant Colonel R G Smithard (CO, 7th King's Shropshire Light Infantry) to Edmonds, 17 August 1938, PRO CAB 45/187; Commander EM Lockwood (CO, Hawke Battalion) to Edmonds, 27 March 1938, with attached 5pp typescript 'Hawke Battalion, 63rd (Royal Naval) Division, August 21 1918 to August 25 1918', PRO CAB 45/186; Douglas Jerrold, *The Hawke Battalion: Some Personal Records of Four Years, 1914–1918*, Benn, London, 1925, p.204. Smithard commented that, in the 7th KSLI, 'compass training proved its value at once and thereafter was never forgotten'. Lockwood wrote that, on 21 August, there was 'a dense mist, but thanks to the skillful leading of the company commanders, direction was kept'. Curiously, and in direct contradiction to the evidence presented by Lockwood and Jerrold, Haldane (GOC VI Corps) complained to Haig, during the afternoon of 21 August, that 'direction was not kept by the leading units of the division' and that the 'young officers will not use their compasses in this, the Naval division': Haig Diary, 21 August, PRO WO 256/35

23 Norman D Cliff, *To Hell and Back with the Guards*, Merlin Books, Devon, 1988, p.96.

24 Major General H Bruce-Williams (GOC, 37th Division) to Edmonds, 10 November 1937, PRO CAB 45/187

25 *OH, 1918, IV*, pp.229–30

26 Lieutenant Colonel E W M Grigg (GSO1, Guards Division) to Edmonds, 23 June 1938, PRO CAB 45/185; H L Aubrey-Fletcher to Edmonds, 15 July 1938, PRO CAB 45/187

27 *OH, 1918, IV*, p.277 and footnote. Follett was killed in action on 27 September 1918. His Brigade Major had been taken ill with appendicitis on the evening of 24 August

28 Coleridge to Edmonds, 15 April 1938, PRO CAB 45/184; Lieutenant Colonel M C C Harrison (CO, 2nd Royal Irish Regiment) to Edmonds, 28 April 1938, PRO CAB 45/185

29 Major General H Bruce-Williams to Edmonds, 10 November 1937, PRO CAB 45/187

30 *OH, 1918, IV*, pp.253–4; Jerrold, *The Royal Naval Division*, pp.305–311; Coleridge to Edmonds, 15 April 1938, PRO CAB 45/184; Commander D M W Beak VC (CO, Drake Battalion) to Edmonds, 21 March 1938, PRO CAB 45/184

31 See, for example, Prior and Wilson, *Command on the Western Front*, pp.292–5, 311–15 and also 'What Manner of Victory?: Reflections on the Termination of the First World War', in *Revue Internationale d'Histoire Militaire*, No.72, 1990, pp.86–7, 95; Bill Rawling, *Surviving Trench Warfare: Technology and the Canadian Corps, 1914–1918*, University of Toronto Press, 1992, pp.189–90, 210–11, 213–14; Jonathan Bailey, 'British Artillery in the Great War', in Paddy Griffith (ed.), *British Fighting Methods in the Great War*, pp.39–43

32 *OH,1918,IV*, pp.181, 183–4; Alan H Maude (ed.), *The 47th (London) Division, 1914–1919*, Amalgamated Press, London, 1922, p.183; Captain G H F Nichols, *The 18th Division in the Great War*, Blackwood, Edinburgh and London, 1922, p.394; Major General Sir Arthur Scott and P Middleton Brumwell, *History of the 12th (Eastern) Division in the Great War, 1914–1918*, Nisbet, London, 1923, p.199

33 *OH, 1918, IV*, pp.213, 222, 274

34 ibid, pp.184, 515–6; Atteridge, *History of the 17th (Northern) Division*, p.386

35 *OH, 1918, IV*, pp.225, 232, 269; Brigadier General W L Osborn (GOC, 5th Brigade) to Edmonds, 24 June 1938, PRO CAB 45/186. Osborn described

the 'rapid barrage advancing 300 yds. a minute on Béhagnies' as 'perfectly useless to the infantry'. The official historian, however, states that the barrage was calculated at 150 yards in two minutes (p.225). It was arranged that when the barrage reached the villages named as the objectives it would pause to allow the infantry to catch up but where, as in the case of Osborn's brigade, the tanks failed to get on, the infantry was left not only without the Whippets but also without the barrage

36 *OH, 1918, IV*, pp.185–6, 302, 377; Stewart, *The New Zealand Division*, p.443
37 *OH, 1918, IV*, p.243
38 Nichols, *The 18th Division in the Great War*, pp.381–2
39 *OH, 1918, IV*, pp.248, 323–4
40 Atteridge, op.cit., pp.380–3
41 P G Yorke to Edmonds, 6 and 19 September 1938, PRO CAB 45/187; Colonel C E Vickery (74th Brigade RFA, Guards Division) to Edmonds, 16 November 1938, PRO CAB 45/187; Major R B Purey-Cust (Brigade Major to CRA, 2nd Division) to Edmonds, 26 August 1938, PRO CAB 45/186
42 Gibbon, *42nd (East Lancashire) Division*, p.160
43 Travers, *How the War was Won*, p.134
44 ibid, pp.134–6, 138
45 Osborn to Edmonds, 24 June 1938, PRO CAB 45/186
46 *OH, 1918, IV*, pp.253, 272, 408–9; Stewart, op.cit., pp.436–42
47 *OH, 1918, IV*, pp.514–17; Travers, op.cit., p.144
48 J P Harris, *Men, Ideas and Tanks: British Military Thought and Armoured Forces, 1903–1939*, Manchester University Press, 1995, p.183
49 Colonel H D Buchanan-Dunlop (2nd Battalion, Machine Gun Corps) to Edmonds, 25 May 1938, PRO CAB 45/184; Gibbon, op.cit., p.165
50 Stewart, op.cit., p.445
51 Gibbon, op.cit., p.165
52 *OH, 1918, IV*, p.269
53 ibid, pp.229, 233
54 ibid, pp.200, 302–3
55 Peter Simkins, 'Co-Stars or Supporting Cast?: British Divisions in the "Hundred Days", 1918', in Paddy Griffith (ed.), *British Fighting Methods in the Great War*, particularly pp.62–6
56 *OH, 1918, IV*, p.323; Atteridge, op.cit., pp.390–1; Gibbon, op.cit., p.164. At least six divisions of V and III Corps attacked at 0100 on 24 August, and 21st Division's zero was 0200 on both 1 and 2 September
57 *OH, 1918, IV*, pp.300, 343–4
58 Smithard to Edmonds, 17 August 1938, PRO CAB 45/187
59 Osborn to Edmonds, 24 June 1938, PRO CAB 45/186
60 *OH, 1918, IV*, p.229
61 Gibbon, op.cit., p.165
62 *OH, 1918, IV*, p.514
63 For example, frequent attempts were made by the Germans to envelop the right flank of the 58th Division, next to the 3rd Australian Division, on 26 August. See *OH,1918,IV*, p.290
64 *OH, 1918, IV*, pp.259–62, 265
65 ibid, p.423

EDWARD M SPIERS
Chemical Warfare in the First World War

Dubbed as 'frightfulness' during the First World War, chemical warfare had already acquired an odious reputation before the end of the conflict. From the first major use on the Western Front (Ypres, 22 April 1915), it was denounced as 'an atrocious method of warfare' which would 'fill all races with a new horror of the German name'.[1] In allied propaganda chemical warfare was branded as inhumane, and the reports of 'Eyewitness', the British government's official war correspondent, highlighted the sufferings of gassed British troops.[2] Wilfred Owen's 'Dulce et Decorum Est', one of the great war poems, was written in August 1917 just after a gas bombardment. It vividly depicts feelings of exhaustion, fear, and choking to death, but compresses the likely period of a gassed soldier's demise.[3] In 1918 John Singer Sargent painted *Gassed*, a memorable portrait of blinded and helpless men on their way to a casualty clearing station – an image which failed to reveal that most victims of mustard gas recovered from temporary blindness after two weeks.[4] Sir Arthur Conan Doyle described the 'agonies of asphyxiation', claiming that the Germans had 'sold their souls as soldiers' by introducing poison gas and inflicting an ordeal that 'seemed mechanical and inhuman . . .'.[5] In short, many of the fears, horror, imagery and revulsion associated with gas warfare were widely disseminated before practitioners and historians began to grapple with the task of reviewing and evaluating its military impact.

Major Samuel J M Auld, the former Chemical Advisor, Third Army, who was later attached to the staff of the American Director of Gas Services, wrote *Gas and Flame in Modern Warfare* (1918). Having already tried to dispel American misconceptions about gas warfare,[6] Auld claimed that it had become the 'most important' method of attacking men, despite the burdens of cylinder installation and the effectiveness of defensive kit. The first gas attack, he affirmed, had suffocated 'thousands of those in support trenches and reserve lines and in billets behind the lines . . . many to die later'. Undaunted by the lack of supporting evidence, he argued that gas could become the weapon of the future, even 'the Achilles' heel of the tank'.[7]

William L Langer, who later became a renowned diplomatic historian, composed a narrative history of his own company, Company E of the 1st Gas Regiment, the American Expeditionary Force (AEF). Written shortly after the end of the war, it recorded the actions of his company without any attempt to exaggerate its role.[8] Throughout 1919 most aspects of the American Chemical Warfare Service (CWS) would be described by scientists and middle-ranking officers in the journal of the American Chemical Society. These articles remain an invaluable quarry for information about the organisation, manning, and activities of the Research, Development, Technical, and Proving Divisions of the CWS, the gases manufactured in the United States, the activities of the First Gas Regiment and the interallied gas organisations.[9] Bereft of any self-criticism, they overlook the duplication caused by the separation of the Development and Proving Divisions, the remoteness of the US-based research from the requirements of the AEF in France, and the inadequacy of the US gas mask designs, which forced the AEF to use British respirators until July 1918.[10]

More substantive accounts of the AEF's gas activities came from Edward S Farrow, a former instructor of tactics at West Point, and Amos A Fries, an engineer, who had risen to the rank of Brigadier-General and Chief of the Gas Service, AEF. In 1919 Fries had returned from France to lobby successfully against the disbandment of the CWS. Having learned the value of publicity for the service, he encouraged Farrow's work, with its useful appendices on the AEF's offensive and defensive gas drills,[11] before compiling a more comprehensive history of chemical warfare. Prone to hyperbole, he argued that gas clouds were more efficient than gas shells 'for at least the first mile of the enemy's territory' and dubbed poison gas as 'the most powerful weapon of war'. Appalled by American unpreparedness in 1917, he insisted that this should never happen again, and that the CWS 'must be recognized as a permanent . . . branch of the Army of every country'.[12]

The origins of the chemical conflict remained an acutely sensitive issue as Professor Fritz Haber, who had pioneered Germany's gas programme, had been indicted as a war criminal after the war (7 February 1920), although he was never brought to trial.[13] The early French writings ignored their usage of tear gas cartridges in 1914 which, though tactically ineffective, probably constituted the first breach of the 1899 and 1907 Hague Conventions.[14] Professor Charles Moureu, former head of the Section des Produits agressifs, described how France had organised its scientific and medical services to respond to the chemical threat, employing 268 chemists throughout the conflict, with thirteen Parisian laboratories examining 'counter aggressives' alone.[15] Unable to produce sufficient quantities of chlorine, France had to import stocks from Britain before it could launch a cloud gas attack in February 1916. The shortage of chlorine had stimulated research upon gas shells, with the French pioneering the use of phosgene shells at Verdun (February 1916) and hydrogen cyanide shells at the Somme on 1 July 1916. General E Vinet, former Colonel-in-Chief of the bureau of Chemical Services, described how the French gas services had exploited the centralisation of laboratories in Paris to facilitate research and development and establish close links between the offensive and defensive gas sections.[16] However, his account of French respirator design is not always accurate, claiming that Professor Paul Labeau spent two years in designing the Appareil Respiratoire Spécial (ARS), which would predate the first chlorine attack,[17] and fails to explain the persistence with the discredited M2 mask, the production delays for the ARS, and the perseverance with hydrogen cyanide, despite its rapid volatilisation and relative ineffectiveness on the battlefield.[18]

In 1921 Victor Lefebure, who had served as a liaison officer with the French forces in 1917–18, produced the first major history of the gas war, *The Riddle of the Rhine: Chemical Strategy in Peace and War*. If not lucidly written, this was a perceptive account of the chemical conflict, with introductions by Marshal Foch and Field Marshal Sir Henry Wilson. Lefebure asserted that 'the history of chemical warfare' was one of 'continual attempts, on both sides, to achieve surprise, and to counter it by some accurate forecast in protective methods. It is a struggle for the initiative'.[19] He emphasised the potential danger from the German chemical industry and urged the dismantling of the German dyestuffs monopoly. Although Sir Edward Thorpe doubted that this was feasible, he accepted Lefebure's charge that the Kaiser Wilhelm Institute had studied the possibilities of gas warfare as early as August 1914.[20] Haber retorted that his institute did not begin its investigations until trench warfare had evolved after the first three months of the war.[21]

In some respects the Germans had relatively little to hide as many manufacturing plants had been opened for allied inspection after the war.[22] Generals Erich von Falkenhayn and Erich Ludendorff also published their memoirs in 1919, revealing snippets of information about their attitudes towards gas warfare. Falkenhayn conceded that the potential of gas was underestimated, and that the first chlorine attack was used to distract attention from his movements on the Eastern Front.[23] Ludendorff claimed that subsequently he 'anticipated great tactical results' from gas, especially during the spring offensive of 1918 once Lieutenant-Colonel Georg Bruchmüller had perfected his gas artillery tactics.[24] In 1920, General M Schwarte produced his vast, edited work, *Die Technik im Weltkriege*. Hastily written, it included only one chapter on Germany's chemical warfare achievements and ignored all allied endeavours.[25] Rudolf Hansilan, a former pharmacist with the XXII Corps, produced the first edition of *Der Chemische Krieg* (1925), a more substantial second edition in 1927 and a partially completed third edition in 1937. In spite of its deficiencies (notably the lack of commentary on research, development and gas organisation, and a ponderous structure and style, prompting L F Haber to describe it as 'vast, badly written and repetitive'),[26] it was widely used in the inter-war years. In a separate account of the first major gas attack, Hansilan revealed the difficulties of cylinder installation, the minimal number of casualties found on the captured ground (rendering claims of 5,000 dead as beyond the bounds of possibility), and the blunder of using this weapon prematurely without additional forces to exploit its effects.[27]

British inter-war writing never emulated this scope or detail, but Brigadier Harold Hartley, former Chemical Adviser to Third Army (1915–17) and later Assistant Director of Gas Services, compared the British and German methods of chemical warfare. Analytically rigorous, he deprecated Germany's choice of gas and mode of attack on 22 April 1915, the lack of concentrated barrages in the shelling of 1916, and the failure to maximise the potential of mustard gas. He conceded, too, that British gas efforts suffered from a shortage of gas, an insufficiency of shells until the attack at Arras (9 April 1917), and the failure to produce mustard gas until the end of September 1918. He still regarded gas as 'a very valuable weapon' since 'it supplements other weapons, offers great opportunities for surprise, and is the most effective means of achieving many tactical objects'.[28]

British (and American) writers, though, were to the fore in interpreting gas casualty statistics.[29] Sir William Pope, who had perfected the British manufacture of mustard gas, claimed that poison gas was a relatively humane weapon because of the paucity of gas fatalities, the shorter periods of hospitalisation for gas casualties, and the lack of evidence proving long-term complications.[30] J B S Haldane, another British scientist, expanded on these views in *Callinicus. A Defence of Chemical Warfare*. Fearful lest poison gas be banned after the first attempt at the Washington Conference (1922), he compared the casualties inflicted by gas and high explosive, concluding that a ban on gas was 'a piece of sentimentalism as cruel as it is ridiculous'.[31] Such protestations were employed by the US Senators who successfully blocked ratification of the Geneva Protocol (1925),[32] and by another notable gas victim, Captain Basil Liddell Hart, who denounced the delegates at Geneva 'for allowing illogical prejudices to outweigh a reasoned deduction from the lessons of history . . .'.[33]

Reasoned argument had never characterised the debates over chemical warfare. Even the prospect of using gas had alarmed British military and naval authorities in 1914. The Earl of Dundonald's suggestion that Britain should try to drive the enemy from fortified positions with clouds of sulphur dioxide was only sustained by Churchill, albeit in the form of naval smoke screens and not as lethal gas clouds.[34] In 1927 the British Official History of the war revealed that the allies had discounted extensive warnings of the first gas attack, and that Sir John French had denounced this 'mean and dastardly practice'. Thereafter, it claimed, man was no longer pitted against man 'but against material'.[35]

The horrific imagery of gas warfare was further boosted by the writing of Erich M Remarque, whose *All Quiet on the Western Front* was

166

translated into English in 1929, selling two and a half million copies in eighteen months. His descriptions of the fear of gas and the suffering of its victims reached a far wider audience than the imagery of Owen or Sargent.[36] English writing compounded these impressions. Edmund Blunden's measured prose (admitting that he suffered no ill effects from gas shelling in 1917, and that several miners only succumbed because they disregarded gas warnings)[37] was eclipsed by the effusive commentary of Robert Graves. Depicting gas as 'a nightmare', he claimed that the respirators aroused little confidence, that the use of 'accessories' (as the cylinders were officially called on the eve of the attack at Loos) evoked scant optimism, and that the actual usage confirmed these fears, with the gas blowing back on British trenches and attracting counter-battery fire. He vividly described the 'yellow-faced and choking' gas victims with the buttons tarnished green, and the 'gas-blood-lyddite-latrine smell' that pervaded the trenches, but was hardly a dispassionate commentator on poison gas. Suffering from a breathing difficulty, he could not wear the respirator issued on the eve of the Somme. Although a nose operation spared him from service on the first day of the battle, Graves retained an obsessive fear of gas, even trembling in later life at the strong scent of flowers.[38] Gas could scar the feelings of sensitive, if uninjured, officers, leaving the impression that war had become, as Siegfried Sassoon observed, 'undisguisedly mechanical and inhuman'.[39] Nor were such feelings confined to the middle-class *literati*. General Peyton C March, who became the US Chief of Staff after the war, was so distressed by the sight of some 100 women and children gas casualties in a Parisian hospital that he suspended anti-gas training in 1919 and favoured abolishing the CWS.[40]

More precise casualty data, as compiled by Colonel Harry L Gilchrist,[41] or more detailed analyses of the gases studied and employed in the war,[42] were unlikely to counteract these impressions. Similarly the claims of J F C Fuller and Liddell Hart that gas was the weapon of the future[43] were far from reassuring. In *The Real War 1914–1918* (1930), Liddell Hart reiterated that gas was the 'least inhumane of modern weapons', but argued that 'it was novel and therefore labelled an atrocity by a world which condones abuses but detests innovations'.[44] If he hardly allayed fears by this reasoning, Liddell Hart perceptively analysed the German errors on 22 April 1915, when they wasted the 'most complete surprise' of the war, disclosing a 'new weapon prematurely and for a paltry prize'.[45] The French General Edmond Ferry, former commander of the 11th Division, asserted that his warnings of the first gas attack had gone unheeded,[46] and the Canadian Assistant Director of Medical Services, V Corps, confirmed that provisions had been made for an extra 1,000 wounded (but not any special arrangements for treating gas casualties).[47] The failure to take more precautions left the 45th Algerians, of whom

Colonel Jean J Mordacq commanded the 90th Brigade, peculiarly exposed when they were engulfed by the first chlorine cloud.[48]

C R M F Cruttwell, another veteran of the trenches, provided a more restrained analysis of attitudes towards chemical warfare. Arguing that soldiers feared the loss of individuality and negation of martial virtues, he claimed that every soldier becomes a fatalist but 'fatalism depends upon the belief that he has a chance. If the very air that he breathes is poison, his chance is gone: he is merely a destined victim for the slaughter'.[49] Once soldiers had efficient respirators, he averred, gas simply became unpleasant and, from a German point of view, counter-productive as the enemy had the advantage of prevailing westerly winds and large potential chemical resources.[50] Brigadier-General Charles H. Foulkes, former Director of Gas Services (1917–18), emphatically agreed that Germany, having sown the seeds of gas warfare, had reaped the whirlwind. In *Gas! The Story of the Special Brigade* (1934), he not only recounted the Brigade's exploits but also contested many of the judgments proffered by post-war commentators. He rejected Hansilan's claims that there was any French provocation for German recourse to gas; disputed that gas failed at Loos (quoting from German sources that the British had achieved surprise and successful results along parts of the front); asserted that gas had effectively harassed the Germans at the Somme; and alluded to German fears of cloud gas attacks, bombardments by Livens projectors, and, in late September 1918, British mustard gas shelling.[51] Gas, he concluded, 'changed the whole *character* of warfare' and 'seriously affected' German morale in the last months of 1918: 'it was certainly one of the factors which led to the Allied victory, and it was increasing in importance and might have played a decisive part in 1919'.[52]

Many of these claims have been disputed by contemporary scholars, arguing that Foulkes grossly exaggerated the Brigade's achievements at Loos, overrated the effectiveness of cloud gas attacks, and presented his case in a chillingly detached manner and in a style reminiscent of the *Boys' Own Paper*.[53] However pertinent, these criticisms need to be placed in perspective. In chronicling the achievements of the Special Brigade, Foulkes had to explain the tactical utility of poison gas, to dispel much of the popular mythology about the risks of deploying and using cylinders, and to explain the efforts expended on reducing the burdens of cylinder installation. Above all, he maintained that Britain dare not ignore the potential of science, that future enemies would not do so, and that there were grave risks in believing that gas warfare could be prevented by disarmament.[54]

As the Geneva Disarmament talks foundered and chemical warfare recurred in Ethiopia, concern about ignoring the 'lessons' of the Great War dominated the gas historiography of the later 1930s. Several scientists sought to allay public fears about aerial gas attack by reviewing the properties and effects of the gases used in the First World War.[55] These writings, though, were overshadowed by the monumental study, *Chemicals in War* (1937), written by Augustin M Prentiss, a Brigadier-General in the CWS who also held a PhD in chemistry. In an immensely detailed work, Prentiss made the first serious attempt to investigate the industrial potential, and provide a cost-benefit analysis, of this mode of warfare. More informative than Hansilan, Prentiss was less polemical than Foulkes. His analysis was careful, systematic, and based upon layers of statistical and empirical data about gas casualties, gas attacks, and the relative effectiveness of various gases. Chemical warfare, he argued, 'is the latest contribution to the science of war. The experience and statistics of the World War both indicate that it is not only one of the most efficient agencies for effecting casualties, but is the most humane method of warfare yet devised by man. All in all,' he added, 'it is clear from the plans of both sides that, had the war continued, the campaign of 1919 would have been largely a chemical war'.[56]

While the British Official History continued producing volumes, chronicling the scale of gas operations in the closing months of the war (including the mustard gas shelling of Armentières, Villers Bretonneux and the approaches to Mount Kemmel in 1918),[57] Major-General Sir Henry Thuillier, a former British Director of Gas Services, wrote *Gas and the Next War* (1939). Although he doubted that 'a recital of the true facts' would convince all of those who held 'deeply prejudiced views on the subject',[58] he asserted that gas remained important for attrition, and that it suited the defender more than the attacker. Convinced that gas abolition was impractical, Thuillier warned of the dangers of being caught in a one-sided gas war, especially if facing an aerial gas attack, and of the demoralising effects of panic caused by ignorance and fear, which could only be obviated 'by teaching the whole population the nature, powers and limitations' of chemical warfare.[59]

Even once the Second World War began, several writers maintained that it was only a matter of time before gas warfare occurred (or more accurately spread, as Japan had already launched chemical attacks in China). Brigadier-General Alden H Waitt, CWS, claimed that the surprise effects of gas had been dissipated at Ypres on 22 April 1915 by the 'congenital stupidity of the Hun'.[60] Reluctant to rely upon this factor unduly, he argued that Ludendorff's spring offensive of March 1918 had shown the full tactical value of gas, and that mustard gas remained highly attractive as a casualty-causing agent. He described how gas could be employed on the battlefield, exploiting the principles of surprise, concentration, persistence (or non-persistence), appropriate choice of target, and co-ordination with other arms.[61] However, allied victory in the Second World War without chemical warfare left a deep impression on gas historiography. This was a rare case of a weapon invented in one war being discarded (other than for deterrence and localised usage in China) in a future war. In the final volume of the Official History, produced in 1947, Brigadier-General Sir J E Edmonds implied that the reasons lay in the tactical failure of gas in the First World War. 'Gas,' he affirmed, 'achieved but local success, nothing decisive; it made war uncomfortable to no purpose.'[62] Widely quoted in post-war writings on chemical warfare, this judgment differed from the conclusions of most inter-war gas historians, reflecting the fact, as Edmonds added, that gas 'was not used in 1939–45'.[63]

Over the next twenty years there was not a major study of what was increasingly regarded as an obsolete weapon. Robert Blake shed some light on Douglas Haig's changing attitudes towards poison gas, namely his disdain for Dundonald's ideas, then the expectation of 'decisive results' from gas in the planning of Loos, immense anxiety about the climatic conditions on the eve of battle, and finally concern about the debilitating effects of wearing respirators over a prolonged period of time.[64] Several brief works appeared, including the wartime memoirs of an American chemist, an article on mustard gas production, a cost-benefit analysis of chemical warfare, a slight descriptive history of Porton Down, a tantalising insight by Sir Maurice Hankey into the deliberations of the Asquith cabinet in the wake of the first gas attack, and further articles on the Special Brigade and the technical problems encountered at Loos.[65] Foulkes continued to defend the role of the Brigade,[66] some referred to the way in which the allies employed gas as an instrument of propaganda,[67] and a biographer of Fritz Haber described his strained relations, as a mere captain, with the German High Command.[68]

In *The Conduct of War 1789–1961* (1961) J F C Fuller highlighted the advantages of gas shell over cylinders and the impact of gas on the Eastern Front and in Ludendorff's spring offensive. He also emphasised that respirators, even if highly efficient, 'reduced the soldier to half a fighting man and gave little protection against mustard gas'.[69] Finally there were some accounts of gas on the Eastern Front, reviewing the first lachrymatory shell attack at Bolimow, the effects of climatic conditions upon gas in the east, and the disregard of protective measures by the Russians in 1917.[70]

Frederic J Brown wrote the first major post-war study, *Chemical Warfare: A Study in Restraints* (1968). Seeking to explain the non-use of gas in the Second World War, he emphasised its lack of assimilation in the Great War.[71] He argued that a pattern of restraints developed as reflected in wartime propaganda, the lack of pre-war preparation by the United States, military resentments (at the logistical burdens of gas, the need for sophisticated unit training and the challenge to the code of martial honour), the dependence on laboratory (and industrial) support, and the belief that gas was only effective as a weapon of surprise. Once the enemy retaliated, he claimed, 'the game did not appear worth the candle'.[72] Though thoughtful, this critique would have been even more useful had Brown explained why allied propaganda failed to sway American opinion, and why, if a two-sided gas war was perceived as ineffectual, the US gas effort expanded from ten per cent of artillery shells in November 1917 to twenty per cent in September 1918, and planned to reach twenty-five per cent by January 1919, with the possibility of aerial gas attacks.[73]

In 1969 Daniel Patrick Jones produced one of the few doctoral theses on chemical warfare, reviewing the organisation and activities of American chemists in support of the US war effort. Jones emphasises that the 1,200 chemists, pharmacologists and physiologists benefited considerably from their wartime collaboration, and that the American Chemical Society remained a loyal ally of the CWS, helping in its post-war battle for survival and in its opposition to chemical disarmament.[74] Two years later the Stockholm Peace Research Institute (SIPRI) produced the first of its six-volume series on *The Problem of Chemical and Biological Warfare.* A monumental work based upon a voluminous bibliography of published scientific, historical and contemporary sources, the first volume reviewed all aspects of the gas war of 1915–18. It noted that chemical weaponry had a strategic potential in 1915, but that as soon as both sides had anti-gas defences poison gas could not be used 'for anything other than limited battlefield objectives'.[75] While accepting that military establishments were often lukewarm towards poison gas, it recognised that gas had attracted large development, procurement and deployment programmes by the end of the war and had become a standard, if not a popular, weapon, with few doubting that it was likely to be used in the future.[76]

In the wake of the SIPRI volume came three strikingly different types of writing. Dr Robert Jones, a biochemist, recounted the history of gas warfare, citing the observations of Conan Doyle, Owen and Sargent as evidence, with a view to justifying the case for disarmament.[77] Conversely, Ulrich Trumpener produced a scholarly account of the first major gas attack based upon meticulous research in the French and German archives, confirming that the estimates of 5,000 dead and 10,000 wounded in this attack were grossly exaggerated, that there had been gas attacks before Ypres, and hence that the latter was simply an 'escalation of a combat technique which had been used before, albeit ineffectually'.[78] Martin Middlebrook also prepared a scholarly account of the first day of the German spring offensive (21 March 1918), examining the extensive use of gas in the initial five-hour, artillery bombardment. Well-dug-in and protected British forces, he noted, restricted the Germans to a fraction of their anticipated objectives, inflicting 39,929 casualties that could not be replaced.[79] Finally, there were more descriptions of the gas experience, including the instruction difficulties of Professor Arthur Smithells,[80] and a study of gas victims, the efficacy of counter-measures, and the fears aroused by poison gas.[81]

As interest in chemical warfare revived in the 1980s (fanned by concerns about the massive Soviet chemical stockpile, the spectre of US chemical rearmament, and the extensive use of poison gas by Iraq), Squadron Leader Graveley reviewed the Great War experience to demonstrate the continuing tactical utility of gas as an instrument of attrition, harassment and area denial.[82] Robert Harris and Jeremy Paxman compiled a journalistic exposé of the 'secret story of gas and germ warfare' but unveiled relatively few secrets about the First World War. They repeated the myth of 5,000 dead after the first chlorine attack, lapsed all too often into hyperbole ('Chemical weapons came to epitomise all that was most disgusting and evil about the war'), and, in trying to refute the arguments of Haldane, simply alleged that there had been a campaign to underestimate the numbers of men killed and wounded by gas.[83] Less controversial were Richard Stevenson's short history of the gas war, John Terraine's review of gas technology and William Moore's popular history of chemical warfare.[84] Major Charles E Heller wrote an excellent study of the AEF's chemical warfare experience. Using a wide array of primary and secondary sources, he examined the way in which chemical warfare had evolved on the Western Front, the tardy response of the US Army, the critical initiatives of the Bureau of Mines, and the way in which the AEF organised itself in the field. In explaining why the AEF suffered disproportionately from gas, Heller blamed a lack of pre-war preparation, a failure to adapt in wartime and defects in education and training. 'For America,' he concluded, 'the real inhumanity of chemical warfare in World War 1 lay in the blindness of US civilian and military leaders who, having ignored the real and present threat posed by gas, deployed the doughboys of the AEF to fight unprepared in a chemical environment.'[85]

James McWilliams and R James (Jim) Steel, two Canadian military historians, prepared a fascinating study of the Second Battle of Ypres, based upon considerable research in the Canadian, British and German archives. Having chronicled the weaknesses of the allied command structure, the system of communications and the use of intelligence, the authors maintained that the real blunder of the Germans lay in their failure to anticipate retaliation-in-kind. Once this began, the Germans incurred ten times as many cloud gas attacks as they inflicted, suffered from gas attacks by projectors, and fell so far behind in chemical warfare that the allies would have achieved an 'overwhelming superiority' had the war lasted into 1919.[86] While Pierre Berton added little in reviewing the Canadian gas attacks at Vimy Ridge beyond the fact that some Canadians and Seaforths became victims of the Canadian gas,[87] Trevor Wilson commented on aspects of the British gas effort, ascribing the failure to heed the warnings of the first chlorine attack to 'sheer disbelief', reviewing the dissension provoked by the Cabinet's decision to retaliate-in-kind, and praising the preparations, if not the outcome, of the gas attack at Loos. Above all, he stressed that a country had to have an industrial infrastructure to engage an adversary in chemical warfare.[88]

This theme is one of many addressed in the magisterial study of the gas war, *The Poisonous Cloud* (1986) by Ludwig Haber, the son of Fritz Haber. Having culled material from British, French, German and American archives, he examined all aspects of the gas war, including the scientific, industrial and operational dimensions (and its use on most fronts, including the Italian). In seeking to explain how Germany repeatedly seized the initiative in chemical warfare but failed to secure decisive successes, he blamed the fitful commitment of the high command to a 'troublesome and unreliable' weapon, the 'mutual incomprehension of officers and scientists', 'manufacturing and organisational weaknesses', and the superiority of gas defences by 1918. Unconvinced by predictions of an allied gas breakthrough in 1919, he declared that the 'gas war of 1918 was no more decisive than the introduction of the chlorine cloud had been three and a half years earlier'.[89]

Though plausible in many respects, this conclusion has been challenged. Edward Spiers has suggested that judgments of success or failure have to be placed in context as gas was only introduced because conventional weapons and tactics had failed to break the trench stalemate. None of the new technological weapons proved war-winners in and of themselves; neither the tank nor the aircraft 'changed the face of war in 1918', as Haber alleged.[90] Moreover, contemporaries never anticipated Haber's judgement; on the contrary, having massively increased their gas investment in 1918, they planned to augment it again in 1919. Accordingly, Spiers has argued that gas ought to be judged – not as a war-winning weapon *per se* – but as an ancillary weapon, which compounded the effects of conventional weapons by attrition, harassment, demoralisation, and area denial.[91] Valerie Adams refined the assessment further by distinguishing between the effectiveness of gas in local situations and its utility overall, while Guy Hartcup accepted that chemical warfare was 'by no means a negligible factor in land operations on the main European fronts'.[92]

In more specialised works, Graden Carter wrote an informative history of Porton Down; Tim Travers reviewed the struggle between the British and Canadian official historians over the interpretation of events at Second Ypres; and Joachim Krause and Charles Mallory elaborated upon the Russian gas experience, using contemporary Russian manuals and anti-gas textbooks.[93] In *Chemical Soldiers* (1992) Donald Richter completed the first major review of the British gas war, focusing upon questions of policy, the Special Brigade and the experience of front-line soldiers. Employing a wide array of archival material, including Foulkes's own papers, he criticises Foulkes for persevering with 'outdated' cylinder attacks, but accepts that the Special Brigade suffered from a 'pervasive spirit of ignorance and obstructiveness on the part of the high command'. In applauding the brigade 'for a job well done', Richter accepts that chemical warfare, if not strategically decisive, was 'manifestly effective as an agent of harassment'.[94]

What then needs to be said about the gas war? The opening of the Russian archives may reveal more about operations on the Eastern Front, and the Italian gas experience could be analysed further to shed light on the subsequent gas war in Abyssinia. The use of gas in particular battles and attitudes towards gas could also be examined, moving beyond the horrific images bequeathed by the war poets and artists. Finally, if gas assimilation suffered, as Haber alleged, because gas 'complicated warfare', how does this accord with his claim that 'gas shells developed naturally . . . within the artillery environment',[95] especially as artillery delivered eighty-five per cent of all toxic gases during the war?[96] Could it be that contemporaries, once they had recovered from the initial shock of chemical warfare and developed methods of response, both defensively and offensively, found gas less burdensome and unpredictable than its critics have alleged?

Notes

1   *The Times*, 29 April 1915, p.9
2   H C Peterson, *Propaganda for War* (New York: Kennikat Press, 1968), p.63; J M Read, *Atrocity Propaganda 1914–1919* (New Haven: Yale University Press, 1941), pp.195–9
3   W Owen, 'Dulce et Decorum Est' in B Gardner, *Up The Line to Death: The War Poets 1914–1918* (London: Methuen, 1964), pp.141–2
4   G B Carter, *Porton Down: 75 Years of Chemical and Biological Research* (London: HMSO, 1992), p.7; for an account of how Sargent came to paint his picture, see M Brown, *The Imperial War Museum Book of The First World War* (London: Sidgwick & Jackson, 1991), pp.76–9
5   Sir A Conan Doyle, *The British Campaign in France and Flanders 1915* (London: Hodder and Stoughton, 1917), vol. 2, pp.49–50, 57
6   Maj. S J M Auld, 'Methods of Gas Warfare', *[The] J[ournal of] I[ndustrial and] E[ngineering] C[hemistry]* 10 (1918), pp.297–301
7   Maj. S J M Auld, *Gas and Flame in Modern Warfare* (New York: G H Doran, 1918), pp.12, 21–5, 59–60, 63–5, 133; and 'Chemical Warfare', *[The] R[oyal] E[ngineers] J[ournal]* xxxv (February 1922), p.69
8   W L Langer, *With 'E' of the First Gas* later reprinted as *Gas and Flame in World War 1* (New York: A A Knopf, 1965)
9   'Gas offense in the United States. A Record of Achievement'; Capt. R F Bacon, 'The Work of the Technical Division Chemical Warfare Service, AEF'; G A Burnell, 'The Research Division, Chemical Warfare Service, USA'; R C Smith, 'Manufacture of Arsenic Trichloride'; Col. B Dewey, 'Production of Gas Defense Equipment for the Army'; Col. F M Dorsey, 'The

Development Division, Chemical Warfare Service, USA'; J H Hildebrand, 'The Organization and Work of Hanlon Field'; Lt. Col. W S Bacon, 'The Proving Division, Chemical Warfare Service, USA'; J C Webster, 'The First Gas Regiment'; Lt. Col. J E Zanetti, 'Interallied Organizations for Chemical Warfare'; Lt. Col. B C Goss, 'An Artillery Gas Attack', *The JIEC* 11/1 (1919), pp.5–12; 13–15; 11/2, pp.93–104; 105–09; 11/3, pp.185–97; 11/4, pp.281–91; pp.291–2; 11/6, pp.513–16; 11/7, pp.621–2; 11/8, pp.721–3; 11/9, pp.829–36

10   L F Haber, *The Poisonous Cloud: Chemical Warfare in the First World War* (Oxford: Clarendon Press, 1986), pp.129, 201; Brig.-Gen. A A Fries and Maj. C J West, *Chemical Warfare* (New York: McGraw-Hill, 1921), p.108

11   E S Farrow, *Gas Warfare* (New York: E P Dutton & Co., 1920)

12   Fries and West (note 10), pp.vii, 17–18, 437; see also A A Fries, 'Chemical Warfare', *JIEC* 12 (1920), pp.423–9

13   M Goran, *The Story of Fritz Haber* (Norman, Oklahoma: University of Oklahoma Press, 1967), p.82

14   U Trumpener, 'The Road to Ypres: The Beginnings of Gas Warfare in World War 1', *Journal of Modern History* 47 (September 1975), pp.463–4

15   C Moureu, *La Chimie et la guerre* (Paris: Masson et C., 1920); see also C Moureu, 'Les gaz de combat employés par l'Allegmagne', *La Nature* (Paris) 48 (1920), pp.300–6, 316–26, 332–4

16   E Vinet, 'La Guerre des Gaz et les travaux des Services Chimiques Français', *Chimie & Industrie* 2/11–12 (November-December 1919), pp.1377–1415

17   ibid., p.1393

18   ibid., p.1406; see also C Moureu (note 15), p.67

19   Maj. V Lefebure, *The Riddle of the Rhine: Chemical Strategy in Peace and War* (London: Collins, 1921), pp.109–10; see also Lefebure, 'Chemical Warfare', *J[ournal of the] R[oyal] U[nited] S[ervices] I[nstitution]* 73 (1928), pp.492–507

20   Lefebure, *The Riddle of the Rhine*, pp.31, 257; T E Thorpe, 'Chemical Warfare', *Nature* 108 (10 November 1921), pp.331–3

21   F Haber, 'Chemical Warfare' in 'Letters to the Editor', *Nature* 109 (12 January 1922), p.40

22   Lt Col. J F Norris, 'The Manufacture of War Gases in Germany', *JIEC* 11 (1919), pp.817–29

23   Gen. E von Falkenhayn, *General Headquarters 1914–1916 and its Critical Decisions* (London: Hutchinson, 1919), pp.84–7

24   Gen. E Ludendorff, *My War Memories 1914–1918*, 2 vols. (London: Hutchinson, 1919) 1., p.141; 2, pp.579, 597

25   M Schwarte (ed.), *Die Technik im Weltkriege* (Berlin: E S Mittler, 1920) ch. XI.

26   Haber (note 10), p.5; R Hansilan, *Der Chemische Krieg* (Berlin: E.S. Mittler, 1927), p.24; (1937), pp.35ff

27   R Hansilan, *Der deutsche Gasangriff bei Ypren am 22 April 1915* (Berlin: Verlag Gasschutz u. Luftschutz, 1934), pp.64, 70, 104; 'The First Gas Attack: A German Expert's View', *Army Quarterly* 30 (1935), pp.302–05; Maj. Charles E Heller, 'Chemical Warfare in World War 1: The American Experience, 1917–1918', *Leavenworth Papers* 10 (September 1984), pp.7–10

28   Brig.-Gen. H Hartley, 'A General Comparison of British and German Methods of Gas Warfare', *Journal of the Royal Artillery* 46 (1919–20), pp.492–509

29   C G Douglas, 'Gas poisoning in Warfare the Task of the Medical Services', *Journal of the Royal Army Medical Corps* xxxv (1920), pp. 79–92; W G Macpherson et al., *History of the Great War: Medical Services Diseases of the War*, 2 Vols. (London: HMSO, 1923) vol. 2, pp.288, 294, 299, 304–8; Lt-Col.

E B Vedder, *The Medical Aspects of Chemical Warfare* (Baltimore: Williams & Wilkins, 1925), pp.xii–xiv

30 Sir W J Pope, 'The Case for Chemical Warfare', *The Chemical Age* IV (7 May 1921), p.526

31 J B S Haldane, *Callinicus. A Defence of Chemical Warfare* (London, 1925, reprinted New York: Garland, 1972), pp.20, 28–9

32 Senator J Wadsworth, *Congressional Record-Senate* lcviii (9 December 1926) pp.144–6; see also Vedder (note 29), pp.20, 28–9

33 Capt. B H Liddell Hart, 'Gas in Warfare: More Humane than Shells', *The Daily Telegraph* (15 June 1926), p.10; and *The Remaking of Modern Armies* (London: John Murray, 1927), pp.80–7

34 The Earl of Dundonald, *My Army Life* (London: Arnold, 1926), pp.331–8 W S Churchill, *The World Crisis 1915* (London: Thornton Butterworth, 1923), pp.81–3

35 Brig. Gen J E Edmonds and Capt. G C Wynne, *Military Operations: France and Belgium 1915* (London: Macmillan, 1927), pp.163–6, 357

36 E M Remarque, *All Quiet on the Western Front* (London: Putnam, 1929, reprinted by Picador, 1993), pp.49–51, 89; see also Haber (note 10), pp. 231–2, 368 n. 66

37 E Blunden, *Undertones of War* (London: Pengiun, 1928), pp.225, 230

38 R Graves, *Goodbye to All That* (London: Cassell, 1929), pp.92–3, 129, 133–5, 137, 140, 173, 237

39 S Sassoon, *Memoirs of an Infantry Officer* (London: Faber, 1930), p.147

40 Gen. P C March, *The Nation at War* (New York: Doubleday, 1932), pp.333–5

41 Col. H L Gilchrist, *A Comparative Study of World War Casualties from Gas and other Weapons* (Washington: US Government Printing Office, 1931)

42 U Müller-Kiel, *Die Chemische Waffe im Weltkrieg und Jetzt* (Berlin: Verlag Chemie, 1932), p.49

43 Col. J F C Fuller, *The Reformation of War* (London: Hutchinson, 1923), pp.108–11, 121–33; B H Liddell Hart, *Paris or the Future of War* (London: Kegan Paul, 1925), pp.50–5

44 B H Liddell Hart, *The Real War 1914–1918* (London: Faber, 1930), p.146

45 ibid., p.195

46 Gen. E Ferry, 'Ce qui s'est passé sur l'Yser', *La Revue Des Vivants* (Paris, 1930), pp.899–900

47 V Corps War Diary, 15 April 1915 quoted by Col. A Fortescue Duguid, *History of the Canadian Forces, 1914–1919*, general series, vol.1 (appendices and maps), (Ottawa: Department of National Defence, 1938), p.232, appendices 323, 326

48 Col. J J Mordacq, *Le drame sur l'Yser* (Paris: Edition des Portiques, 1933), pp.69, 75–7

49 C R M F Cruttwell, *A History of The Great War 1914–1918* (Oxford: Clarendon Press, 1934), pp.153–4

50 ibid., pp.154–5

51 Brig-Gen. C H Foulkes, *Gas! The Story of the Special Brigade* (Edinburgh: Blackwood, 1934), pp.24–8, 72–84, 116, 126–7, 136–9, 152–5, 172–3, 326

52 ibid., pp.334, 336, 345

53 Haber, *Poisonous Cloud*, pp.57, 90, 279; D Richter, *Chemical Soldiers: British Gas Warfare in World War I* (London: Leo Cooper, 1992), pp.3, 91–2; P Griffith, *Battle Tactics of the Western Front: The British Army's Art of Attack, 1916–18* (New Haven: Yale University Press, 1994), pp.116–19

54 Foulkes (note 51), pp.184–5, 345

55 E C McDowell, 'Poison Gas: myth and menace', *Current History* 44 (July 1936), pp.59–64; J Kendall, *Breathe Freely! The Truth about Poison Gas* (London: G Bell, 1939), pp.51–66; M Sartori, *The War Gases: Chemistry and Analysis* (London: Churchill, 1940), p.viii; F A Hessel and M S Hessel, *Chemistry In Warfare* (New York: Hastings House, 1940), p. 115; C Wachtel, *Chemical Warfare* (Brooklyn, New York: Chemical Publishing Co., 1941), pp.3, 5

56 A M Prentiss, *Chemicals in War: A Treatise on Chemical Warfare* (New York: McGraw-Hill, 1937), pp.680, 684

57 Brig.-Gen. Sir J E Edmonds, *Military Operations: France and Belgium, 1918* (London: Macmillan, 1937), pp.163–4, 383, 390, 412–13

58 Maj.-Gen. Sir H F Thuillier, *Gas in the next war* (London: G. Bles, 1939), p.3

59 ibid., pp.69–73, 107, 174–5; see also Maj.-Gen. Sir H F Thuillier, 'Can Methods of Warfare be Restricted?', *JRUSI* lxxxi (1936), pp.264–79

60 Brig.-Gen. A H Waitt, *Gas Warfare The Chemical Weapon, Its Use, and Protection Against It* (New York: Duell, Sloan and Pearce, 1942), p.19; see also Wachtel (note 55), p.3

61 Waitt (note 60), pp.20–1, 50–3, 138–45

62 Brig.-Gen. Sir J E Edmonds and Lt.-Col. Sir J Maxwell-Hyslop, *Military Operations: France and Belgium 1918*, vol. V (London: HMSO, 1947), p.606

63 ibid.

64 R Blake (ed.), *The Private Papers of Douglas Haig 1914–1919* (London: Eyre & Spottiswoode, 1952), pp.87, 103, 104, 296

65 E E Reid, 'Reminiscences of World War 1', *A[rmed] F[orces] C[hemical] J[ournal]* 9/4 (1955), pp.37–9; J K Senior, 'The Manufacture of Mustard Gas in World War 1', *AFCJ* 12/5 (1958), pp. 12–14, 16–17, 29; D K Clark, *Effectiveness of Chemical Weapons in World War 1* (Staff paper ORO-SP-88, Bethesda Maryland: Tactics Division, Operations Research Office, Johns Hopkins University, 1959, DTIC AD-233081); Lt.-Col. A E Kent, *A Brief History of the Chemical Defence Experimental Establishment Porton* (Porton, 1961); Sir M P Hankey, *The Supreme Command 1914–1918*, 2 Vols. (London: Allen & Unwin, 1961), 1, pp.306–7; M S Fox, 'The Special Brigade, RE', *REJ* lxxix (December 1965), pp.377–82; 'The First British Gas Attack', *Chemistry and Industry* 46 (1960), p.1395

66 Maj.-Gen. C H Foulkes, 'Chemical Warfare Now, and in 1915', *REJ* lxxvi (1962), pp.177–84

67 Lt. S D Fair, 'The Ghost of Ypres', *Army* (February 1967), pp.51–5; Peterson (note 2), p.63

68 Goran (note 13), pp.66–79

69 J F C Fuller, *The Conduct of War 1789–1961* (London: Eyre Methuen, 1961, reprinted 1972), pp.172–4

70 I Hogg, 'Bolimow and the First Gas Attack', *The History of the First World War* (London: Purnell, 1970) 2/6 (1970), pp.609–11; N Stone, *the Eastern Front 1914–1917* (London: Hodder and Stoughton, 1975), p.112; W Rutherford, *The Ally The Russian Army in World War 1* (London: Gordon & Cremonesi, 1975), p.191

71 F J Brown, *Chemical Warfare: A Study in Restraints* (Princeton: Princeton University Press, 1968), p.6

72 ibid., pp.12–37

73 ibid., pp.31, 45

74 D P Jones, 'The Role of Chemists in Research on War Gases in the United States during World War 1', unpublished PhD thesis (University of Wisconsin, 1969), pp.164–5, 186–8, 211–12, 214

75 Stockholm International Peace Research Institute, 'The Rise of CB Weapons', vol. 1 of *The Problem of Chemical and Biological Warfare*, 6 vols. (Stockholm: Almqvist & Wiskell, 1971), p.52

76 ibid., pp.58–9, 140–1

77 R Jones, 'Chemical warfare – the initial horror' and 'Chemical warfare – the peacetime legacy', *New Scientist* 66 (17 April 1975), pp.142–4 and 66 (24 April 1975), pp.202–4

78 Trumpener, 'The Road to Ypres', p.480

79 M Middlebrook, *The Kaiser's Battle 21 March 1918: The First Day of the German Spring Offensive* (London: Allen Lane, 1978), pp.52–3, 152, 322, 341

80 A J Flintham 'Gas warfare in World War 1', *Education in Chemistry* 15 (1978), pp.175–7

81 D Winter, *Death's Men. Soldiers of the Great War* (London: Penguin, 1978), pp.123–6

82 Squadron Leader A F Graveley, 'The Voices of Experience: Learning for the Future from the Chemical War of 1915–1918', *The Army Quarterly and Defence Journal* 110 (1980), pp.410–35

83 R Harris and J Paxman, *A Higher Form of Killing: The secret story of gas and germ warfare* (London: Chatto & Windus, 1982), pp.3, 20, 34

84 R Stevenson, 'Chemical warfare: A history of horror', *Chemistry in Britain* 19/4 (April 1983), pp.277–8; J Terraine, *White Heat: The New Warfare 1914–18* (London: Sidgwick & Jackson, 1982), pp.155–61; W Moore, *Gas Attack! Chemical Warfare 1915 to the Present Day* (London: Leo Cooper, 1987)

85 Heller (note 27), p.94

86 J McWilliams and R J Steel, *Gas! The battle for Ypres, 1915* (St Catherines, Ontario: Vanwell Publishing, 1985), pp.220–1

87 P Berton, *Vimy* (Markham, Ontario: Penguin, 1986), pp.60–1, 126–8, 130

88 T Wilson, *The Myriad Faces of War: Britain and the Great War, 1914–1918* (Cambridge: Polity Press, 1986), pp.127, 255–6, 785; see also E David (ed.), *Inside Asquith's Cabinet: From the Diaries of Charles Hobhouse* (London: John Murray, 1977), p.239; S G Hewitt, 'Aspects of the Social History of Chemical Warfare in World War One', unpublished M.Sc. thesis (University of Sussex, 1972), pp.79–84

89 Haber (note 10), pp.227, 262, 270–1, 274, 278

90 ibid. p.270

91 E M Spiers, *Chemical Warfare* (London: Macmillan, 1986), pp.29–30, 33 and *Chemical Weaponry: A Continuing Challenge* (London: Macmillan, 1989), pp.80–2

92 V Adams, *Chemical Warfare, Chemical Disarmament: Beyond Gethsemane* (London: Macmillan, 1989), p.44; G Hartcup, *The War of Invention: Scientific Developments 1914–18* (London: Brassey's, 1988) pp.114–17

93 G B Carter (note 4); T H E Travers, 'Allies in Conflict: The British and Canadian Official Historians and the Real Story of Second Ypres', *Journal of Contemporary History* 2 (1989), pp.301–25; J Krause and C K Mallory, *Chemical Weapons in Soviet Military Doctrine* (Boulder, Colorado: Westview Press, 1992), pp.15–29

94 Richter (note 53), pp.3, 114, 169–71, 191, 193–4, 220, 224, 228

95 Haber (note 10), pp.268–9, 279

96 Prentiss (note 56), pp.657 and 660

Index

179